"*Flight of the Garuda*"

A COMPLETE EXPLANATION OF THOROUGH CUT BY ZHABKAR

BY TONY DUFF
PADMA KARPO TRANSLATION COMMITTEE

This text is secret and should not be shown to those who have not had the necessary introduction and instructions of the Thorough Cut system of meditation. If you have not had the necessary instructions, reading this text can be harmful to your spiritual health! Seal! Seal! Seal!

First edition, November 2011
ISBN: paper book 978-9937-572-05-7
ISBN: e-book 978-9937-572-04-0

Janson typeface with diacritical marks and
Tibetan Classic typeface
Designed and created by Tony Duff
Tibetan Computer Company
http://www.pktc.org/tcc

Produced, Printed, and Published by
Padma Karpo Translation Committee
P.O. Box 4957
Kathmandu
NEPAL

Committee members for this book: translation and composition, Lama Tony Duff; editorial, Lama Richard Roth, Tom Anderson; cover design, Christopher Duff.

Web-site and e-mail contact through:
http://www.pktc.org/pktc
or search Padma Karpo Translation Committee on the web.

CONTENTS

INTRODUCTION

Presented here is the text *Song of the View of the Thorough Cut of Luminosity Great Completion Called "Flight of the Garuda Capable of Quickly Traversing All the Levels and Paths"* by the Tibetan master Tshogdrug Rangdrol, who was also known as Zhabkar. A summary to facilitate study of the text, written by the present-day Tibetan master Ontrul Tenpa'i Wangchug, has also been included.

Zhabkar's text, commonly known as *Flight of the Garuda*, has become one of the important texts of the Nyingthig teachings of the Great Completion system of dharma that came down through Padmasambhava. Therefore, we begin with an explanation of the Great Completion system in general and its Nyingthig teachings in particular.

Great Completion

The Great Completion system of dharma came from a land called Uddiyana, which early writings say was "north-west of the vajra seat", the vajra seat being the place where the Buddha attained enlightenment, now in Bodhgaya, India. The name of Great Completion in the language of Uddiyana is "mahāsaṅdhi" literally meaning "great juncture". The Tibetans translated this name with "rdzogs pa chen po" (Dzogpa Chenpo), commonly abbreviated simply to "rdzogs chen" (Dzogchen) literally meaning "great completion".

The words "juncture" and "completion" have the same meaning in this case; they refer to that one all-encompassing space, that one juncture, in which all that there could be—whether enlightened or unenlightened, whether belonging to nirvana or samsara—is complete.

The name Great Completion refers both to an all-inclusive space that beings including humans could realize and to a system of instruction designed to bring beings to the realization of it[1]. When a being does realize it, there is nothing more to be realized or done because all is complete within that being's space of realization and the work of spiritual practice is complete. In a Buddhist way of talking, Great Completion is the final realization in which that being has manifested truly complete buddhahood.

Great Completion is often called "Great Perfection" in English but that presents an incorrect understanding of the name. The final space of realization is not a state of perfection but one that contains both perfection and imperfection. The name is not intended to connect us with the idea of perfection but with the idea of the juncture of all things perfect and imperfect, to the idea of a state of realization in which all things are complete. There is also the problem that the incorrect translation "Great Perfection" feeds into the theistic habits of the West and can easily mislead people into thinking of a godly state of perfection. Last but by no means least is the unavoidable point that Longchen Rabjam's definitive explanations in his revered text *The Dharmadhatu Treasury*[2] make it clear beyond a doubt that the meaning of the name is Great Completion and not Great Perfection. He mentions in several places that the

---

[1] For realization, see the glossary.

[2] Tib. chos dbyings mdzod. This is one of the seven treasuries written by Longchenpa. It concerns the practice of Thorough Cut. An exceptionally large commentary to it is currently being translated by Padma Karpo Translation Committee.

name is intended to convey the inclusion—just as the original name from Uddiyana states—of all dharmas within dharmadhatu wisdom.

Completion in Great Completion means that all phenomena are included at once in a single space of realization. *Great* is used to distinguish something known by wisdom in direct perception from the same thing known by dualistic mind as a concept. Thus *Great Completion* is not the completion understood through the use of concept, but the greater version of that, the actual state of completion known through wisdom.

Levels of Great Completion Teaching

The Great Completion teaching is divided into three main sections, arranged in a sequence of increasing profundity. The three main sections are Mind, Space, and Foremost Instruction sections, with the Foremost Instruction Section containing the most profound teaching of Great Completion. The Foremost Instruction section can be further divided into outer, inner, and secret sections. There is also a section literally called "more secret again" which contains the most profound teaching of Great Completion. Because the name "more secret again" is cumbersome in English and because this is the most profound level of teaching of all, its name is usually translated as "innermost". This innermost section is not surpassed by any other level of Great Completion teaching, therefore it is also called "unsurpassed". The two names are usually put together with the result that this most profound level of Great Completion teaching is referred to as "innermost, unsurpassed Great Completion".

There is a second, equally common name for the innermost, unsurpassed level of the Great Completion teaching. The original Indian name for it is "hridaya tilaka" which was literally translated into Tibetan with "snying thig" (Nyingthig). The literal translation into English is "heart drop" but it will be misleading to use that given that, in actual use in the Indian language, it does not mean "heart drop" but "the very essence of all", which corresponds exactly to the English "quintessence". It is a mistake then to think of and to translate the name as "heart drop" or "heart essence" as is commonly been done; the name means "quintessence" or "quintessential" level.

Thus, "innermost, unsurpassed" and "quintessential" are alternative names for the most profound level of teaching of Great Completion that has appeared in our current era of human society.

Lineage of the Teaching

The quintessential Great Completion teaching came into Tibet from India via Padmasambhava and Vimalamitra. Several lines of transmission appeared within Tibet following on from their teachings. The main line of teaching from Padmasambhava came down through his consort, Yeshe Tshogyal, and was known as the Khadro Nyingthig or Dakini Quintessence because of it.

This lineage came down to Longchen Rabjam [1308–1363] who then transmitted it to others in a number of ways. For example, he transmitted the teaching to Jigmey Lingpa [1730–1798] in a series of visions and this transmission became known as the Longchen Nyingthig or Longchenpa's teaching of the Quintessence. This transmission was very powerful and spread through Tibet, though it flourished strongly in Eastern Tibet, where it caused a major resurgence of the quintessence teaching.

Many great practitioners of the quintessence teaching appeared in East Tibet following Jigmey Lingpa. The author of the *Flight of the Garuda* text, commonly known as Tshogdrug Rangrol [1781-1850], was one of them. He was born in the far eastern Tibetan province of Amdo where he later became an important figure in the Quintessence Great Completion movement of East Tibet.

Tshogdrug Rangrol had many gurus, though the three most important ones were the king of Urge in Mongolia, whom he considered to be his principal guru and whom he therefore called "King of Dharma"—Chokyi Gyalpo—and two gurus from the Amdo region, Ngagchang Dorje, and Jamyang Gyatso. He pays homage to the three of them in the verses that show his lineage at the very beginning of *Flight of the Garuda*.

Tshogdrug Rangrol lived the life of a wandering yogin, embodying one of the important ideals of the Nyingthig teaching, and achieved great mastery. His name Tshogdrug Rangdrol, meaning "he who has achieved the level of attainment in which his six senses are entirely self-liberating", is a name given to those of very high attainment. With his knowledge and realization he became a major lineage holder of the Quintessence teaching. He taught and wrote extensively and his *Collected Works* encompasses several volumes. A number of his works are used regularly today to transmit the Quintessence teaching, though the *Flight of the Garuda* remains the most popular. Its popularity can be judged by the fact that two translations of it have already been made into English[3].

The teaching in *Flight of the Garuda* was widely transmitted in the Quintessential Great Completion community in Tibet. Amongst other places, it went to the great home of Great Completion teachings in East Tibet, Dzogchen Monastery, and was passed down through the main lineage holders there. After some generations it reached the Dzogchen Monastery master Jigmey Yontan Gonpo [first half of the 20th century] and then after that, in recent times, reached his two main lineage holders, Padma Kalzang Rinpoche and the great siddha Lodro Gyatso. The lineage then went from Lodro Gyatso to his main disciple, Ontrul Tenpa'i Wangchug of Golok who is still alive at the time of writing. He transmitted it, as part of his entire lineage transmission, to his disciples, myself included, in 2011.

---

[3] One is by Eric Kunzang Schmidt, the other by Keith Dowman.

The Close Lineage

Lodro Gyatso of Dzogchen Monastery lived during the twentieth century and was one of the greatest Dzogchen practitioners in Tibet in recent times. He stayed in retreat in the mountains, gained the realization of Great Completion, and in doing so kept the practice tradition alive despite the calamities that accompanied and followed on from the Communist Chinese invasion starting in 1959. He was one of the very important few who maintained the continuity of realization and practice through the calamities. At the time of his death in 2003, the seven signs of a manifest buddha appeared—the same signs that appeared when Longchen Rabjam attained enlightenment—and he was understood to be someone who attained buddhahood in his lifetime through the profound practices discussed in this book. He became very famous for the power of his practice and realization, and his memory is cherished today.

At the time of the Communist Chinese invasion, Lodro Gyatso and Ontrul Tenpa'i Wangchug were gaoled and put in the same cell where they stayed together for seventeen years. Lodro Gyatso passed his entire lineage to Tenpa'i Wangchug during that time and Tenpa'i Wangchug developed great mastery and scholarship. After their release, they went to their respective places in East Tibet—Lodro Gyatso to Dzogchen Monastery and Tenpa'i Wangchug to his two monasteries in Golok, including The Sanctuary of Elaboration-Free Alpha Purity. Each of them worked unceasingly to ensure that the Quintessence Great Completion teaching was properly re-established in Tibet and fully transmitted to the next generation, with the result that this jewel of a teaching is still flourishing in Tibet today.

Lodro Gyatso has passed into nirvana but Tenpa'i Wangchug is still alive. In his early 70's, he is regarded as the most learned of the

Dzogchen masters in Tibet, not to mention one of the most realized. Interestingly, he is also a terton or treasure revealer.

In recent years, Tenpa'i Wangchug has written a series of commentaries on important subjects of Great Completion, and these commentaries are known for being accompanied by an unusual clarity and transmission of blessing. For example, his commentary on Longchen Rabjam's all-important *Dharmadhatu Treasury*, which is the only commentary ever written on this key text except for Longchenpa's own commentary, is exceptionally clear, settling many points that cannot be settled even using Longchenpa's own commentary.

Tenpa'i Wangchug's commentaries are contemporary writings which come from high realization. These two factors mean that the blessings associated with them are very strong. Moreover, they are a direct conduit to the extraordinary level of realization of his guru Lodro Gyatso who also is very close to us in time. All together, the level of blessings available through Tenpa'i Wangchug's writings and teachings is very high, which is an exceptionally important point for anyone who is practising this material. This is not just mouthing words of flattery, but something which I have directly experienced repeatedly both when reading his works at a distance and being with him and receiving his teachings.

The lineage was passed from Ontrul Tenpa'i Wangchug to his disciples, including myself, in 2011. As a matter of interest, I went through great hardship to receive his lineage, including the teaching on the text in this book. Living under extremely difficult conditions with Tibetans only, and with no special arrangements at all made to accommodate my Western self, I was able to receive the teachings very purely, directly in Tibetan, and at the end was kindly given permission to translate not only this text but all of Ontrul Tenpa'i Wangchug's writings.

This permission, I would like to note, did not come easily; Tibetans in these remote places with their very pure transmission of Great Completion have seen the state of so-called Dzogchen teaching in the West and are very un-impressed by it. When I first met Ontrul Tenpa'i Wangchug, he simply dismissed the idea that a Westerner could successfully translate the innermost, unsurpassed Great Completion teaching into English. However, by staying with him and his people and slowly showing them that I could sit with them, understand the teaching, and practice with them without any special arrangements at all, it was collectively acknowledged within his inner circle that here was, rather unexpectedly, a Westerner who could understand and practise the teaching as a Tibetan would. Because of that, in my final meeting with Ontrul Tenpa'i Wangchug, he did, without my asking, not only reverse his doubtful stance about Westerner's capabilities but offered his permission to translate the entirety of his works. This was a significant moment indeed for all present because with it he was expressing to his people a major change in attitude towards what Westerners might accomplish. It was also a very moving moment because, in front of his previously doubting inner circle, he had fully entrusted a Westerner with the family jewels and encouraged that they be translated and fully presented to the West.

The close lineage details, including a brief version of my own involvement, are not told not out of pride but to instill faith in the reader. The story here shows that a very pure transmission of Great Completion is still alive, that the blessings of it are available in this book, and that an authentic bridge to it has been made by a Westerner. It will help readers to have faith in the purity of the lineage and, with that, in the reliability of the translations provided in this book. It will also help, I think, to open readers to the blessings that come with the translation of the text.

About the Text

The Text is the First Part of a Trilogy

The earlier English translations present *Flight of the Garuda* as though it were a single text, when in fact it is the first part of a trilogy. The Quintessence teaching of Great Completion consists of two main practices, called Thorough Cut and Direct Crossing[4]. *Flight of the Garuda* teaches only Thorough Cut, the second part of the trilogy teaches only Direct Crossing, and the third part of the trilogy contains special supporting instructions for both practices.

Westerners have wanted to obtain a translation of the second and third parts because they explicitly show the teaching of Direct Crossing. However, the few who could translate these last two parts of the trilogy have shied away from doing so because it is very dangerous to attempt to learn the Direct Crossing practices reading a book. It might help to point out that the second part is simply a re-arrangement of the Direct Crossing section of *The Guidebook called "Highest Wisdom"*[5]; the only difference is that the order of the teachings has been re-arranged and that some of Jigmey Lingpa's commentary has been removed. Given that we have already translated and published *The Guidebook called "Higher Wisdom"*, I see no need to translate the second part. The third part is private, oral instructions on the practice of Direct Crossing given to support the second part. These instructions have to be obtained in person from a qualified master, for them to be of any use and also are highly secret; I see no point in translating them at the moment.

---

[4] For Thorough Cut and Direct Crossing, see the glossary.

[5] Tib. khrid yig ye shes bla ma. A translation of this text by Jigmey Lingpa has been published by Padma Karpo Translation Committee, author Tony Duff, 2010, ISBN: 978-9937-8386-0-3.

The first part of the trilogy, *Flight of the Garuda*, stands on its own. It is a very complete set of Thorough Cut teachings that cannot be found in any other one place—you can see in the colophon to the text the many texts that Zhabkar used as a basis for the teachings. It is this unusual comprehensiveness that has made it one of the main texts used to teach Thorough Cut.

The Meaning of the Title

The title is *Song of the View of the Thorough Cut of Luminosity Great Completion Called "Flight of the Garuda Capable of Quickly Traversing All the Levels and Paths"*.

The teaching for his disciples in the form of a *song*. This is emphasized in the colophon where Zhabkar indicates what the song is about, who it was composed for, who should sing it, and how it should be sung; readers are directed to the colophon now to understand these points.

The song concerns the *view of the Thorough Cut* of Luminosity Great Completion. Teachings intended for practice are usually given using the "view, meditation, conduct, and fruition" presentation and that is how the teachings in *Flight of the Garuda* are given, as can be clearly seen in Ontrul Tenpa'i Wangchug's summary of the topics of the song. Nevertheless, the key feature of Thorough Cut always is the view, so the view alone is mentioned in the title.

The name *Luminosity Great Completion* is one of several, more complete names for Great Completion. Although it has often been translated as "Luminous Great Completion" that is mistaken; the name does not mean that Great Completion is luminous. Innermost unsurpassed Great Completion teaches that mindness[6] has three characteristics: empty entity, luminosity nature, and

---

[6] For mindness, see the glossary.

compassionate activity[7]. Of the three, this level of Great Completion focusses on the nature[8], luminosity, as the way to buddhahood. Therefore, Great Completion is called Nature Great Completion and also Luminosity Great Completion.

The poetic portion of the title[9], *Flight of the Garuda Capable of Quickly Traversing All the Levels and Paths*, indicates that these instructions have the ability to take a practitioner quickly and easily through all of the levels and paths of the journey to truly complete enlightenment. The levels and paths can be explained in a number of ways. The common explanation would be that they are the ten levels of a bodhisatva and the five paths to enlightenment as taught in the more general teachings of Prajnaparamita. However, that is an explanation from sutra which does not really apply here. What is applicable is the four levels of the vidyadharas and the paths of Thorough Cut and Direct Crossing taught in the teachings of Great Completion.

Figure 1. The Garuda Bird

The Garuda bird is the mythical king of birds of ancient Indian culture. One of its features is that it hatches fully-fledged and ready for flight, a feature which is used to illustrate the style of the Great Completion teaching. Another of its features is that it has

[7] For compassionate activity, see the glossary.

[8] For the nature, see the glossary.

[9] Tibetan literary style allows for titles to have two parts: a descriptive title and a poetic title.

enormous size and power, and this too is to illustrate the Great Completion teachings—the Garuda bird has the ability to swoop down and effortlessly pluck a whole poisonous plant from the ground then immediately carry it off into the vastness of space. This is like the Great Completion teaching which, unlike all of the teachings of the lesser vehicles below it, makes no effort at all to deal with the samsaric mind with its nasty baggage of afflictions, karmic latencies, and so on that keep beings in samsara, but simply carries the whole thing off, immediately returning it back into its primordial state, the over-arching space of enlightened reality[10].

Content of the Text

The song consists of a title, a single prefatory section of homages and so on, the main part, a brief conclusion, and a colophon. The main part, with the actual instructions of Thorough Cut, consists of twenty-three smaller songs.

The Instructions

The twenty-three songs present the important topics of Thorough Cut in a carefully arranged sequence. They are not songs sung at various times that have been randomly lumped together to make a text on Thorough Cut. To the contrary, they are songs that have been carefully crafted to build on each other to show the key points of the Thorough Cut teaching. Each is a chapter in the larger song, with all of them precisely woven together to create a tightly-knit presentation of Thorough Cut.

The topics and sub-topics presented within the song will be apparent to those who are very familiar with the details of the Thorough Cut teaching. However, there will be many who will not be able to see them just by reading the text. Therefore, Ontrul Tenpa'i Wangchug wrote a short but very clear summary of the contents of the song called *A Summary of the Guidebook to the Thorough Cut*

---

[10] For afflictions and for latencies, see the glossary.

View, Flight of the Garuda, Called "A Key to Unravel the Treasury of the Three Lineages' Instructions". This aid to study has been placed after *Flight of the Garuda*.

The Special Quality of the Instruction

The teachings of quintessential Great Completion are presented only through a very special form of oral instruction called foremost instruction[11].

The particular quality of a foremost type of instruction is that it goes right to the heart of the person being instructed and connects the person very directly to the meaning being presented. It is not just a "pith" or "key" or "oral" instruction as so often translated, but it is specifically the foremost of all types of instruction, the one that has the ability to get right into and move the mind of the person who is being instructed.

The Ultimate Quality of the Instructions

It is common in to use the introduction of a book to pick out a number of the interesting topics in the text and expand on them. I have not done that here for two reasons.

Firstly, foremost instruction obtained in person and followed by practise is the essential method of these teachings. By not writing extensive explanations of the various topics in the book, I hope to create a circumstance that will guide the reader to obtaining these foremost instructions in person from a qualified teacher.

---

[11] Foremost instruction is "upadeśha" in the Sanskrit language, with "deśha" meaning "verbal instruction", simple as that, and "upa" meaning the one above the others, the one that is better in every way, the one that comes at the front of all other types of instruction. It was translated into the Tibetan language with "man ngag", where *ngag* means the type of verbal instruction and *man* means the one that comes before all others. In English it is exactly, *foremost instruction*.

Secondly, one of the essential features of this text is the blessings of the Quintessence transmission that come with it. I have always found that studying these writings in general leads to an interesting transmission of both meaning and blessings. This text comes with strong blessings of quintessential Great Completion because of the power and purity of the lineage connected with it, as described earlier, and there is a very real possibility of connecting with those blessings directly. I strongly encourage the reader to be open to that level of transmission.

About the Transmission of Great Completion

In our human world, there are three main ways that the innermost unsurpassed or quintessential Great Completion teaching is transmitted: direct mind to mind transmission which only occurs between buddhas and tenth level bodhisatvas; transmission via symbolic means which occurs mainly between beings who are advanced on the path—the vidyadharas as they are known in this system; and aural transmission which is the main means for transmitting Great Completion to ordinary beings. The aural system of transmission is said to be comprised of two parts: Word Great Completion, which is the use of concept-based speech to convey the meaning from one person to another, and Factual Great Completion, which is the direct transmission of the meaning using the method called "introduction to the nature of mind"[12].

It is a fundament of the tantras as a whole that no-one should hear the tantra teachings or be exposed to their profound methods for directly transmitting the ultimate meaning without first receiving what is called empowerment[13]. And Great Completion is extremely

---

[12] For introduction, see the glossary.

[13] A clear explanation of empowerment in general and how it connects with quintessential Great Completion can be found in the book (continued...)

particular about these two points of secrecy and correct procedure. The tantras of Great Completion clearly state that, before any formal teaching of the system can be given to a person, the person must have the introduction mentioned just above in which Factual Great Completion has been directly shown. In other words, the introduction must be received before a person can be given any explanations of the system using Word Great Completion.

Zhabkar himself says this early in *Flight of the Garuda* and clearly states the reason for it:

> Thus, this sort of introduction must first be received
> while sitting in front of the guru
> So that it is determined based on what is real—then you
> won't go down a mistaken path.

In other words, the fact of Great Completion must be shown by someone qualified to transmit the meaning directly to the disciple before any teaching of Great Completion is given. This has to be done so that the disciple "gets it" based on what is real, what is fact. If it is not done that way, the disciple will not be able to avoid going down a mistaken path.

Zhabkar also makes the point that this introduction to the fact of Great Completion must be done in person. These days teachers are offering the introduction to Factual Great Completion over the internet or by similar means, with the claim that their students can obtain a valid introduction that way. Zhabkar's words indicate that it is not true. At the aural level of transmission—which is what we are talking about here—the transmission has to happen in person.

---

[13](...continued)
Empowerment and Atiyoga by Tony Duff, published by Padma Karpo Translation Committee, second edition, 2010, ISBN: 978-9937-8244-5-3. It also contains the root empowerment text for the Longchen Nyingthig Great Completion and instructions by Dilgo Khyentse Rinpoche on the practise of Thorough Cut, making it a useful support for this book.

Note that the tantras offer no alternatives or escape clauses on this point!

Someone might think that I am taking a few words from the midst of one song and overstating the matter. Well, Jigmey Lingpa says the same in his *Guidebook called "Highest Wisdom"*, which is regarded as the ultimate text on the practices of quintessential Great Completion:

> In order ... to be turned into a vessel for meditation on the quick path, the activities that perform the entrance into and ripening within a great empowerment mandala are, at this juncture, to be obtained at the factual [meaning non-conceptual] level. In regard to this, it would not be appropriate at this point simply to continue the instruction [on the preliminaries which has been given as a short pre-amble up to this point] on to completion [in which all the details of Thorough Cut and Direct Crossing would be exposed]; to do so would mean that the disciples would not be able to access the fact shown by empowerment and what goes with it during further instruction and that they would be seeing the meaning of the [seventeen Ati] tantras without empowerment [which is proscribed within the tantras themselves].

He is saying that the necessary introduction to Factual Great Completion—which occurs in the great empowerment mandala—must be obtained before any instruction on the actual practices—Thorough Cut and Direct Crossing of quintessential Great Completion—are explained. The sections following the quote given above make it clear that this has to happen in person, with the disciples actually present before the guru.

The incomparable vidyadhara Chogyam Trungpa Rinpoche, regarded by most as the best of Tibetan Buddhist teachers to have taught tantra to Western students, followed these instructions of the tantras to the letter. No-one in his community of students was allowed to study tantra until they had been through years of preparation. After they had prepared themselves, they had to receive the introduction to the nature of mind from Chogyam Trungpa in person before they could hear anything about tantra. Trungpa Rinpoche never once attempted to circumvent the commands of the tantras—for example, he never attempted to use internet or telephone or other such means to give the introduction; it was always given in person in a very closed environment to ensure both the secrecy and sacredness of the introduction. This single point of his willingness to follow the commands of the tantra had a great deal to do with why his students were in general very successful at their practise of the path.

Thus, there are two main points here. First is a spiritual health warning that the tradition itself is giving you: do not to even attempt to read the material in this or any other book on Great Completion unless you have already received the introduction to Factual Great Completion or have been given explicit permission to do so by someone in a position to give that permission. Study of the words without the introduction to Factual Great Completion will lead you astray and could, as the tradition warns, even prevent you from connecting to the actual fact of Great Completion in this life. In conjunction with this, there are many instructions which explain that the introduction has to be, at this aural level of transmission, given in person.

Second is the command concerning the process: first obtain the necessary introduction and then study the oral instructions on how to practice. The oral instructions will be delivered in language of Word Great Completion. This language has a unique vocabulary and a unique style of expression, which together are capable of expressing profound levels and shades of meaning. We will examine each of them in relation to Zhabkar's song.

Terminology

Zhabkar's song is composed using the unique vocabulary of Great Completion. This vocabulary has not been part of the English language, leaving us with the task of understanding it and translating it into English. To assist the reader with this, I have over the last thirty years gradually developed a vocabulary in English which for the most captures the vocabulary of the Great Completion tantras. Of that, the vocabulary needed for this book is explained in the notes to the song and an extensive glossary.

An important point of vocabulary is that it is used consistently. I do not take the simplistic approach in which several important terms, each with its own specific shade of meaning, are translated with one English term, and eschew the approach of inconsistent translation where an important term will be translated with varying English words throughout a text. Instead and just like in the original Tibetan, every single term is given its own unique equivalent in the English translation and the equivalents are used consistently throughout. This has two effects: firstly, it opens the door to the reader being able to follow the many and profound threads of meaning in a text in the same way that a Tibetan would be able to do; and secondly, merely by reading the translation the reader is educated in the use of the vocabulary of Great Completion in a manner which is completely consistent with its use in the original Tibetan texts.

Note that this consistency of translation is not only maintained on a text by text basis but is maintained across all of our translations. This has the effect that a library of texts made using this approach has appeared through the work of Padma Karpo Translation Committee, giving readers access to a consistently-translated range of literature. It is pleasing to note that readers have been remarking on the great value of this consistent use of vocabulary throughout our publications and that knowledgeable Tibetan teachers who know sufficient English have expressed joy on seeing this approach, which is rarely found these days but which accurately presents the language involved.

Style of Expression

Great Completion also has its own, unique style of expression. Compared to many texts on Great Completion, Zhabkar's song uses a style of expression that is generally straightforward, and that is certainly one reason why it is so popular. However, there are several places where he is deeply involved with presenting the actual state of being of Great Completion, all of which are marked by the very intense style of expression which is a hallmark of quintessential Great Completion. In these places, key terms of the system are piled one on top another, without consideration of ease of comprehension. For anyone who does not know the language of Great Completion and how it is used to transmit the factual meaning, these sections will seem to be gibberish and they certainly are a way, as I well know, to make an editor yell "This is not English!" However, for Great Completion practitioners who know both the vocabulary and style of expression of the system, these places are cherished because they are understood to be places where language is being bent to its limit in a push to connect to something which cannot be expressed in words. Here is a sample from Zhabkar's song which is not too difficult to follow:

> That non-dual appearing-while-empty self-arising
>   rigpa,
> Self-illumining, clearly present, vividly present,
> Three kayas spontaneously-existing type of mind …

This type of expression is just as much outside the limits of the accepted ways of composition in Tibetan as it is in English. Any attempt to fix either the Tibetan or English would be a case of trying to impose logical order on words which are being spoken at the edge of logical process in order to get past logical, that is, dualistic, understanding. In both cases, the expression is part of the transmission of the system and that cannot be changed under any circumstance. So, be warned that there will be places in this song where the English seems to be gobbledygook but in fact is not. I have many times experienced Westerners who, even with this explained, will indicate that there is still something wrong with the translation and that it should be fixed. They have missed the point completely, which is that this type of wording is not intended to follow the rational-minded rules of any language; to the contrary, it is supposed to provoke a breakthrough past a rational way of thinking. What has to change here is our level of knowledge of the system and our closeness to it. And this has to happen, as this section began by pointing out as clearly as possible, in the presence of someone who himself has received the transmissions of the system, who knows how it works, and who can pass it on to the listener aurally, as has been clearly explained. There is a famous saying in the Great Completion tradition, which is very pertinent here: "It is not Dzogchen that has to change, it is the person who has to change!"

The Great Value of Word Great Completion

One of the wonderful aspects, and I do mean that literally, of studying the language of Great Completion is that, once one knows its vocabulary and expression, merely hearing or reading it can open the door to glimpses of realization. Deep faith can suddenly arise because of it, a faith which has the three features of lucidity, admiration, and trust needed to bring on an actual transmission of blessings from the mind of the author to the reader. I myself have experienced this many times during years of translation and study of Great Completion. For beginners, there can be a tendency not to trust or believe it when it happens but, later, as one feels at home in the tradition, deeper connections can and do take place even on reading the language of Great Completion, and real confidence in the magical connections that happen begins to dawn.

The magic of connecting with reality is always possible because, despite the darkness of our dualistic perceptions that would have us believe otherwise, reality is always switched on. Once again though, we have to come back to the point made in the beginning of this section that, generally speaking, not just anyone can read texts like this and have realization dawn in the way just described. Because of good fortune accumulated in the past or because of vast amounts of prayers and accumulation of merit in the present, you have to meet with someone who introduces you, even if only for the briefest of moments, to Factual Great Completion. Following that, you can listen to the basic oral instructions needed to start the practice. As you practise, you continue to learn the language of Great Completion by hearing more teachings and reading books like this. As your connection with Factual Great Completion develops, it becomes possible to access to the magic through the words, because those words can connect you back to fact of Great Completion which you were shown initially. Without having the introduction and precious foremost instructions that go with it to begin with, it is very difficult for this magic to happen. Perhaps some people who have a very strong connection from the past might have something happen on hearing the words of the system, but they still must have the in-person human contact of a guide who can show the teaching properly according to the tantras of Great Completion.

Points of Translation

Translations compared

Some might wonder why this publication was made, given that there are two other translations of the song in English already. The answer essentially stated is that there is an outstanding need for an accurate translation of this text for serious practitioners of Great Completion.

Flight of the Garuda is a series of songs which are inspiringly beautiful and the translation by Eric Schmidt captures this aspect of the text quite well. However, the songs are much more than just beautiful poetry—they also are very precise presentations of the profound meaning of Great Completion. In regard to this point, Eric himself says in his translation:

> … this English translation reflects little of the depth and beauty of the songs in the Tibetan original …

Eric has explained to me personally that he eliminates the subtleties of meaning and also the technical terminology in favour of more easy-to-read English in order to make his translations accessible to a wider audience, one that does not care about the subtleties of Great Completion view as expressed by its unique terminology. Here is a single verse of Eric's translation that has lost meaning in several ways due to glossing over details of the Tibetan wording in order to make it simpler to read:

> If a tree is cut down at the root
> Its thousands of leaves and branches will all simultaneously wither.
> Similarly, cutting the root of one's mind
> Dries up all the appendages of samsara, such as grasping and fixation.

Compare this to what the original text says:

> As an example, if the one root of a tree trunk is cut,
> A thousand million branches and leaves wither at once,
> And likewise, if the one root of mind is cut,
> Samsara's leaves and petals—grasped-grasping[14], and so on—all wither.

Note how the first and third lines use the word "one" as an important part of the meaning being conveyed and how this has been simply lost in the first translation. Note how the large number given in the second line in order to indicate the vast extent of samsaric mind has been reduced in the first translation, with loss of meaning. Note how the fourth line refers to "leaves and petals" to make the poetic image complete but that this has been altered and the meaning lost in the first translation. As an example of technical

---

[14] For grasped-grasping, see the glossary.

vocabulary, note the term grasped-grasping (which can be looked up in the glossary here for an explanation) in the fourth line and how that term has been roughly translated in the first translation. These are small points but they add up very quickly to a translation which does lose the depth of meaning available in the original. Surprisingly, Eric's translation also loses a number of lines of the original. Nevertheless, it is a worthy effort.

The other translation, by Keith Dowman, is hard to praise. It distorts the original song in many ways. Most obviously, it invents a style of expression that is simply not found in the songs, then it makes up meanings not in the songs, and on top of that it is simply mistaken in places. It is not a translation but an interpretation, and one which often exceeds both the feeling and meaning of the original.

The translation here was made to overcome the problems mentioned above. It follows the Tibetan text as closely as possible and uses a consistent and carefully worked out vocabulary that comes as close as possible to presenting all of the meaning of the original in English. The Tibetan text has been included for ease of comparison with the English translation and as an aid to study for those who need it.

Poetry or Prose?

Flight of the Garuda is, like many Tibetan teachings, composed in verse. Tibetan verse is not composed by ensuring that certain lines of the verse are in rhyme, but by ensuring that a set number of words (usually 5, 7, 9, or 11 though it can be more) are written words to a line. This opens the door to writing prose which has a verse form imposed on it as it is written, simply by cutting the prose into lines of a certain length, and Buddhist teachings are commonly composed in this versified prose form.

An English speaker might say, "That seems forced! Why not just leave the prose as prose?" and that would be a good point in relation to English composition. However, Tibetan language works a little differently to English language with the result that, in Tibetan language, this sort of versified prose comes with some significant advantages. It allows the full and complete expression that is possible with prose to be packaged in a form that makes it interesting to the listener, easy to sing as a song, and much easier to remember than the prose form. All of these points are important to a yogin. He can hear teachings that have great depth of meaning fully expressed yet in a form that he can sing to keep his mind happy and that he can easily remember while in secluded places away from all books, let alone today's modern devices of computers and so on. *Flight of the Garuda* has this quality of prose turned into poetry with all of the advantages that come with it.

There is a very interesting point here: if the translation into English of this song which was composed in verse is perfect, the verse and prose forms will be perfectly interchangeable, even down to the last detail of punctuation. I was very happy with the translation, which had been completed in Tibet under very auspicious circumstances, but was surprised when I found that the verse form could be transposed into the prose form with not a single change having to be made to the wording let alone the punctuation! This was truly gratifying, for it showed how well the English translation represents the flow and expression of the original Tibetan song.

Thus both verse and prose forms of the song have been included in the book. The original, verse form of the song is presented first, and that transferred to the prose form is presented immediately after that. Note again that the *only* difference between the two is that one is in verse where the other is in prose.

There are advantages to each form. The verse form has its own rhythm and that rhythm helps to get a feel for the subject that the prose form cannot. Personally, I prefer to the verse form for that reason. I would offer a hint here, which is that the verse form in English can be made to read well if you adopt a rhythm similar the "rap" style of current day music—though it is important to keep the delusions of desire, aggression, and so on out of it. Zhabkar offers his own hint on how to read it in the colophon of the song and that should be combined with my own hint just given. The prose form does not have the advantages of verse and rhythm but is very suited to study of the song because of the ease of reading that goes with it.

Footnotes and Endnotes

Copious notes have been provided to ensure the clearest possible understanding of the song. Notes are usually provided in our publications as footnotes. However, footnotes seemed to clutter the verse too much, so notes to the texts have been provided in this book as endnotes. The notes to the song are marked in both the verse and prose versions of the song.

Use of the Second Person

I have often abandoned the use of the more formal English "one" in favour of the less formal but much more personal "you" simply because that is the tone of *Flight of the Garuda*; its style of composition is very personal and goes straight to the heart.

Sanskrit and diacriticals

Sanskrit terminology is properly transliterated into English with the use of diacritical marks. These marks often cause discomfort to less scholarly readers and can distance them from the work. The texts here deal with Thorough Cut with great precision but are intended for the use of practitioners, so diacritical marks have not been used in the translations unless diacritical marks were used in the Tibetan text—something which does happen occasionally.

Health Warning

The texts here are about a subject that is normally kept secret. Anyone who has had these teachings in person will be able to understand them or at least go to his teacher and ask for further explanation. As mentioned in the earlier section on the transmission of Great Completion, anyone who has had the introduction to the nature of mind upon which the teachings hinge, please use and enjoy the text as you will! However, if you have not heard these teachings and especially have not had the requisite introduction to the nature of his mind, you would be best iff not reading this book but seeking out someone who could teach it to you according to the ways of transmission laid out in the lineage itself. Nowadays there are both non-Tibetans and Tibetans who can do that for you and who are available in many countries across our planet. In short, the contents of this book could be dangerous to your spiritual health if you are not ready for it, so exercise care.

Garuda swoops down unexpectedly
Carrying off the whole of mind—
Thorough Cut!
What's left? That's it!

Lama Tony Duff,
The Sanctuary of Elaboration-Free Alpha Purity,
Golok, Tibet,
Summer, 2011

Plate 1. Mahasiddha Lodro Gyatso of Dzogchen Monastery.
Taken at Dzogchen Monastery, around 2001.

Plate 2. Ontrul Tenpa'i Wangchuk at the Sanctuary of
Elaboration-Free Alpha Purity,
Golok, Tibet, 2007.

Song of the View of the Thorough Cut of Luminosity Great Completion Called "Flight of the Garuda Capable of Quickly Traversing All the Levels and Paths"

by Tshogdrug Rangdrol

Namo guruvyaḥ[1]

Your seven-horsed disk of all-illuminating knowledge and love
Radiates the light rays of immeasurable compassionate activity
Dispelling at once all of the darkness of ignorance of the
 migrators of the three realms—
I bow down to you Chokyi Gyalpo[2].
In the vast heavens of your empty-luminous dharmakaya,
Moisture-laden clouds of loving-kindness and love amass
And you expertly pour down a rain of dharma on the vessels who
 will hold it, the fortunate ones[3] to be tamed—
I bow down to you Ngagchang Dorje.

Amidst your ship of the view, the great sail of the special wish is
 hoisted[4]
And, propelled by the wind of perseverance, you set the
 migrators
Drowning in the ocean of becoming down on the jewel island of
 the three kayas[5]—
I bow down to you captain Jamyang Gyatso.

The warm rays of potent blessings radiated from
These three seven-horsed disks of knowledge and love,
Strike myself, the white lotus of a fortunate one who has abandoned activities[6],
Making my bud of rigpa blossom into a thousand petals of experience and realization[7].

This melodious song of the view, a nectar which liberates on tasting,
Having descended nicely into the centre of the fresh flower of my intellect,
Is offered to the swarm of bees, my fortunate students;
Please, respectfully drink to your heart's content!

———— ◆◆◆ ————

E MA HO
I, abandoned of activities, spacious and carefree, happy of mind,
Sing Flight of the Garuda, a melodious song of the view
Which will quickly take you through all the levels and paths without exception;
Fortunate mind sons, listen attentively!

The loud sound of "buddha" is, like the roar of thunder,
Heard everywhere throughout both samsara and nirvana.
That buddha is perpetually present in the mindstreams of the six migrator sentient beings,
An alliance which never fails even for an instant—how amazing!

Not knowing that buddha exists in themselves,
They seek it elsewhere outside themselves—how amazing!
It is directly visible, being like the pure brilliance
Which is the essence of the sun, yet few see it—how amazing!

One's own mind, buddha itself, having no parents
Never knows birth so has no cause of death—how amazing!
No matter what it experiences of the diverse joys and sufferings,
It is not bettered or worsened in the slightest—how amazing!

This unborn primally-pure mindness[8]
Uncontrived, primordially comes spontaneously into existence—how amazing![9]
This primordially-liberated self-knowing, its nature,
Is liberated by leaving what arises to be as it pleases—how amazing!

❁ ❁ ❁

E MA HO
Fortunate sons[10] of the family[11] listen undistractedly!

All of the conquerors of the three times without exception
Give teachings—the eighty-four thousandfold dharma heap, and so on[12].
These, equal to the limits of space, are unfathomable in extent
Yet are for the one purpose of realizing your own mind.
The conquerors do not give teaching for any purpose other than that.

As an example, if the one root of a tree trunk is cut,
A thousand million branches and leaves wither at once,
And likewise, if the one root of mind is cut,
Samsara's leaves and petals—grasped-grasping[13], and so on—all wither.

An empty house might be in darkness for a thousand years
But a lamp dispels it in an instant and likewise

In the instant of realizing your own mind, luminosity[14],
The evil deeds and obscurations accumulated over countless
aeons are purified.

The pure brilliance which is the nature of the sun's essence
Cannot be obscured by the darkness of a thousand aeons
And, likewise, the luminosity which is the essence of your own
mind
Cannot be obscured by the confusion of aeons[15].

Like the sky's nature beyond measure of colour and shape
Does not become tainted by black and white clouds,
Mind's nature beyond measure of colour and shape
Does not become tainted by the black and white of evil and
virtue.

For example, like milk is the cause of butter but,
Until it has been churned, the butter does not arise,
All migrators are the cause, sugatagarbha[16], but,
If they do not practise it, sentient beings do not become buddhas.
If they do practise it, all of them will be liberated
Regardless of the sharpness or dullness of their faculties—
If it is practised, even a cowherd will be liberated[17].

If the fact of your own mind, luminosity, is realized in direct
perception,
There is no need for someone expert in its verbal explanation,
Just as, when you put sugar[18] in your own mouth,
There is no need for an explanation of the taste of sugar.
When just this is not realized, even master scholars remain
confused;
They might be totally expert at explaining the nine vehicles
But their explanations will be like tales of unseen, far away places,
And buddhahood will be even further away for them than the sky
is from the earth[19].

If the authentic[20], your own mind, luminosity, is not realized,
You might keep the disciplines for as long as an aeon and
Might practise patience for a very long time but
Will not lift yourself out of the abodes of three-realmed samsara.
Therefore, you must work hard to cut mind at the root and
eliminate it completely!

❁ ❁ ❁

E MA HO
Now, listen once more, all you excellent fortunate sons!

If the root of your own mind is not resolved,
Any spiritual practice you do will not get to the key point[21].
To give examples: it would be like putting a target before you,
Yet firing the arrow in a direction far from it;

It would be like leaving a thief behind in your house,
While making a strong effort to get rid of him outside;
It would be like leaving a harmful spirit at the eastern door,
While putting the payment to get rid of him to the west;

It would be like a poor man who, not knowing that his
Hearth stones are gold goes begging for alms from others.
Thus, those who are going to resolve the root of mind
Must go about it like this, fortunate heart sons!

The flickering knowing and moving called "mind"
If pursued cannot be captured—it vanishes and vanishes elusive as mist—
And if set in place does not stay put—restless, it flitters about all over the place.
There's no showing it as "this" for it is definitely empty.

This agent who experiences the diversity of happiness and suffering, your mind—
Where initially does it come from, what is its source?
Ask yourself and try to resolve, "Does it have a basis in outer appearances such as
Rocky mountains, rivers, trees, the wind of the sky, and so on
Or is it without such basis—from where does it come?"
Alternatively, you might think, "Did it come from
The semen and blood of the two parents[22]?" in which case you should analyse just how that would occur.

When analysing like that yields no source for it,
Next ask where in the interim of the present moment does it dwell?
Is it dwelling in the upper or lower part of your body,
In your sense faculties, internal organs, heart, and so on?
If it is dwelling in the heart, then, top to bottom, where exactly is it dwelling?
What sort of shape, colour, and so on does it have?

When, having analysed well, you find no dwelling place for it,
Try to resolve at the end when it goes, through which door
Of the object faculties[23] it goes, and, for the mere instant that
It takes to arrive at the external objects, during that time,
Whether it went via the body or via only the mind itself,
Or via body and mind as a combination? Resolve it in these and other ways.

Moreover, when affliction or discursive thought arises[24],
Look to see, "First, from where did it arise?", then for the present time
"Where does it dwell?" and "What colour and shape does it have?"
At the end, when subsiding in its own place it vanishes,
Ask, "Where did it vanish and go?" Try to resolve it in those and other ways.

At the time of death, carefully research to find out what exactly
happens when it departs?
And continue to analyse for as long as you have not arrived at a
certain determination
Of an inexpressible, cleared-out, empty state[25] free of
Birth and death, coming and going, and the identification of
things[26].

The dry examples and verbal explanations of others
Tell you "It is emptiness", but this does not help.
For example, in a place where there are said to be tigers,
Others can tell you that there are no tigers but
That will not be enough to make you believe it,
Leaving you consumed with doubt—it's like that.[27]

When you yourself have determined
The root of your mind through careful research,
It is, for example, like going yourself to that area
Where there are said to be tigers and looking everywhere,
High and low, asking "Are there tigers here?" When, having
resolved the matter like that,
You find no tigers, you trust in that yourself and
Henceforth have none of the doubt that thinks
"Are there tigers there?"—it's like that.

❁ ❁ ❁

E MA HO
Now, listen here once more you fortunate sons!

When you examine and analyse mind as described above,
At the point when you have failed to find so much as a speck of
substantially existing "mind"
That you could point to and say, "This is it",
That not finding is the supreme finding.

Initially, our minds have no source, no place of arising,
Because, being primordially empty, they have no entity that could be identified[28].
In the interim, they have no dwelling place, no shape and colour.
In the end, there is no place to which they go nor a trace left that shows where they went—
Their movement is empty movement, their being empty is empty appearance[29].

This mindness[30] initially was not created by causes
And at the end will not be destroyed by external circumstances.
It has no rise and fall, no being filled and emptied.
Wholly pervading samsara and nirvana, it has no partiality.
Not demonstrable as "This", it shines forth[31] without stoppage[32] as everything whatever;
Not existing as anything whatever, it is beyond the extremes of existence and non-existence.
It is without going and coming, without birth and death, and without clearing and obscuration.

Mind's nature is like a stainless crystal ball—
It sits clearly present[33] as entity empty, nature luminous,
And compassionate activity stoppageless.
It is not tainted at all by the faults of samsara;
Mindness is ascertained to be the primordial buddha.

This has been the introduction which determined
The nature of the actuality[34] of the ground's mindness.

❁ ❁ ❁

E MA HO
Now, listen once more you fortunate mind sons!

First, there is the way that dharmakaya Samantabhadra was liberated
Without having done so much as a speck of meditation,
Then the way that the six migrators wandered into samsara
Without having done so much as a whisker of non-virtue and evil deeds.

In the original primordial beginning prior to all,
Samsara and nirvana, nameless, resided in the primal ground.
This is how rigpa arose from the ground at that time:
As with crystal which has its own light become externally visible[35] on being struck by sunlight,
Propelled by the life-wind of rigpa wisdom[36]
The seal of the youthful vase body was torn open
And spontaneous existence, luminosity[37], became visible as the
Field realms of kayas and wisdoms, like the sun rising in the sky.
At that time, dharmakaya Samantabhadra,
By knowing it to be own appearance[38], in an instant
Had the externalized luminosity kayas and wisdoms dissolve back
Inside and on the alpha purity[39] primal ground was buddha.

We, not knowing the appearances of the nature,
Spontaneous existence, to be our own offput[40],
Developed a blacked-out[41] awareness[42] without thought process
Called "co-emergent ignorance".
Then an awareness which grasped dualistically
At that ground appearance luminosity was produced
Called "nothing-but-conceptualization ignorance"[43]
Now we were in the cocoon of ignorance with dualistic grasping.
Then latencies[44] gradually grew and due to them
All these functions of samsara began.
Then, the afflictions—the three, five,
Eighty-four thousand, and so on poisons—grew and due to them

We began to cycle like a water-wheel through the places of samsara[45]
Where we have till now suffered the misery of pleasure and pain.
If you'd like a longer explanation, look at All-Knowing's *Supreme Vehicle Treasury*[46],
Billowing Clouds of An Ocean of Profound Meaning, and so on.

Now, through the guru's profound foremost instructions,
You have understood the faults inherent in samsara
Then seen your own essence, your own mind of buddha.
You have met the primal guardian face to face.
You are equal in fortune to Samantabhadra.
Cultivate gladness at this deep in your hearts, mind sons!

This has been the introduction which determined confusion.

❀ ❀ ❀

E MA HO
Now, listen once more you fortunate heart sons!

The loud sound of "mind" is universally heard.
As for how it exists, it has not a single existence.
As for how it occurs, it occurs as the whole variety of happiness and suffering of samsara and nirvana.
As for how it is asserted, it is asserted in many ways in the enumerations of the vehicles.
As for how is it named, it is given an inconceivable number of differing names:
Ordinary beings call it "I";
Some tirthikas[47] give it the name "self";
Shravakas call it "selflessness of persons";
Mind Only followers give it the name "mind";
Some call it "prajnaparamita";
Some give it the name "sugatagarbha";

Some give it the name "mahamudra";
Some give it the name "madhyamaka";
Some give it the name "single unique sphere";
Some give it the name "dharmadhatu"[48];
Some give it the name "alaya"[49];
Some give it the name "common awareness"[50].
Regardless of which of the inconceivable names it is given,
Know that what is really being referred to is exactly this:[51]
Set yourselves into mindness relaxed in its own place
And that right there is common awareness naked,
Looking but nothing to be seen's clear presence[52],
Rigpa in direct perception's vividly[53] clear presence,
The non-existence of anything at all empty yet panoramically seen,
The non-duality of luminosity and emptiness sticking out as one thing,
Not permanent, having no existence as anything at all,
Not nihilistic, being clearly present, vividly present,
Not singular, being known and visible as many,
Not many, being inseparability, one taste;
There is nothing else, just exactly this is self-knowing rigpa!

You are seeing the face of the primal guardian
Seated at your heart centre in direct perception.
Do not separate from this, heart sons!

Anyone who asserts that it is not this but something special obtained somewhere else
Is like someone who has the elephant but continues to search for it by following its tracks;
Though he combs the entire third-order world[54],

It will be impossible for him to find so much as the name buddha[55].

This has been the main part's factual introduction to actuality[56].

❁ ❁ ❁

E MA HO
Now, once more, sons of the family listen well!

In this self-knowing self-illumination of the present,
The three kayas—entity, nature, and compassionate activity—
And the five kayas, five wisdoms, and so on all are complete.
Rigpa's entity, with no existence at all as colour, shape, and so on, is empty dharmakaya.
That empty aspect's natural offput, luminosity, is the sambhogakaya.
Its being an unstopped basis from which the variety shines forth is the nirmanakaya[57].
The example used to illustrate this is that
A glass mirror is analogous to the dharmakaya;
Its nature, purity and luminosity[58], shows the sambhogakaya;
Its being an unstopped basis from which the reflections shine forth exemplifies the nirmanakaya.

Migrators are mindness primordially abiding as
The three kayas; if that is self-recognized, then
They, without needing to do so much as a speck
Of meditation, at once become buddhas.

The introduction to the three kayas shows them as separate,
But in fact they are one; other than that, taking them
To be separate is confusion—do not go there, heart sons!
The three kayas being primordially empty are alpha purity—

Understanding them to be a single entity of unified luminosity-emptiness,
Act in the state without grasping!
Threefold entity, nature, and compassionate activity moreover
Are equivalent to dharmakaya, sambhogakaya, and nirmanakaya;
Understanding the three together to be great unified luminosity-emptiness,
Act in the state without grasping!

Then again, this self-arising rigpa wisdom:
By appearing as everything is the Vairochana kaya;
By being changeless is the Akshobyavajra kaya;
By being without centre and edge is the Amitabha kaya;
By being comparable to a jewel that is the source of all
Supreme and ordinary siddhis is the Ratnasambhava kaya;
By being the accomplisher of all purposes is the Amoghasiddhi kaya[59].
Those are not something apart from rigpa's liveliness[60].

Rigpa's wisdom as an unstopped entity:
By being directly perceiving luminosity is mirror wisdom;
By being all-pervasive is equality wisdom;
By being the variety shining forth from liveliness is individually discriminating wisdom;
By being the accomplisher of all purposes is all-accomplishing wisdom;
By containing their entities in alpha purity,
Is dharmadhatu wisdom.
All of them have not a speck of existence apart
From one's own rigpa's liveliness.

If the three kayas of entity, nature, and compassionate activity,
The five kayas, and five wisdoms are introduced
All together at once in direct perception by pointing them out,
Then just this awareness of the present, unmanufactured and unaltered,

Not modified by conditions, not spoiled by grasping—
This clearly present, vividly present rigpa is it!
This is the source of all the buddhas of the three times,
This is the enlightened mind of the buddhas of the three times,
So do not separate from this, all you fortunate ones!

This is uncontrived self-illumination exactly,
So how can you complain that you do not see your own mind, buddha?
Here, there is no meditation is to be done at all,
So how can you complain that your meditation has failed?
This is exactly rigpa directly seen,
So how can you complain that you do not find your own mind?
This is uninterrupted vividly present luminosity exactly,
So how can you complain that you do not see mind's essence?
Here, not so much as a speck of work is to be done,
So how can you complain that your efforts have failed?
This is non-dual abiding and not abiding,
So how can you complain that you are not getting to abiding?
Here is self-knowing's three kayas of spontaneous existence not having conceived endeavours,
So how can you complain that your endeavours at accomplishment yield no result?
Here, with nothing to be done, setting yourself just so[61] is sufficient,
So how can you complain that you are unable to do that?
This here is thought shining forth and being liberated simultaneously,
So how can you complain that antidotes are not working?
This is awareness of the present exactly,
So how can you complain that you do not know it?

❁ ❁ ❁

E MA HO
Now, once more fortunate sons listen with respect!

One's own mind is like the non-thing empty space[62];
To see whether that is so or not all you fortunate sons,
Look straight at your own minds with the approach
That there is nothing to be looked at and let go into vast evenness, then know how it is!

It is not only decided on as empty,
For it is ascertained to be self-knowing wisdom, primordially luminous[63].
It is self-arising self-illumination like the sun's essence;
To see whether that is so or not, look straight at
Your own mindness and let go into vast evenness, then know how it is!

It is ascertained that it cannot be identified as the movement and thinking of discursive thought,
For such movements appear with uncertainty, like breezes;
To see whether that is so or not, look straight at
Your own mindness and let go into vast evenness, then know how it is!

It is ascertained that all of its appearances are own appearance,
All of what appears being like the images in a mirror;
To see whether that is so or not, look straight at
Your own mindness and let go into vast evenness, then know how it is!

There is nothing somewhere other than mind,
So there is no view to be viewed elsewhere.
There is nothing somewhere other than mind,
So there is no meditation to be done anywhere else.
There is nothing somewhere other than mind,
So there is no conduct to be done anywhere else.

There is nothing somewhere other than mind,
So there is no samaya to be kept anywhere else.
There is nothing somewhere other than mind,
So there is no fruition to be accomplished anywhere else.

Look again and look again at your own mind!
Send your mind into the external space of the sky and
Look to see, "Is there coming and going in my own mindness?"
When you have looked, if you find that mind does not have
going and coming,
Look inwardly at your internal mind and
Look to see, "Is there an agent who emits the emitted thoughts?"
If there is no agent who emits the emitted thoughts,
Look to see, "Does mind have colour, shape, and so on?"
When you connect with its being empty of colour and shape,
Look to see, "Does the emptiness have centre and edge?"
When you find no centre and edge, look to see, "Does it have
inside and outside?"
Rigpa without outside and inside is vast like space,
Transparent[64] in its freedom from delimitation and falling into
sides,
A vast great interior space of self-knowing, everywhere-spread.
Within it, the whole variety of the phenomena of samsara and
nirvana appear like rainbows floating in space,
Yet that whole variety is the play of mind.
Look out from this state without moving from self-knowing
rigpa and see that
All phenomena, like illusions and moons in water,
Are an appearance-emptiness not separable into parts.
In the state of rigpa, samsara and nirvana are non-dual;
Look out from this state without moving from self-knowing
rigpa and see that
The phenomena of samsara and nirvana, like images in a mirror,
Appear as they do but primally never know existence.
All phenomena of samsara and nirvana, nameless, are the
dharmakaya.

The migrators who wander in three-realmed samsara,
Not realizing their own entity, the wisdom in which
All the phenomena of samsara and nirvana are equally present,
Are under the control of the confusion of dualistic grasping.
Thus they apprehend phenomena individually and because of dualistic grasping are not liberated into the non-dual fact.
Every one of them has a mind which is samsara and nirvana inseparable
Yet their engagement in abandonment-adoption, rejection-adoption[65] causes them to wander in samsara.

All the migrators who, in their stupidity and lack of knowledge, seek the levels and paths
Using methods which are not this self-knowing rigpa, three kaya, conceived-endeavours-less spontaneous-existence,
Methods that take them elsewhere very far way,
Do not ever arrive at the level of a buddha.

It is ascertained that all that appears is own appearance.
Look out from a state not moving from self-knowing rigpa
And see that all of appearance and existence[66] is like reflected images—
Sights seen yet empty and sounds heard yet empty, it has the nature of being primordially empty.

Look in like that at the mind doing the looking and
The thoughts of the thought process self-vanish, leaving an empty experience like space
Which is elaboration-less, elaboration-free[67], beyond verbal and mental expression.

All that appears is mind's trickery[68];
All of the trickery is baseless, empty.
If you realize that all of it is your own mind,
All appearances seen are empty, the dharmakaya.

One is not bound by appearance, one is bound by clinging;
Sever the confusion of clinging and attachment, heart sons!

❀ ❀ ❀

E MA HO
Excellent mind sons of good fortune:
Since a horse not struck with a whip
Does not reach the speed of a donkey,
Milk not churned a great deal
Does not produce butter,
And nothing is determined without precise explanations,
This song comes with many words.
However, do not be irritated, listen with a glad mind!

If you do not know that all appearances are mind
You will never realize the meaning of emptiness,
So examine and analyse well, all you fortunate sons:
Where initially do these appearances arise,
Where in the interim do they dwell, and where at the end do they go?

When examined, you will find that, like mist in the sky
Arises from the sky and goes back again to the sky,
Appearances, mind's trickery,
Shine forth in one's mind and go back into mind.

To give an example for this: a person whose eye faculty is impaired
Will, on looking up into the sky, see floaters[69]—
There appears to be something there in the sky but
There is not, it is just the eye's trickery.
Similarly, the bad latencies of grasping at things
In tandem with the mind faculty being impaired,
Make it seem as though every one of the fictional[70] phenomena

Seen and heard do truly exist there,
Yet primally they do not have so much as a speck of existence as things—
All are the trickery of one's own mind.
All this trickery is baseless, empty.
It does not exist yet obviously appears, like an illusion and a moon in water,
So put yourself in equipoise on the fact of appearance-emptiness inseparable!

Now, in our dreams during sleep we directly see
The appearances of homeland, dwelling, close ones, and so on
And so experience happiness and sadness, yet
At the time not a single one of those things dear to us is present.
We have not moved even a little from our beds, yet
We experience them as directly as we would in our waking day.
Similarly, all of the appearances of this life
Are like the experiences of last night's dream.
One's own mind labels everything, grasps at that, and then
Appearance happens accordingly; everything is experienced because of mind.
Dreams occurring during sleep are without nature[71] and
Similarly, appearances, however they occur, are empty.

❁ ❁ ❁

E MA HO
Only sons of mind, you of good fortune!

All appearances are indefinite;
Where for some there is brightness, for others there is darkness.
Moreover, for some sentient beings and this world:
There are sentient beings who perceive earth as earth,
There are sentient beings who perceive earth as a fire,
There are sentient beings who perceive earth as useful,

There are sentient beings who perceive earth as suffering.
There are sentient beings who perceive water as water,
There are sentient beings who perceive water at fire,
There are sentient beings who perceive water as nectar,
There are sentient beings who perceive water as a dwelling,
There are sentient beings who perceive water as earth.
There are sentient beings who perceive fire as fire,
There are sentient beings who perceive fire as useful,
There are sentient beings who perceive fire as a dwelling,
There are sentient beings who perceive fire as food.
There are sentient beings who perceive space as space,
There are sentient beings who perceive space as a dwelling,
There are sentient beings who perceive space as earth.
Thus appearances are not definite and the reason is that
Controlled by latencies they appear as they do.
Correspondingly, humans perceive each
Of the four elements as they do.

Moreover, other migrators perceive this world
As hell's fires, a place for the use of farmers, and,
For those with a depressed mind, as suffering.
Similarly, fire is perceived as something for the fire god's use,
Pretas having a body of fire perceive it as a dwelling,
And fireflies perceive it as something to eat.
Similarly, water is perceived by hell's migrators as fire,
By preta sentient beings as pus and blood,
By elephants as the ground, and by gods as nectar.
For the Gods who Control Other's Emanations it is jewels and
Rains of flowers, and for nagas a dwelling.
When space is treated like that, it is an abode
Which all the gods perceive as a ground.
That being so, everything is labelled by oneself
Then appears in accordance with however it was labelled.

Moreover, when Devaputra asked the Buddha[72]
"Who made Mt. Meru, the sun, moon, and so on?",

The Buddha replied,
"They have no other creator at all.
The concretization of the latencies of one's own thoughts
Labels that, grasps at that, and then it appears as such.
Everything has been made by one's own mind".
When Devaputra further asked the Buddha,
"Aside from how one's own thoughts are concretized,
Where did this sort of solid and firm
Mt. Meru, sun, moon, and so on come from?"
The Buddha replied,
"In Vāraṇāsi, an old woman imagined her body
As a tiger and the village,
On seeing her as such, was emptied.
If she could make that appearance happen in a short time,
Habituation to the mind of latencies since births without beginning
Could indeed produce this sort of appearance!" So said the Capable One[73].
That being so, everything has been made by mind.

Moreover, there is the story of one outsider tirthika who,
In order to stop the distractions of worldly entertainments,
Imagined an isolated place thereby actually producing
An isolated place that could be seen by other humans.
And there is the story of a person who meditated on space being solid as rock
and, it having turned into rock, his body was trapped.
That being so, everything has been made by mind's thoughts,
So all of it is mind's own appearance and
All own appearance in fact is empty.

Moreover, the sentient beings of the transient hells
Perceive their bodies as form—doors, pillars, stoves, ropes,
And so on—and experience suffering because of it.
That being so, however mind's thought
Makes a label, it appears like that to others.[74]

All of the happinesses and sufferings of the six migrator
Sentient beings are made solely by their own minds.
Thus, everything is the trickery of one's own mind.
Therefore, decide with total confidence that all of it is
Non-existent appearance, emptiness's own forms, and let go into vast evenness!

Moreover, it was taught, "The Capable One Great Snow Lake
Has on a single pistil of the lotus in his hand
The third-order world Endurance[75]."
It was taught that at the time of Direct Crossing's rigpa having reached full measure[76],
"In each body pore of one's own body
Immeasurable buddha field realms will be seen and
Limitless six migrator sentient beings' abodes also will be seen.
Migrator-taming emanations will be distributed to them
And will act in a dream-like way to benefit them."
That being so, the phenomena of samsara and nirvana are own appearance
And all of own appearance is groundless, empty.
Develop a concept-based assurance of the empty yet luminous grasping-less state[77].

Furthermore, it was taught, "On one single atom there are
As many as there atoms—unfathomable numbers—of buddha field-realms
And there are also countless six migrators' abodes."
The conqueror taught that, "None of them
Mix with, contaminate, or damage any of the others."

Furthermore, it was taught, "In the interior of each insect,
There are unfathomable cities of insects."

It was taught, "In the space element there are
An unfathomable number of cities where
Many cities face downwards and

Similarly many face sideways and also upwards."
If you wonder who made these kinds of things,
The conqueror taught that everything has been made by mind.

Know that mind's nature primally is like space
And that all phenomena are likewise!
Every one of all the fictional phenomena—sights and sounds[78]—
Are the own appearance solely of one's own mindness;
Therefore, when at death one's mindstream changes,
It is not a change in external appearances but a change in own appearance.
That being so, everything is mind's own appearance and
All the own appearance is groundless, empty.
Its non-existent yet evident appearance is like a reflected image and moon in water;
Preserve the experience of the state of non-dual luminous-empty rigpa![79]

All appearance seen is mind's own appearance.
The appearance of the material container worlds is mind.
The appearance of the six classes of contained sentient beings also is mind.
The appearance of the happiness of the gods and men in the upper levels also is mind.
The appearance of suffering of the three bad migrations[80] also is mind.
The appearance of ignorance's afflicted five poisons also is mind.
The appearance of self-arising wisdom rigpa also is mind.
The appearance of the latencies of bad-thought samsara also is mind.
The appearance of good-thought buddha field realms, also is mind.
The appearance of obstacles created by maras and demons also is mind[81].
The appearance of good deities and spiritual attainments also is mind.

The appearance of various discursive thoughts also is mind.
The appearance of no-thought one-pointed meditation also is mind.
The appearance of things, concept tokens[82], and colours also is mind.
The absence of concept tokens and elaborations also is mind.
The appearance of non-duality of one and many also is mind.
The appearance of there being no establishment at all of existence and non-existence also is mind.
Except for what comes from mind, there is no appearance whatsoever.

Mind is comparable to an artist:
One's own body is made by mind
And moreover all the third-order world realms,
As many as there are, are drawn by mind.
Furthermore, these drawings made by one's own thought
Deceive all migrators with their childish rational minds[83].
That being so, it is very important to develop the certainty
Of having decided that everything is the trickery of mind.

This has been the introduction to discursive thought as mind.

❁ ❁ ❁

E MA HO
Now, listen once more, all you supreme mind sons!

Even the buddhas did not teach that
The agent, one's own mindness,
Has an identifiable entity of colour, shape, and so on.
Mindness is ascertained to be empty, groundless,
Like primordially empty, grasping-less, space.
Mindness is illustrated with the example of space but
That serves only to illustrate the empty side.

Mindness, which has knowing rigpa, is empty and shines forth in every which way.
Space, without knowing rigpa, is a cut-off emptiness, a blankness[84];
Therefore, mindness cannot fully be illustrated by space.
This has been the introduction to mindness being empty.

From the self-liveliness of that luminous-empty mindness
The whole variety of appearance shines forth.
It shines forth but, like the images in a mirror,
It is non-dual, one with the state of being empty.
This has been the introduction to the empty aspect being apparent.

Primordially it is non-dual appearance-emptiness;
One's own mind being empty, appearance occurs without stoppage, and
Appearance without grasping glitters while being the empty state.
Appearances do not stop the empty aspect and
Even as they appear their nature is one of being primordially empty.

For the yogin who realizes non-dual appearance-emptiness
Like a rainbow in the sky and the form of a moon in water,
The phenomena of samsara and nirvana are an illusory spectacle.
When viewing this non-dual apparent while empty spectacle,
The rational mind of the yogin whose mind is changeless is at ease.
To see whether it is so or not, all you fortunate sons
Look to see "Can the two aspects, the emptiness and appearance,
Of your minds be separated out?" and know how it is!
Primordially they are appearance-emptiness non-dual.
This has been the introduction to non-dual appearance-emptiness.

That non-dual appearing-while-empty self-arising rigpa,
Self-illumining, clearly present, vividly present,
Three kayas spontaneously-existing type of mind,
Must, mind sons, be preserved day and night in
Around the clock practice without division into sessions and breaks!
This has been the introduction to non-dual self-liberation.

❁ ❁ ❁

E MA HO
Now, listen once more to this song of mine, a man who has abandoned activity!

There is the way that the three kayas are complete in ground's rigpa and
The way that the three kayas are complete at the time of ground appearances,
And when this pair of distinctions has been properly comprehended,
Samsara and nirvana will be understood to be the field of the three kayas.[85]

Although the way that the three kayas are complete in ground's rigpa
Was explained earlier, it will be explained here again.
The self-knowing ground is comparable to a crystal ball:
Its being empty is the dharmakaya's nature;
Its natural offput of luminosity is the sambhogakaya; and
Its being an unstopped basis of shining forth is the nirmanakaya.
That is the way in which the three kayas are complete within the ground's rigpa.
In this, there is never any meeting and parting[86].

Then, as in the example of five lights shining forth from a crystal,
At the time of ground appearances shining forth from it[87], all of whatever shines forth—
Purity, the appearances of the conquerors' field-realms,
And impurity, the appearances of containers and contents—
Has an empty entity which is the dharmakaya,
A nature of appearance which is the sambhogakaya,
And an unstopped variety which is the nirmanakaya.
And that is the way that the three kayas are complete at the time of ground appearances.
This distinction, which is not much made in other places,
Is a key point that must be properly understood.
For myself, I've understood it through the kindness of All-Knowing's excellent explanations.

When known like that, the whole of appearance and existence
Primordially is the spontaneously existing mandala of the three kayas and
There is no seeking the three kayas in some other field realm.
The six migrator sentient beings moreover abide as
The three kayas and if they are able to self-recognize this,
Then, without needing to do so much as a speck of meditation,
The migrators all will become buddhas.

Moreover, in actual fact, the ground's three kayas also are
The dharmakaya, so do not conceive of them as separate!
The three kayas of the time of ground appearance also are
The form kayas, so do not conceive of them as separate!
The dharma and form kayas are two but in actual fact they are not separate,
They are one taste in the state of empty dharmakaya.

Ultimately, ground appearances dissolve of themselves back into the ground then
Ground dharmakaya's mind becomes manifest
At which time the factual fruition has become manifest.

Then, while not wavering from dharmakaya's space,
Both types of form kaya are shown just like rainbows,
And the enactment of benefit for migrators goes on continuously.

❀ ❀ ❀

E MA HO
Now, listen once more to this song of mine, a man who has abandoned activity!

In the past you have been harmed.
Bring to mind in detail all the ways that others
Have done this to you, mulling over
How they have bullied, hit and beaten, and
Humiliated you, and acted to make you feel bad.
Allow yourself to become angry and then,
Looking straight at what it is, ask,
"This agent[88] anger, first from where does it arise? And then in the present time
Where does it dwell? And at the end, where does it go?
Does it have colour, shape, and so on?"
When you look, it is primordially empty, grasping-less.
Un-abandoned, anger is mirror wisdom.

Bring to mind in detail and mull over the ways in which
You so badly want a beautiful woman,
And want meat and foods which you find tasty,
And want clothes and good things nice to wear,
And want the wealth of horses and other fine possessions.
Allow yourself to become desirous and then,
Looking straight at what it is, ask,
"This agent desire, first from where does it arise? And then in the present time
Where does it dwell? And at the end, where does it go?

Does it have colour, shape, and so on?"
When you look, it is primordially empty, grasping-less.
Un-abandoned, desire is discriminating wisdom.

Allow yourselves to become deluded as you do in sleep,
Sinking and dullness, and so on, and then,
Looking straight at what it is, ask,
"This agent delusion, first from where does it arise? And then in the present time
Where does it dwell? And at the end, where does it go?
Does it have colour, shape, and so on?"
When you look, it is primordially empty, grasping-less.
Un-abandoned, delusion is dharmadhatu wisdom.

Bring to mind in detail the extent of your qualities—
The strength of your family line,
Your very fine form and beautiful tone of voice,
Your ability at threefold hearing, contemplation, and meditation, and reading and writing,
Your great knowledge and your ability to perform village rites, and so on.
Allow yourself to have the pride of thinking
"I am a little better than others" and then,
Looking straight at what it is, ask,
"This agent pride, first from where does it arise? And then in the present time
Where does it dwell? And at the end, where does it go?
Does it have colour, shape, and so on?"
When you look, it is primordially empty, grasping-less.
Un-abandoned, pride is equality wisdom.

Allow the jealousy of being concerned that others are higher than you to arise
Through bringing to mind in detail all the good qualities of others—
Those whose family strengths are greater than yours,

Who are filled with good qualities and who have more disciples,
Who are more knowledgeable, better at reciting aloud, and have
a finer voice,
Who understand dharma, know worldly stories, and so on.
Then, looking straight at what it is, ask,
"This agent jealousy, first from where does it arise? And then in
the present time
Where does it dwell? And at the end, where does it go?
Does it have colour, shape, and so on?"
When you look, it is primordially empty, grasping-less.
Un-abandoned, jealousy is all-accomplishing wisdom.

If you realize it like that, affliction is wisdom.
On the other hand, casting aside the realization of affliction
Then seeking emptiness and wisdom from there is just ludicrous;
I feel pity for anyone who seeks it like that then does not find it!
It is this way: after knowing that the five poisons are empty,
The five poisons henceforth shine forth as realized five poisons,
Removing the need for the analysis explained in this introduction
Of birthplace, dwelling-place, destination, and colour and shape.
The five poisons already having been understood to be empty,
Immediately they shine forth, set yourself in not following them
But letting them relax in their own place in the state of mindness;
There is no doubt that they will go on to vanish of themselves.
This has been both introduction and training[89].

It is like this: if training has been done beforehand,
Then when the five poisonous afflictions do shine forth,
The force of having already understood their faults
Will cause both emptiness and wisdom to shine forth
simultaneously, with the result that
The afflictions will enter a process of shining forth and being
liberated at the same time!
Understand this to fit with what has been said
In the life stories of the forefather gurus—
"Many afflicted thoughts, many chances for dharmakaya!"

For the beginner, when afflicted minds appear intensely,
It is good to do analysis then resting—
This is my personal instruction, so keep it in mind!

This has been the introduction to the self-liberation of the five poisons.

❁ ❁ ❁

E MA HO
Now, listen once more sons who are like my heart!

Wrap smooth things like clothing, and so on around your body and
Look at your mind's thought "It is smooth".
Wrap rough things like serge, and so on around your body and
Look at your mind's thought "It is rough".
On looking, both are equal taste in being empty.

Look at beautiful forms like golden statues, and so on and
Look at your mind's thought "It is beautiful".
Look at ugly forms like frogs, and so on and
Look at your mind's thought "It is ugly".
On looking, both are equal taste in being empty.

Take good-tasting things into your mouth, like sugar, and so on and
Look at your mind's thought "It is sweet".
Take things into your mouth like ginger, and so on and
Look at your mind's thought "It is foul".
On looking, both are equal taste in being empty.

Smell nice smells like sandalwood incense, and so on and
Look at your mind's thought "It is nice".
Smell bad smells such as asafoetida, garlic, and so on and

Look at your mind's thought "It is rank".
On looking, both are equal taste in being empty.

Listen to the sounds of a bell, vina[90], and flute and
Look at your own mind's thought "It is pleasant".
Listen to the sounds of stones and hands being clapped together and
Look at your mind's thought "It is unpleasant".
On looking, both are equal taste in being empty.

Meditate on being born as a wheel-wielding king who
Governs a realm of the four continents[91] and is
Surrounded by a retinue of many queens and ministers
And, in a palace made of the five precious substances[92],
Eats food having one hundred flavours.
When this appears in mind,
Look at your mind's thought "It is pleasant".
Meditate on having become poor, without a single helper,
With a bed in a broken down shack with earthen walls,
The rain coming in from above and moisture coming up from the ground beneath,
Your body struck by many illnesses, such as leprosy, and the like,
And your hands and feet gone. You have so many difficulties
That you experience unremitting suffering.
When that sort of appearance has been brought to mind,
Look at your mind's thought "It is suffering".
On looking, pleasure and pain are equal taste in being empty.

It is like this: the sixfold group is known to be empty beforehand[93]
Then after that, however it shines forth, whether good or bad,
Analysis as explained in this introduction will be unnecessary.
Because it is groundless, primordially liberated, empty,
Just as it shines forth, do not follow after it but

Set yourself into letting it relax in its own place in the state of mindness;
There is no doubt that it will go on to vanish of itself.

This has been the introduction to the sixfold group self-liberating.

❁ ❁ ❁

E MA HO
Now, once more listen well sons of the family!

Set yourselves so that your minds are relaxed, allowed to be themselves, then
Look at how they are when they abide!
Fortunate mind sons, having looked, understand that,
Because this is abiding in rigpa's state,
This is the abiding yet empty state of rigpa!
That was the introduction to how abiding is an ornament of mind.

For the elaboration of discursive thoughts, look at
The way in which they are emitted and then
Fortunate sons of the family understand that,
Because there is not so much as the slightest shift
Away from that state of empty-luminous rigpa,
This is the emitting but empty state of rigpa!
That is the introduction to emitting, the play of mind.

For example, a wave that appears on an ocean
Does not shift in the slightest from being the ocean;
Likewise, mind whether it abides or moves does not
Shift in the slightest being from rigpa-emptiness.

Thus, whichever way mind abides, take that as being the state of rigpa;
Whichever way it shines forth, take that as being the offput of rigpa!

The assertions that mind when abiding is meditation and
That mind when emitting is not meditation,
With their failure to appreciate the faults inherent in both abiding and movement,
Signify that threefold abiding, movement, and knowing rigpa have not been merged into one.
Therefore, all of you excellent fortunate mind sons,
For us there is the state of rigpa in which abiding and movement are equally fine.
Thus, with these points absorbed beforehand,
Practise threefold abiding, moving, and knowing rigpa as one!

This has been the introduction to emitting and abiding being non-dual.

❁ ❁ ❁

E MA HO
Only mind sons, you who are fortunate,
Listen here with undistracted and attentive ears!

The singer of this song, I, Tshogdrug Rangrol who has abandoned activities,
Have a melodious song pleasant to hear, so take it into your snow-white minds.

When all phenomena have been determined to be one-taste in being empty,
Samsara and nirvana are freed of abandonment-adoption,
The confusion of grasping at enemies and friends is destroyed,

And there are none of the appearances that come with
dualistically grasping at self and other,
Because everything has been realized to be one-taste in being
empty.

Here is a summation of the essential points of extensive
explanations:
In the pinnacle of vehicles, Great Completion,
All of samsara and nirvana are free of ground and root;
Primordially buddhahood, they are one taste in the dharmakaya.
In the state of Great Completion, there is no duality of gods and
demons;
In the land of Great Completion, there are no buddhas and
sentient beings;
In the ground of Great Completion, there is no good and bad;
In the path of Great Completion, there is no near and far;
In the fruition of Great Completion, there is no attained and not
attained;
In the dharma of Great Completion, there is no doing and not
doing the conduct;
In the fact of Great Completion, there is no meditating and not
meditating;
Stay like that, which is the Great Completion king of views.

When you realize that sort of Great Completion view,
All of the coarse and subtle thoughts of the three doors are
pacified
And you remain, like wool to which water has been applied[94],
In a state in which your three doors are pacified and tamed.
The samadhis of bliss, luminosity, and no-thought arise and,
For all the migrators wandering in samsara who have not realized
such,
An uncontrived compassion like the love a mother has for an
only son is produced.
Those are special features of the Great Completion view[95], so
know that too!

After you have firmly decided that everything is emptiness,
If you develop a conduct in which you abandon virtue and do not avoid evil deeds,
That will be the view of the mara of bad action run wild.
Keep yourself falling under the control of the view of that sort of mara!
These are the introductions of Great Completion.

These introductions are extremely important:
While you have not realized that every one of
All the external fictional visible and audible phenomena are emptiness,
You might think you are meditating in the view but what meditation is it?
Therefore, first you should proceed like this:
Sometimes look while supplicating the guru and
Sometimes look carefully while relaxing and tightening.
When you look in that way, your mind will be glad and
Everything will be shining forth while obviously empty.
There will definitely be the birth of a deep certainty in which you
Think "I can touch the objects of external appearances
With my hand but there is nothing to apprehend there"
And "This is definitely the view."
This is the time of discovering certainty of the view.
Do not spoil it with grasping; relax into a state without grasping.

Even if you do not practise after having received the introduction[96],
At the time of death no matter which fears arise in the bardo,
You will know that everything is own appearance, the own forms of emptiness, and
You will become buddha in the alpha purity ground.
To practise without having received the introduction
Will be like the example of someone who is mistaken on the first day of the month
Being still being mistaken on the fifteenth day of the month.

When you have not realized that all fictional phenomena are truthless,
What a huge lie it is to say, "I have realized emptiness."

Thus, this sort of introduction must first be received while sitting in front of the guru
So that it is determined based on what is real—then you won't go down a mistaken path.
Therefore, fortunate sons keep this advice in your hearts!

❁ ❁ ❁

E MA HO
Now, once more fortunate sons of the family, listen!

When you have taken in that actuality of the view,
Sever all ties of attachment and aversion to people and homeland.
Alone in forest tracks and mountain valleys,
Give up endeavours of the body and let it be natural;
Cut talk and other expressions of speech, and stay silent;
Allow mind to be like space, beyond the realm of thinking.
Relax in that state without addition or subtraction[97].

If there is no focus in mind, that is the view[98].
Stay in the state in which there is no meditation to be done!
Attain the fruition of attainment-less Great Completion!
Moreover, when you set yourself in equipoise on the view,
Do not catch yourself in nets of thought such as
"This is how to rest in the state of rigpa!" or
"I am falling under the control of sinking and agitation!"
Instead, set yourself relaxed in the state absent of the things of referenced focus, a state clear and open, free of restrictions,
A state of transparency, free to be as it pleases[99].

You cannot see the fact beyond rational mind using the stuff of rational mind and
You cannot reach the activity-less place with the stuff of activity,
So, if you want to attain the beyond rational mind, activity-less fact,
Instead of engaging in the spoilage of contrivance, set yourself in naked rigpa[100].

That is the supreme, free of all grasped-grasping view.
That is the supreme, absent of abandonment-adoption meditation.
That is the supreme, beyond conceived-endeavour conduct.
That is the supreme, hope-free self-abiding fruition.

It is not seen by looking at a view, so put aside all searching for the view!
It is not discovered by meditation, so cast away the referenced foci of thinking with grasping.
It is not accomplished by conduct, so let go of grasping at illusions.
It is not gained by seeking it, so leave aside hopes of a fruition.

The awareness of the present is un-manufactured and hanging loose, so
Do not engage in biasses, do not spoil it with grasping!

This rigpa of non-thing which is luminous—
Just this is the pinnacle of all views.
This freedom from rational mind smeared all over with referenced foci—
Just this is the pinnacle of all meditation.
This placement in uncontrived grasping-less looseness—
Just this is the pinnacle of all conduct.
This unsought primordially spontaneously-existing situation—
Just this is the pinnacle of all fruition.

Look at the heart of the view, empty luminosity without grasping!
Preserve the heart of meditation, self-liberation without grasping!
Set yourself in the heart of conduct, the sixfold group left loose!
The heart of the fruition is the collapse of hope and fear.

If you are free of bounding extremes, that is the supreme king of views.
If you are free of vacillatory foci[101], that is the supreme king of meditation.
If you are free of accepting and rejecting, that is the supreme king of conduct.
If you are free of hope and fear, that is the supreme king of fruition.

Since there is nothing to view, cast off referenced foci of the view.
Since there is nothing to meditation on, let whatever arises do as it pleases.
Since there is no conduct to be done, release suppression and furtherance[102], abandonment and adoption.
Since there is nothing to be attained, leave aside hopes for a fruition.

By letting what it[103] is be, do not engage in grasping on its account.
By being without "This is it", do not engage in suppression and furtherance.
By being without vacillatory foci, do not engage in biasses.

In primal purity's self-knowing self-illumination,
Because it is beyond rational mind's objects of thought, there is nothing to view;
Because its entity is free of a ground, there is nothing to meditate on;

Because it is self-liberation beyond extremes, there is no conduct to be done;
Because it is beyond the clinging that goes with conceived endeavours' accomplishment, there is no fruition.

Because the entity is emptiness, there is no abandonment and no attainment.
Because the nature is luminosity-emptiness, conceived endeavours' accomplishment has collapsed.
Because everything is stoppageless, there are no biasses.
No matter which way it shines forth, do not grasp at it being so!

A yogin's awareness is comparable to a bird's path in the sky.
As with a bird's trace which is not visible because of having ceased to begin with,
Thinking and thought cannot be seen because of having ceased to begin with,
So do not attempt to continue them by grasping at following after them!
As with a bird's trace which is nothing because of not happening afterwards,
Do not go out to greet thinking and thought afterwards!
As with a bird's trace which in the present has no colour and shape,
The thinking and thought of the present in the end goes its own way,
So do not create the spoilage of contrivance by using an antidote directed at "it".

No matter how it shines forth, do not grasp at it being like that!
This is the ultimate heart instruction for bringing it to the path:
No matter which way it shines forth, if you do not grasp at it being like that,
Affliction, vanishing of itself, is great wisdom.

It is a birthless beyond-thought primordially-liberated view,
So if you work hard at it, there will be no view of it.
It is a relaxation-into-being-left-to-be-itself naturally-occurring meditation,
So if you work hard at it, there will be no meditation on it.
It is a non-duality of abandonment-adoption illusory conduct,
So if you work hard at it, there will be no conduct of it.
It is a non-duality-of-hope-and-fear nature of fruition,
So if you work hard at it, there will be no fruition.

This mindness, being free of root of the three times,
Unmeditated, directly appears—what a happy event!
Phenomena from beginning to end are by nature pure,
Primordially liberated, wholly liberated, with all conceived effort-endeavours collapsed—how wondrous!

This common awareness left un-manufactured and hanging loose
Is the conqueror's mind, extreme-free, a wide-open interior space.
Moreover, analysis and meditation done with conceived efforts
Will not make mindness, actuality, the innate, become visible.
In the uncontemplated, unanalysed, common dharmata[104],
There is no meditating and not meditating, no being distracted and not distracted—
It is through unmeditated looseness that many have been liberated.

Liberation and non-liberation are non-dual in its fact.
If you know actuality, whether you make conceived endeavours or not, mind remains at ease.
If you are bound by thought that wants to be without thought,
Discursive thought having risen up, it will try its best to go all over the place.
If, on the basis of the innate character which is rigpa without coming and going,

You relax into letting it do what it wants, then, having given it the freedom to do as it pleases,
It will stay put, unmoving, steady as a mountain.
Sons, understand its perverse ways!

The point to be most highly treasured is that, for this, there is no reference to even a speck of meditation to be done,
Nevertheless, it must be kept in place, without distraction, by mindfulness.

❁ ❁ ❁

E MA HO
Now, listen here once more, fortunate sons!

This own-form of appearance-emptiness without external object,
Because it is primordially empty, comparable to a moon in water, does not need to be cleansed.
The internal thoughts of the thinking process vanish of themselves, without trace,
So it is not necessary to apply the antidotes of effort-filled endeavours to them.
The appearing mind, which is primordially-liberated hanging-loose wisdom,
Does not need the superimposition of any abandonment-adoption, hope and fear, at all.
For this directly seen, naked, rigpa,
Do not dress it in the clothes of mental analysis's elaborations[105] but
Relax yourself into its being just as it is, just what it is, evanescent, and traceless[106],
In bias-less great equality.

In that state, whichever ideas of the thought process shine forth,
Know all of them to be bias-less self-arising rigpa's own offput,

And then, instead of following after them,
If you let the jingling and jangling, blaring on and off,
Elusive comings and goings of appearing mind[107]
Be a vast sameness of the dharmata's shifting events[108],
You will have arrived at Samantabhadra's mind space.
That is referred to as "Great Completion, the yoga of self-liberation
Of the whole variety produced in primordially-liberated spontaneous-existence".

You have not gone anywhere, yet have arrived at the level of a buddha.
You have not accomplished anything, yet your fruition is spontaneously existing.
You have left the afflictions un-abandoned, and now they purified in their own place.
Your mind is equal to the mind of the holy gurus.
You have followed after them and completed all works.
There is this key point, so sons, you should know it!

Through the kindness of the old father, Chokyi Gyalpo,
I, Tshogdrug Rangrol, the man whose sixfold group is self-liberated, have arrived
At the mind of activity-free spontaneous existence.

There is this key point, though some do not understand it.
Everything is already primordially done but they say "I will do it!"
Everything is already primordially liberated but they say "I will liberate it!"
Everything is already primordially in equipoise but they say "I will enter equipoise on it!"
Everything is already primordially in meditation but they say "I will meditate on it!"
Everything is already primordially seen but they say "I will see it!"

Everything is already primordially traversed but they say "I will traverse it!"
Speaking like that, they are people who put their hopes in a mental analysis type of view.
They have learning, but being theoretical, dead words only, it is discursive thought;
They have realization, but being a result of can-do meditation[109], it is a product of rational mind;
They have analysis but being a dualistic accomplishment, it is samsaric.
These people who approach dharmata through mental analysis
Certainly have no karmic connection to Quintessence Great Completion.
Engaging in activity is not necessary; doing so does not achieve it.
It is beyond the accounting of acting and not acting.
In non-meditation beyond meditation, meditation only ruins it.
In non-viewing beyond viewing, what will be viewed?
In non-seeking beyond seeking, there is no finding.
Rigpa is present with transparency; that's how it is.
The person who has that explained but does not listen,
Has no karmic connection to Great Completion, how ridiculous!

Wherever you look, since it is the mind of alpha purity great space
Shining forth, samsara and nirvana are without duality.
Having put the mind of that sort into song,
The conquerors of the three times will be pleased, no doubt!

If you ask, "But, having given confusion's externally appearing objects
The freedom to go to their own place,
Won't one return to being confused again?"
An ordinary person grasps at a self in them and so is confused;
A yogin, knowing them to be groundless, root-free,

Does not treat them with contrivance-spoiled adoption and rejection but
Leaves them to be themselves, without grasping, and so is unconfused.
If you then ask, "Is there a point in this where one could deviate?"
The answer is no, there is not a single point of deviation nor mistake in it.
Points of deviation happen when there is clinging and attachment[110];
If there is no grasping at what shines forth,
Where could there be a point of deviation to fall into?
Still, there is the point that, at the time when rigpa shines forth as an object,
The meditation of viewing the entity of the discursive thinking is not what is proclaimed;
What is to be preserved is the rigpa of that time's
Factor of being naked and clearly present.
Furthermore, when rigpa is not emitting-withdrawing[111],
When it is abiding, it is not the no-thought abiding factor
Itself that is the actual meditation—
At that time, the factor which is the strength of the luminous pure part
Which at that time is vividly present and clear is what is to be preserved.
Not having understood this key point, if you think
"The viewing of both abiding and shining forth is the entity of meditation",
Then you have become confused, heart sons!
Mere abiding is the same as the dhyana of the gods[112] and
Mere shining forth is the same as ordinary thought.
You could meditate in those ways but you would not attain buddhahood.
In short, for as long as the rigpa factor
Being naked, transparent, and comparable to a crystal ball

Has not become interior space, you must preserve its clear presence!
When it has, do not be separated from that state!

The main issue of Thorough Cut's view stated as
"Rigpa is to be stripped naked then have its clear presence preserved",
Is the particular key point that is of the greatest importance—
It is the central issue of a hundred statements about the subject because of which
You fortunate heart sons must know it!

❁ ❁ ❁

E MA HO
Now, once more fortunate sons listen with respect!

The four great spotlights that unmistakenly illuminate are as follows[113].
The great spotlight of view without mistake
Is exactly this awareness of the present clearly present;
Because it illuminates this un-mistakenly it is called "a spotlight".
The great spotlight of meditation without mistake
Is exactly this awareness of the present clearly present;
Because it illuminates this un-mistakenly it is called "a spotlight".
The great spotlight of conduct without mistake
Is exactly this awareness of the present clearly present;
Because it illuminates this un-mistakenly it is called "a spotlight".
The great spotlight of fruition without mistake
Is exactly this awareness of the present clearly present;
Because it illuminates this un-mistakenly it is called "a spotlight".

The four great nails that make an unchanging situation are as follows.
The great nail of changeless view

Is exactly this awareness of the present clearly present;
Because it is steady through the three times, it is called "a nail".
The great nail of changeless meditation
Is exactly this awareness of the present clearly present;
Because it is steady through the three times, it is called "a nail".
The great nail of changeless conduct
Is exactly this awareness of the present clearly present;
Because it is steady through the three times, it is called "a nail".
The great nail of changeless fruition
Is exactly this awareness of the present clearly present;
Because it is steady through the three times, it is called "a nail".

There are a vast number of differing views,
But in the self-knowing rigpa self-arising wisdom of the present
There is no duality of view and viewer.
Do not look at the view but seek the viewing agent.
If the viewing agent having been sought is not found,
At that time, the view is reaching the exhaustion point.
This view in which there is nothing at all to be viewed
Does not go into the primordial absence of a cut-off emptiness, a blankness—
This awareness of the present, uncontrived and clearly present,
Is Great Completion's view exactly.

There are a vast number of differing meditations,
But in transparent common awareness of the present
There is no duality of meditated on and meditator.
Do not meditate but seek the agent of meditation.
Having been sought, if the agent of meditation is not found,
At that time, meditation is reaching the exhaustion point.
This meditation in which there is no meditation at all to be done
Does not fall under the control of agitation, dullness, and absence of knowing—
Uncontrived equipoise on the awareness of the present, uncontrived and self-luminous,
Is the meditation.

There are a vast number of differing conducts,
But in the single unique sphere of self-knowing wisdom
There is no duality of conduct to be done and doer of it.
Do not engage in conduct but seek the agent of the conduct.
Having been sought, if the agent of the conduct is not found,
At that time, conduct is reaching the exhaustion point.
This conduct in which there is no conduct at all to be done
Does not fall under the control of latencies' confusion—
In the awareness of the present, uncontrived and self-luminous,
Not engaging at all in contrivance-spoiled adopting and rejecting
Exactly is the conduct of complete purity[114].

There are a vast number of differing fruitions,
But in the self-knowing three kayas conceived endeavour-less spontaneous existence,
There is no duality of accomplishment and accomplisher.
Do not engage in accomplishment of a fruition but seek the agent of the accomplishing.
Having been sought, if the agent of accomplishing the fruition is not found,
At that time, fruition is reaching the exhaustion point.
This fruition in which there is no accomplishment at all to be made
Does not fall under the control of adoption-rejection, hope and fear—
The awareness of the present, self-luminous spontaneous existence,
The manifest three kaya self-illuminating emptiness
Is itself the fruition of primordial buddhahood.

❁ ❁ ❁

E MA HO
Now, once more sons of the family listen well!

If like that, first you have preserved being without distraction,
Then later, even if you allow everything without inhibition,
Based on the factual state it all will be left normal but there will be no coming and going.

When both appearance and emptiness are inseparable,
At that time the view has become internalized.
When both dream and day times are without difference,
At that time the meditation has become internalized.
When both happiness and suffering are without difference,
At that time the conduct has become internalized.
When both this and the next life are without difference,
At that time the actuality has become internalized.
When both mind and space are without difference,
At that time dharmakaya has become internalized.
When your mind and buddha are without difference,
At that time the fruition has become internalized.

❁ ❁ ❁

E MA HO
Still, sons of the family, please listen to me!

View this material body as a moon in water!
Let your verbal expressions of speech be as echoes!
Allow mind's mass of thoughts to be cleared out in their own place!

Seeing all visible, audible, and mental phenomena as though they were illusions,
Mirages, dreams, reflections, moons in water,
Gandharva's cities, visual distortions, apparitions,

Bubbles, or echoes, do your conduct without grasping;
Do all types of behaviour within that state!
Conduct yourself like that day and night around the clock
without cutting it up into sessions and breaks.
Stay in a state without the spoilage of contrivance of the thought
process, where everything is left to be itself;
There, self-complexion self-liberated without grasping is
luminous and empty[115]—
Stay in truthless, meditation-less, conceived endeavour-less,
tracelessness.
Treat all discursive thinking that goes by
As the traceless flight of a bird in the sky.
With the awareness of the present like a dustless space and
Future thoughts like a mill with its water cut off,
In tranquil relaxation without manufacturing or altering,
Set yourself loose in the state where thought is left to be itself,
free of all restriction.

Leave coarse and subtle thoughts, the three poisons, five poisons,
and so on alone,
Treating them like a thief who has arrived in an empty house.
Leave all appearing objects of the sixfold group to be traceless,
Treating them as a city of illusion which has collapsed.

In short, threefold birth, cessation, and dwelling, ground, path,
and fruition,
View, meditation, and conduct, fruition, time, place, and words
expressed,
That to be placed and placer of it, that to be liberated and
liberator of it, and so on
Are in self-illumination bias-less, without the grasped endeavours
of abandoning and adopting.
Like streamlets merging with a great ocean,
All phenomena are, in mind's expanse, alpha purity;
Having developed assurance in this, cross over into being
without grasping.

At the time of meditating like that, many thoughts will be elaborated,
But there is no need for the suffering that comes from thinking "Meditation is not happening!"
Mind elaborates but is empty and abides but is empty.
Whichever way it shines forth, it is rigpa's state,
So, not engaging in suppression and furtherance, adoption and rejection at all,
Put yourself into relaxation in the state of the uncontrived innate.
By doing so, it is certain that discursive thought will be liberated in its own place.

If you are a person of lesser ability, unable to stay in the state,
You should alternate analysis and resting as described earlier in the introductions.
Alternatively, you can force the issue to a resolution with discursive thought like this:
Provoke discursive thoughts needed or otherwise
Till all sorts of thoughts are being produced, one after another,
And keep it up until mind becomes tired of the process.
Then, when mind has become being tired of it, enter relaxation.
Alternatively, meditate on the genuine guru in the centre of your heart;
Keep your mind on him for a long time, then,
After that, set yourself in the state of grasping-less rigpa.
Alternatively, meditate on a sphere in the centre of your heart
And imagine that it descends down
Until reaching the place of Great Indra;
Doing so will definitely sever agitation.
When the agitation has been cut, put yourself in the state of rigpa.

If there is a greater level of dullness, intensify your gaze then,
Having stripped rigpa naked, preserve its clear presence.
Alternatively, with your own mindness visualized as a sphere,
Exclaim the sound of PHAṬ and immediately expel it

From the Brahma aperture as though shot by a mighty archer
And think that it has thoroughly merged with space,
Then make your mind into the characteristic of space.
It is impossible that doing so will not clear away the sinking.
When the sinking has been cleared, put yourself into the grasping-less state.
These are my personal oral instructions, so understand them!

Not being bound by thoughts of wanting to be without thought,
Make your rigpa vast, let go into an infinite reach of elevated scope,
Then remain at ease and happy, open and unhindered.

First discursive thought is like water rushing through a ravine,
In the middle, it is like the slow-flowing Ganges,
In the end, like all rivers having become one taste with the ocean,
Abide in the state of mother and child luminosities having met.

In particular, whatever trickery of sickness and dons[116] arises,
Do not try to solve the problem using various rituals[117];
Instead, take the upper hand using equalization of taste.
Go to frightening, anxiety-inducing places such as
Forests, charnel grounds, islands, productive groves[118],
Rock caves, deserted houses, the foot of a single tree[119], and so on,
Transform your body and containers and contents, appearance and existence, into nectar
And offer it to all of the conquerors together with their sons in the ten directions.
Having been pleased, they show a loving appearance.
You visualize that they melt into light and that the whole of samsara and nirvana,
All of it, is totally filled with luminosity nectar.
Then the ones of good qualities who have become guests, the samaya'd dharma protectors[120],

The excellent field of compassion—the six classes of sentient beings,
And those with retribution to make[121]—all the dons, obstructors, and elementals[122],
All of the migrators equal to the limits of space
Are satisfied by this nectar which liberates on being tasted.
Then, having firmly decided that samsara and nirvana are of one taste,
From the state of mindness, uncontrived dharmakaya,
Engage in the conducts of going, staying, jumping, running,
Talking, laughing, crying, singing, and
Being alternately subdued and agitated, the behaviour of a madman.
At the end, stay in a peaceful and happy state.

At night-time, sleep peacefully being just as you are,
Free of all the discursive thoughts that come from the emitting and withdrawing of the thought process.
Sleep in the state of the birthless, complete as you remember it, innate.

If you do that, sickness and dons will be pacified of themselves, then
View and meditation will be enhanced, you will have a realization like space,
Meditation will be self-illumining, and conduct will be like that of a small boy.
Through the state free of all vacillatory foci, you will be like a madman.
Without the duality of self and other, you will be like a noble person.
Whatever you say, being without grasping, will be like a melodious echo.
With no attachment to anything, you will be like a garuda.
You will be like a lion who has no anxiety or concern.

Everything being primordially liberated, you will be the sky
cleared of clouds.

That sort of yogin is a real sugata vidyadhara
Worthy of the prostrations the come with being placed above the
crowns of hundreds of faithful beings,
Superior in greatness to even a wish-fulfilling jewel.

❁ ❁ ❁

E MA HO
Now, listen once more fortunate ones to this song of one who
has abandoned activities!

Vairochana does not exist outside, he exists within.
Mindness free of elaboration, dharmadhatu wisdom,
The very entity of delusion purified in its own place
Is the actual bhagavat Vairochana.

Vajrasatva does not exist outside, he exists within.
Rigpa liveliness's unstopped basis of shining forth, mirror-like
wisdom,
The very entity of anger purified in its own place,
Is the actual bhagavat Vajrasatva[123].

Ratnasambhava does not exist outside, he exists within.
Without adoption-rejection, stoppage-furtherance, equality
wisdom,
The entity of pride purified in its own place,
Is the actual bhagavat Ratnasambhava.

Amitabha does not exist outside, he exists within.
Discriminating wisdom, subsidence into the bliss-empty expanse,
The entity of desire purified in its own place,
Is the actual bhagavat Amitabha.

Amogasiddhi does not exist outside, he exists within.
Rigpa unimpededly-occurring self-liberated, all-accomplishing wisdom
The entity of jealousy purified in its own place
Is the actual bhagavat Amogasiddhi.

❁ ❁ ❁

E MA HO
Now, listen once more fortunate only mind sons,
Glad and thankful, to this vajra song!

When you have realized it that way, the whole of appearance and existence, all of it,
Is a mandala showing the meaning of the books of oral instruction.
On papers of the various red and white appearances[124],
The pen of self-arising wisdom, rigpa, writes
Groundless, primordially liberated, grasping-less letters.
Having looked at these books in the state of non-dual appearance-emptiness,
All of the third-order thousand worlds are a spontaneous-existence mandala.
Their rain sprinkles the mandala with the water of things left to be themselves,
Their straight roads have the nature of the baselines laid out,
Their foot marks are the coloured sand drawing.
Your body is the apparent-empty body of the yidam deity,
Your verbal expressions are the empty sounds of vajra recitation and
Your thoughts grasping-less self-liberated are the deity's mind.
Your limbs' movements all are prostrations,
Your food and drink are dharmata offerings.
Everything apparent in form is the deity's body.

All sounds and expressions you make are music.
This is the without keeping, without corruption, left-to-be-itself samaya.

For that sort of yogin, no matter what he does
Oral instructions together with development stage and
Samaya are completed in the state of luminosity dharmata
And that being so, he does not need to rely on the cause-and-effect conceived-endeavour dharma.

Fortunate heart sons, the attainment of wondrous and marvellous siddhis
Quickly and without application of conceptual efforts is
One of the special features of Great Completion!

If your practice turns into that kind of certainty,
Samsara-nirvana's masses of thoughts will have been purified in the primal ground
Like clouds having vanished in the state of the sky and
Self-knowing luminosity, the dharmakaya, will have been manifested
Like the sun's disk which is luminous without obscuration.
Then you will be able to revive the dead and understand the secret[125],
And will tame migrators by showing various miracles.

Having perfected all good qualities of the levels and paths without exception,
Those of you with the best of faculties will be liberated in this life,
Those with intermediate ones at the point of death, and those with inferior ones in the bardo.
Having been liberated in the alpha purity ground,
You will be perpetually seated in the inner expanse without disconnection from the wisdom three kayas.

Then you will distribute the taming emanations and they
Will enact benefit for migrators uninterruptedly.

Hold the meaning of these words in your minds and
The sun of happiness will surely shine from within!

The singer of this song of the understanding expressed here
Is Activities Abandoned Sixfold Group Self-Liberated[126].
By its virtue, may many fortunate ones to be tamed
Quickly purify all the stains of ignorance's afflicted thoughts
Into alpha purity's primal expanse,
Then attain the fruition in this very life!

This "Song of the View of the Thorough Cut of Luminosity Great Completion Called 'Flight of the Garuda Capable of Quickly Traversing All the Levels and Paths'" is based on many Great Completion treasures—"Introduction which Brings Naked Sight of Rigpa" by Orgyan Rinpoche, All-Knowing's "Seven Treasuries" and "Three Chariots" and his support dharmas for Great Completion "The Space Trilogy" and "Billowing Clouds of An Ocean of Profound Meaning", his "Great Completion Dakini Quintessence", "Buddha in the Palm of the Hand", and so on—and ornamented with notes from my guru's foremost instructions and my own experience. It was spoken to benefit the many faithful disciples by [7]Activities Abandoned Tshogdrug Rangdrol[127]. May it also become a cause that holds unfathomable benefit for the teaching and for sentient beings.

This vajra song was roused in order to benefit all the fortunate ones who seek emancipation, so the time to sing it is when yogins are preserving the view. The way to sing it is contained in the words of the eminent vidyadhara Saraha[128] *who said,*

> *Buddhas' enlightened mind is pervasively present;*
> *Sentient beings' rigpa is partially present;*
> *Making it as vast as space is the great way to enhance it.*

According to that, making your rigpa vast as space, let go into an infinite reach of elevated scope, then bring this vajra song forth from the state of mindness wide open and pervasively spread, and that will enhance view and meditation.

"Flight of the Garuda" written as prose

Namo guruvyaḥ[1]

Your seven-horsed disk of all-illuminating knowledge and love radiates the light rays of immeasurable compassionate activity, dispelling at once all of the darkness of ignorance of the migrators of the three realms—I bow down to you Chokyi Gyalpo[2].

In the vast heavens of your empty-luminous dharmakaya, moisture-laden clouds of loving-kindness and love amass and you expertly pour down a rain of dharma on the vessels who will hold it, the fortunate ones[3] to be tamed—I bow down to you Ngagchang Dorje.

Amidst your ship of the view, the great sail of the special wish is hoisted[4] and, propelled by the wind of perseverance, you set the migrators drowning in the ocean of becoming down on the jewel island of the three kayas[5]—I bow down to you captain Jamyang Gyatso.

The warm rays of potent blessings radiated from these three seven-horsed disks of knowledge and love, strike myself, the white lotus of a fortunate one who has abandoned activities[6], making my bud of rigpa blossom into a thousand petals of experience and realization[7].

This melodious song of the view, a nectar which liberates on tasting, having descended nicely into the centre of the fresh flower of my intellect, is offered to the swarm of bees, my fortunate students; please, respectfully drink to your heart's content!

E MA HO
I, abandoned of activities, spacious and carefree, happy of mind, sing Flight of the Garuda, a melodious song of the view which will quickly take you through all the levels and paths without exception; fortunate mind sons, listen attentively!

The loud sound of "buddha" is, like the roar of thunder, heard everywhere throughout both samsara and nirvana. That buddha is perpetually present in the mindstreams of the six migrator sentient beings, an alliance which never fails even for an instant—how amazing!

Not knowing that buddha exists in themselves, they seek it elsewhere outside themselves—how amazing! It is directly visible, being like the pure brilliance which is the essence of the sun, yet few see it—how amazing!

One's own mind, buddha itself, having no parents never knows birth so has no cause of death—how amazing! No matter what it experiences of the diverse joys and sufferings, it is not bettered or worsened in the slightest—how amazing!

This unborn primally-pure mindness[8] uncontrived, primordially comes spontaneously into existence—how amazing![9] This primordially-liberated self-knowing, its nature, is liberated by leaving what arises to be as it pleases—how amazing!

❁ ❁ ❁

E MA HO
Fortunate sons[10] of the family[11] listen undistractedly!

All of the conquerors of the three times without exception give teachings—the eighty-four thousandfold dharma heap, and so on[12]. These, equal to the limits of space, are unfathomable in extent yet are for the one purpose of realizing your own mind. The conquerors do not give teaching for any purpose other than that.

As an example, if the one root of a tree trunk is cut, a thousand million branches and leaves wither at once, and likewise, if the one root of mind is cut, samsara's leaves and petals—grasped-grasping[13], and so on—all wither.

An empty house might be in darkness for a thousand years but a lamp dispels that in an instant and likewise in the instant of realizing your own mind, luminosity[14], the evil deeds and obscurations accumulated over countless aeons are purified.

The pure brilliance which is the nature of the sun's essence cannot be obscured by the darkness of a thousand aeons and, likewise, the luminosity which is the essence of your own mind cannot be obscured by the confusion of aeons[15].

Like the sky's nature beyond measure of colour and shape does not become tainted by black and white clouds, mind's nature beyond measure of colour and shape does not become tainted by the black and white of evil and virtue.

For example, like milk is the cause of butter but, until it has been churned, the butter does not arise, all migrators are the cause, sugatagarbha[16], but, if they do not practise it, sentient beings do not become buddhas.

If they do practise it, all of them will be liberated regardless of the sharpness or dullness of their faculties—if it is practised, even a cowherd will be liberated[17].

If the fact of your own mind, luminosity, is realized in direct perception, there is no need for someone expert in its verbal explanation, just as, when you put sugar[18] in your own mouth, there is no need for an explanation of the taste of sugar.

When just this is not realized, even master scholars remain confused; they might be totally expert at explaining the nine vehicles but their explanations will be like tales of unseen, far away places, and buddhahood will be even further away for them than the sky is from the earth[19].

If the authentic[20], your own mind, luminosity, is not realized, you might keep the disciplines for as long as an aeon and might practise patience for a very long time but will not lift yourself out of the abodes of three-realmed samsara. Therefore, you must work hard to cut mind at the root and eliminate it completely!

❁ ❁ ❁

E MA HO
Now, listen once more, all you excellent fortunate sons!

If the root of your own mind is not resolved, any spiritual practice you do will not get to the key point[21]. To give examples: it would be like putting a target before you, yet firing the arrow in a direction far from it; it would be like leaving a thief behind in your house, while making a strong effort to get rid of him outside; it would be like leaving a harmful spirit at the eastern door, while putting the payment to get rid of him to the west; it would be like a poor man who, not knowing that his hearth stones are gold, goes begging for alms from others.

Thus, those who are going to resolve the root of mind must go about it like this, fortunate heart sons!

The flickering knowing and moving called "mind" if pursued cannot be captured—it vanishes and vanishes elusive as mist—and if set in place does not stay put—restless, it flitters about all over the place. There's no showing it as "this" for it is definitely empty.

This agent who experiences the diversity of happiness and suffering, your mind—where initially does it come from, what is its source? Ask yourself and try to resolve, "Does it have a basis in outer appearances such as rocky mountains, rivers, trees, the wind of the sky, and so on or is it without such basis—from where does it come?" Alternatively, you might think, "Did it come from the semen and blood of the two parents[22]?" in which case you should analyse just how that would occur.

When analysing like that yields no source for it, next ask where in the interim of the present moment does it dwell? Is it dwelling in the upper or lower part of your body, in your sense faculties, internal organs, heart, and so on? If it is dwelling in the heart, then, top to bottom, where exactly is it dwelling? What sort of shape, colour, and so on does it have?

When, having analysed well, you find no dwelling place for it, try to resolve at the end when it goes, through which door of the object faculties[23] it goes, and, for the mere instant that it takes to arrive at the external objects, during that time, whether it went via the body or via only the mind itself, or via body and mind as a combination? Resolve it in these and other ways.

Moreover, when affliction or discursive thought arises[24], look to see, "First, from where did it arise?", then for the present time ask "Where does it dwell?" and "What colour and shape does it have?" At the end, when subsiding in its own place it vanishes, ask, "Where did it vanish and go?" Try to resolve it in those and other ways.

At the time of death, carefully research to find out what exactly happens when it departs? And continue to analyse for as long as you have not arrived at a certain determination of an inexpressible, cleared-out, empty state[25] free of birth and death, coming and going, and the identification of things[26].

The dry examples and verbal explanations of others tell you "It is emptiness", but this does not help. For example, in a place where there are said to be tigers, others can tell you that there are no tigers but that will not be enough to make you believe it, leaving you consumed with doubt—it's like that.[27]

When you yourself have determined the root of your mind through careful research, it is, for example, like going yourself to that area where there are said to be tigers and looking everywhere, high and low, asking "Are there tigers here?" When, having resolved the matter like that, you find no tigers, you trust in that yourself and henceforth have none of the doubt that thinks "Are there tigers there?"—it's like that.

❁ ❁ ❁

E MA HO

Now, listen here once more you fortunate sons!

When you examine and analyse mind as described above, at the point when you have failed to find so much as a speck of substantially existing "mind" that you could point to and say, "This is it", that not finding is the supreme finding.

Initially, our minds have no source, no place of arising, because, being primordially empty, they have no entity that could be identified[28]. In the interim, they have no dwelling place, no shape and colour. In the end, there is no place to which they go nor a trace left that shows where they went—their movement is empty movement, their being empty is empty appearance[29].

This mindness[30] initially was not created by causes and at the end will not be destroyed by external circumstances. It has no rise and fall, no being filled and emptied. Wholly pervading samsara and nirvana, it has no partiality. Not demonstrable as "This", it shines forth[31] without stoppage[32] as everything whatever; not existing as anything whatever, it is beyond the extremes of existence and non-existence. It is without going and coming, without birth and death, and without clearing and obscuration.

Mind's nature is like a stainless crystal ball—it sits clearly present[33] as entity empty, nature luminous, and compassionate activity stoppage less. It is not tainted at all by the faults of samsara; mindness is ascertained to be the primordial buddha.

This has been the introduction which determined the nature of the actuality[34] of the ground's mindness.

❁ ❁ ❁

E MA HO
Now, listen once more you fortunate mind sons!

First, there is the way that dharmakaya Samantabhadra was liberated without having done so much as a speck of meditation, then the way that the six migrators wandered into samsara without having done so much as a whisker of non-virtue and evil deeds.

In the original primordial beginning prior to all, samsara and nirvana, nameless, resided in the primal ground. This is how rigpa arose from the ground at that time: as with crystal which has its own light become externally visible[35] on being struck by sunlight, propelled by the life-wind of rigpa wisdom[36] the seal of the youthful vase body was torn open and spontaneous existence, luminosity[37], became visible as the field realms of kayas and wisdoms, like the sun rising in the sky. At that time, dharmakaya Samantabhadra, by knowing it to be own appearance[38], in an instant had the externalized luminosity kayas and wisdoms dissolve back inside and in the alpha purity[39] primal ground was buddha.

We, not knowing the appearances of the nature, spontaneous existence, to be our own offput[40], developed a blacked-out[41] awareness[42] without thought process called "co-emergent ignorance". Then an awareness which grasped dualistically at that ground appearance luminosity was produced called "nothing-but-conceptualization ignorance"[43]. With that, we were in the cocoon of ignorance with dualistic grasping. Then latencies[44] gradually grew and due to them all these functions of samsara began. Then the afflictions—the three, five, eighty-four thousand, and so on poisons—grew and due to them we began to cycle like a water-wheel through the places of samsara[45] where we have till now have suffered the misery of pleasure and pain. If you'd like a longer explanation, look at All-Knowing's *Supreme Vehicle Treasury*[46], *Billowing Clouds of An Ocean of Profound Meaning*, and so on.

Now, through the guru's profound foremost instructions, you have understood the faults inherent in samsara then seen your own essence, your own mind of buddha. You have met the primal guardian face to face. You are equal in fortune to Samantabhadra. Cultivate gladness at this deep in your hearts, mind sons!

This has been the introduction which determined confusion.

❁ ❁ ❁

E MA HO
Now, listen once more you fortunate heart sons!

The loud sound of "mind" is universally heard. As for how it exists, it has not a single existence. As for how it occurs, it occurs as the whole variety of happiness and suffering of samsara and nirvana. As for how it is asserted, it is asserted in many ways in the enumerations of the vehicles. As for how is it named, it is given an inconceivable number of differing names:

ordinary beings call it "I";
some tirthikas[47] give it the name "self";
shravakas call it "selflessness of persons";
Mind Only followers give it the name "mind";
some call it "prajnaparamita";
some give it the name "sugatagarbha";
some give it the name "mahamudra";
some give it the name "madhyamaka";
some give it the name "single unique sphere";
some give it the name "dharmadhatu"[48];
some give it the name "alaya"[49];
some give it the name "common awareness"[50].

Regardless of which of the inconceivable names it is given, know that what is really being referred to is exactly this:[51] set yourselves into mindness relaxed in its own place and that right there is common awareness naked, looking but nothing to be seen's clear presence[52], rigpa in direct perception's vividly[53] clear presence, the non-existence of anything at all empty yet panoramically seen, the non-duality of luminosity and emptiness sticking out as one thing, not permanent, having no existence as anything at all, not nihilistic, being clearly present, vividly present, not singular, being known and visible as many, not many, being inseparability, one taste; there is nothing else, just exactly this is self-knowing rigpa!

You are seeing the face of the primal guardian seated in your heart centre in direct perception. Do not separate from this, heart sons!

Anyone who asserts that it is not this but something special obtained somewhere else is like someone who has the elephant but continues to search for it by following its tracks; though he combs the entire third-order world[54], it will be impossible for him to find so much as the name buddha[55]. This has been the main part's factual introduction to actuality[56].

❁ ❁ ❁

E MA HO

Now, once more, sons of the family listen well!

In this self-knowing self-illumination of the present, the three kayas—entity, nature, and compassionate activity—and the five kayas, five wisdoms, and so on all are complete. Rigpa's entity, with no existence at all as colour, shape, and so on, is empty dharmakaya. That empty aspect's natural offput, luminosity, is the sambhogakaya. Its being an unstopped basis from which the variety shines forth is the nirmanakaya[57]. The example used to illustrate this is that a glass mirror is analogous to the dharmakaya; its nature, purity and luminosity[58], shows the sambhogakaya; its being an unstopped basis from which the reflections shine forth exemplifies the nirmanakaya.

Migrators are mindness primordially abiding as the three kayas; if that is self-recognized, then they, without needing to do so much as a speck of meditation, at once become buddhas.

The introduction to the them as separate, but in fact they are one; other than that, taking them to be separate is confusion—do not go there, heart sons! The three kayas being primordially empty are alpha purity—understanding them to be a single entity of unified luminosity-emptiness, act in the state without grasping! Threefold entity, nature, and compassionate activity moreover are equivalent to dharmakaya, sambhogakaya, and nirmanakaya; understanding the three together to be great unified luminosity-emptiness, act in the state without grasping!

Then again, this self-arising rigpa wisdom: by appearing as everything is the Vairochana kaya; by being changeless is the Akshobyavajra kaya; by being without centre and edge is the Amitabha kaya; by being comparable to a jewel that is the source of all supreme and ordinary siddhis is the Ratnasambhava kaya; by being the accomplisher of all purposes is the Amoghasiddhi kaya[59]. Those are not something apart from rigpa's liveliness[60].

Rigpa's wisdom as an unstopped entity: by being directly perceiving luminosity is mirror wisdom; by being all-pervasive is equality wisdom; by being the variety shining forth from liveliness is individually discriminating wisdom; by being the accomplisher of all purposes is all-accomplishing wisdom; by containing their entities in alpha purity, is dharmadhatu wisdom. All of them have not a speck of existence apart from one's own rigpa's liveliness.

If the three kayas of entity, nature, and compassionate activity, the five kayas, and five wisdoms are introduced all together at once in direct perception by pointing them out, then just this awareness of the present, unmanufactured and unaltered, not modified by conditions, not spoiled by grasping—this clearly present, vividly present rigpa is it! This is the source of all the buddhas of the three times, this is the enlightened mind of the buddhas of the three times, so do not separate from this, all you fortunate ones!

This is uncontrived self-illumination exactly. so how can you complain that you do not see your own mind, buddha? Here, there is no meditation is to be done at all, so how can you complain that your meditation has failed? This is exactly rigpa directly seen, so how can you complain that you do not find your own mind? This is uninterrupted vividly present luminosity exactly, so how can you complain that you do not see mind's essence? Here, not so much as a speck of work is to be done, so how can you complain that your efforts have failed? This is non-dual abiding and not abiding, so how can you complain that you are not getting to abiding? Here is self-knowing's three kayas of spontaneous existence not having conceived endeavours, so how can you complain that your endeavours at accomplishment yield no result? Here, with nothing to be done, setting yourself just so[61] is sufficient, so how can you complain that you are unable to do that? This here is thought shining forth and being liberated simultaneously, so how can you complain that antidotes are not working? This is awareness of the present exactly, so how can you complain that you do not know it?

❁ ❁ ❁

E MA HO

Now, once more fortunate sons listen with respect!

One's own mind is like the non-thing empty space[62]; to see whether that is so or not all you fortunate sons, look straight at your own minds with the approach that there is nothing to be looked at and let go into vast evenness, then know how it is!

It is not solely determined as empty, for it is ascertained to be self-knowing wisdom, primordially luminous[63]. It is self-arising self-illumination like the sun's essence; to see whether that is so or not, look straight at your own mindness and let go into vast evenness, then know how it is!

It is ascertained that it cannot be identified as the movement and thinking of discursive thought, for such movements appear with uncertainty, like breezes; to see whether that is so or not, look straight at your own mindness and let go into vast evenness, then know how it is!

It is ascertained that all of its appearances are own appearance, all of what appears being like the images in a mirror; to see whether that is so or not, look straight at your own mindness and let go into vast evenness, then know how it is!

There is nothing somewhere other than mind,
So there is no view to be viewed elsewhere.
There is nothing somewhere other than mind,
So there is no meditation to be done anywhere else.
There is nothing somewhere other than mind,
So there is no conduct to be done anywhere else.
There is nothing somewhere other than mind,
So there is no samaya to be kept anywhere else.
There is nothing somewhere other than mind,
So there is no fruition to be accomplished anywhere else.

Look again and look again at your own mind! Send your mind into the external space of the sky and look to see, "Is there coming and going in my own mindness?" When you have looked, if you find that mind does not have going and coming, look inwardly at your internal mind and look to see, "Is there an agent who emits the emitted thoughts?" If there no agent who emits the emitted thoughts, look to see, "Does mind have colour, shape, and so on?" When you connect with its being empty of colour and shape, look to see, "Does the emptiness have centre and edge?" When you find no centre and edge, look to see, "Does it have inside and outside?" Rigpa without outside and inside is vast like space, transparent[64] in its freedom from delimitation and falling into sides, a vast great interior space of self-knowing, everywhere-spread. Within it the whole variety of the phenomena of samsara and nirvana appear like rainbows floating in space yet that whole variety is the play of mind. Look out from this state without moving from self-knowing rigpa and see that all phenomena, like illusions and moons in water, are an appearance-emptiness not separable into parts. In the state of rigpa, samsara and nirvana are non-dual; look out from this state without moving from self-knowing rigpa and see that the phenomena of samsara and nirvana, like images in a mirror, appear as they do but primally never know existence. All phenomena of samsara and nirvana, nameless, are the dharmakaya.

The migrators who wander in three-realmed samsara, not realizing their own entity, the wisdom in which all the phenomena of samsara and nirvana are equally present, are under the control of the confusion of dualistic grasping. Thus they apprehend the phenomena individually and, because of dualistic grasping, are not liberated into the non-dual fact. Every one of them has a mind which is samsara and nirvana inseparable, yet their engagement in abandonment-adoption, rejection-adoption[65] causes them to wander in samsara.

All the migrators who, in their stupidity and lack of knowledge, seek the levels and paths using methods which are not this self-knowing rigpa, three kaya, conceived-endeavours-less spontaneous-existence, methods that take them elsewhere very far way, do not ever arrive at the level of a buddha.

It is ascertained that all that appears is own appearance. Look out from a state not moving from self-knowing rigpa and see that all of appearance and existence[66] is like reflected images—sights seen yet empty and sounds heard yet empty, it has the nature of being primordially empty.

Look in like that at the mind doing the looking and the thoughts of the thought process self-vanish, leaving an empty experience like space which is elaboration-less, elaboration-free[67], beyond verbal and mental expression.

All that appears is mind's trickery[68]; all of the trickery is baseless, empty. If you realize that all of it is your own mind, all appearances seen are empty, the dharmakaya. One is not bound by appearance, one is bound by clinging. Sever the confusion of clinging and attachment, heart sons!

❁ ❁ ❁

E MA HO

Excellent mind sons of good fortune: since a horse not struck with a whip does not reach the speed of a donkey, milk not churned a great deal does not produce butter, and nothing is determined without precise explanations, this song comes with many words. However, do not be irritated, listen with a glad mind!

If you do not know that all appearances are mind, you will never realize the meaning of emptiness so examine and analyse well, all you fortunate sons: where initially do these appearances arise, where in the interim do they dwell, and where at the end do they go? When examined, you will find that, like mist in the sky arises from the sky and goes back again to the sky, appearances, mind's trickery, shine forth in one's mind and go back into mind.

To give an example for this: a person whose eye faculty is impaired will, on looking up into the sky, see floaters[69]—there appears to be something there in the sky but there is not, it is just the eye's trickery. Similarly, the bad latencies of grasping at things in tandem with the mind faculty being impaired, make it seem as though every one of the fictional[70] phenomena seen and heard do truly exist there, yet primally they do not have so much as a speck of existence as things—all are the trickery of one's own mind. All this trickery is baseless, empty. It does not exist yet obviously appears, like an illusion and a moon in water, so put yourself in equipoise on the fact of appearance-emptiness inseparable!

Now, in our dreams during sleep we directly see the appearances of homeland, dwelling, close ones, and so on and so experience happiness and sadness, yet at the time not a single one of those things dear to us is present. We have not moved even a little from our beds, yet we experience them as directly as we would in our waking day. Similarly, all of the appearances of this life are like the experiences of last night's dream. One's own mind labels everything, grasps at that, and then appearance happens accordingly; everything is experienced because of mind. Dreams occurring during sleep are without nature[71] and similarly, appearances, however they occur, are empty.

❀ ❀ ❀

E MA HO

Only sons of mind, you of good fortune!

All appearances are indefinite; where for some there is brightness, for others there is darkness. Moreover, for some sentient beings and this world:

> there are sentient beings who perceive earth as earth,
> there are sentient beings who perceive earth as a fire,
> there are sentient beings who perceive earth as useful,
> there are sentient beings who perceive earth as suffering.
> there are sentient beings who perceive water as water,
> there are sentient beings who perceive water at fire,
> there are sentient beings who perceive water as nectar,
> there are sentient beings who perceive water as a dwelling,
> there are sentient beings who perceive water as earth.
> there are sentient beings who perceive fire as fire,
> there are sentient beings who perceive fire as useful,
> there are sentient beings who perceive fire as a dwelling,
> there are sentient beings who perceive fire as food.
> there are sentient beings who perceive space as space,
> there are sentient beings who perceive space as a dwelling,
> there are sentient beings who perceive space as earth.

Thus appearances are not definite and the reason is that Controlled by latencies they appear as they do. Correspondingly, humans perceive each of the the four elements as they do.

Moreover, other migrators perceive this world as hell's fires, a place for the use of farmers, and, for those with a depressed mind, as suffering. Similarly, fire is perceived as something for the fire god's use, pretas having a body of fire perceive it as a dwelling, and fireflies perceive it as something to eat. Similarly, water is perceived by hell's migrators as fire, by preta sentient beings as pus and blood, by elephants as the ground, and by gods as nectar. For the Gods who Control Other's Emanations it is jewels and rains of flowers, and for nagas a dwelling. When space is treated like that, it is an abode which all the gods perceive as a ground. That being so, everything is labelled by oneself then appears in accordance with however it was labelled.

Moreover, when Devaputra asked the Buddha[72] "Who made Mt. Meru, the sun, moon, and so on?", the Buddha replied, "They have no other creator at all. The concretization of the latencies of one's own thoughts labels that, grasps at that, and then it appears as such. Everything has been made by one's own mind". When Devaputra further asked the Buddha, "Aside from how one's own thoughts are concretized, where did this sort of solid and firm Mt. Meru, sun, moon, and so on come from?" the Buddha replied, "In Vāraṇāsi, an old woman imagined her body as a tiger and the village, on seeing her as such, was emptied. If she could make that appearance happen in a short time, habituation to the mind of latencies since births without beginning could indeed produce this sort of appearance!" So said the Capable One[73]. That being so, everything has been made by mind.

Moreover, there is the story of one outsider tirthika who, in order to stop the distractions of worldly entertainments, imagined an isolated place thereby actually producing an isolated place that could be seen by other humans. And there is the story of a person who meditated on space being solid as rock and, it having turned into rock, his body was trapped. That being so, everything has been made by mind's thoughts, so all of it is mind's own appearance and all own appearance in fact is empty.

Moreover, the sentient beings of the transient hells perceive their bodies as form—doors, pillars, stoves, ropes, and so on—and experience suffering because of it. That being so, however mind's thought makes a label, it appears like that to others.[74]

All of the happinesses and sufferings of the six migrator sentient beings are made solely by their own minds. Thus, everything is the trickery of one's own mind. Therefore, decide with total confidence that all of it is non-existent appearance, emptiness's own forms, and let go into vast evenness!

Moreover, it was taught, "The Capable One Great Snow Lake has on a single pistil of the lotus in his hand the third-order world Endurance[75]."

It was taught that at the time of Direct Crossing's rigpa having reached full measure[76], "In each body pore of one's own body immeasurable buddha field realms will be seen and limitless six migrator sentient beings' abodes also will be seen. Migrator-taming emanations will be distributed to them and will act in a dream-like way to benefit them." That being so, the phenomena of samsara and nirvana are own appearance and all of own appearance is groundless, empty. Develop a concept-based assurance of the empty yet luminous grasping-less state[77].

Furthermore, it was taught, "On one single atom there are as many as there atoms—unfathomable numbers—of buddha field-realms and there are also countless six migrators' abodes." The conqueror taught that, "None of them mix with, contaminate, or damage any of the others."

Furthermore, it was taught, "In the interior of each insect, there are unfathomable cities of insects."

It was taught, "In the space element there are an unfathomable number of cities where many cities face downwards and similarly many face sideways and also upwards."

If you wonder who made these kinds of things, the conqueror taught that everything has been made by mind.

Know that mind's nature primally is like space and that all phenomena are likewise! Every one of all the fictional phenomena—sights and sounds[78]—are the own appearance solely of one's own mindness; therefore, when at death one's mindstream changes, it is not a change in external appearances but a change in own appearance. That being so, everything is mind's own appearance and all the own appearance is groundless, empty. Its non-existent yet evident appearance is like a reflected image and moon in water; preserve the experience of the state of non-dual luminous-empty rigpa![79]

All appearance seen is mind's own appearance. The appearance of the material container worlds is mind. The appearance of the six classes of contained sentient beings also is mind. The appearance of the happiness of the gods and men in the upper levels also is mind. The appearance of suffering of the three bad migrations[80] also is mind. The appearance of ignorance's afflicted five poisons also is mind. The appearance of self-arising wisdom rigpa also is mind. The appearance of the latencies of bad-thought samsara also is mind. The appearance of good-thought buddha field realms, also is mind. The appearance of obstacles created by maras and demons also is mind[81]. The appearance of good deities and spiritual attainments also is mind. The appearance of various discursive thoughts also is mind. The appearance of no-thought one-pointed meditation also is mind. The appearance of things, concept tokens[82], and colours also is mind. The absence of concept tokens and elaborations also is mind. The appearance of non-duality of one and many also is mind. The appearance of there being no establishment at all of existence and non-existence also is mind. Except for what comes from mind, there is no appearance whatsoever.

Mind is comparable to an artist: one's own body is made by mind and moreover all the third-order world realms as many as there are are drawn by mind. Furthermore, these drawings made by one's own thought deceive all migrators with their childish rational minds[83]. That being so, it is very important to develop the certainty of having decided that everything is the trickery of mind.

This has been the introduction to discursive thought as mind.

❁ ❁ ❁

E MA HO

Now, listen once more, all you supreme mind sons!

Even the buddhas did not teach that the agent, one's own mindness, has an identifiable entity of colour, shape, and so on. Mindness is ascertained to be empty, groundless, like primordially empty, grasping-less, space. Mindness is illustrated with the example of space but that serves only to illustrate the empty side. Mindness, which has knowing rigpa, is empty and shines forth in every which way. Space, without knowing rigpa, is a cut-off emptiness, a blankness[84]; therefore, mindness cannot fully be illustrated by space. This has been the introduction to mindness being empty.

From the self-liveliness of that luminous-empty mindness the whole variety of appearance shines forth. It shines forth but, like the images in a mirror, it is non-dual, one with the state of being empty. This has been the introduction to the empty aspect being apparent.

Primordially it is non-dual appearance-emptiness; one's own mind being empty, appearance occurs without stoppage, and appearance without grasping glitters while being the empty state. Appearances do not stop the empty aspect and even as they appear their nature is one of being primordially empty.

For the yogin who realizes non-dual appearance-emptiness like a rainbow in the sky and the form of a moon in water, the phenomena of samsara and nirvana are an illusory spectacle. When viewing this non-dual apparent while empty spectacle, the rational mind of the yogin whose mind is changeless is at ease. To see whether it is so or not, all you fortunate sons look to see "Can the two aspects, the emptiness and appearance, of your minds be separated out?" and know how it is! Primordially they are appearance-emptiness non-dual. This has been the introduction to non-dual appearance-emptiness.

That non-dual appearing-while-empty self-arising rigpa, self-illumining, clearly present, vividly present, three kayas spontaneously existing type of mind, must, mind sons, be preserved day and night in around the clock practice without division into sessions and breaks! This has been the introduction to non-dual self-liberation.

❁ ❁ ❁

E MA HO
Now, listen once more to this song of mine, a man who has abandoned activity!

There is the way that the three kayas are complete in ground's rigpa and the way that the three kayas are complete at the time of ground appearances, and when this pair of distinctions has been properly comprehended, samsara and nirvana will be understood to be the field of the three kayas.[85]

Although the way that the three kayas are complete in ground's rigpa was explained earlier, it will be explained here again. The self-knowing ground is comparable to a crystal ball: its being empty is the dharmakaya's nature; its natural offput of luminosity is the sambhogakaya; and its being an unstopped basis of shining forth is the nirmanakaya. That is the way in which the three kayas are complete within the ground's rigpa. In this, there is never any meeting and parting[86].

Then, as in the example of five lights shining forth from a crystal, at the time of ground appearances shining forth from it[87], all of whatever shines forth—purity, the appearances of the conquerors' field-realms, and impurity, the appearances of containers and contents—has an empty entity which is the dharmakaya, a nature of appearance which is the sambhogakaya, and an unstopped variety which is the nirmanakaya. And that is the way that the three kayas are complete at the time of ground appearances. This distinction, which is not much made in other places, is a key point that must be properly understood. For myself, I've understood it through the kindness of All-Knowing's excellent explanations.

When known like that, the whole of appearance and existence primordially is the spontaneously existing mandala of the three kayas and there is no seeking the three kayas in some other field realm. The six migrator sentient beings moreover abide as the three kayas and if they are able to self-recognize this, then, without needing to do so much as a speck of meditation, the migrators all will become buddhas.

Moreover, in actual fact, the ground's three kayas also are the dharmakaya, so do not conceive of them as separate! The three kayas of the time of ground appearance also are the form kayas, so do not conceive of them as separate! The dharma and form kayas are two but in actual fact they are not separate, they are one taste in the state of empty dharmakaya.

Ultimately, ground appearances dissolve of themselves back into the ground then ground dharmakaya's mind becomes manifest at which time the factual fruition has become manifest. Then, while not wavering from dharmakaya's space, both types of form kaya are shown just like rainbows, and the enactment of benefit for migrators goes on continuously.

❁ ❁ ❁

E MA HO

Now, listen once more to this song of mine, a man who has abandoned activity!

In the past you have been harmed. Bring to mind in detail all the ways that others have done this to you, mulling over how they have bullied, hit and beaten, and humiliated you, and acted to make you feel bad. Allow yourself to become angry and then, looking straight at what it is, ask, "This agent[88] anger, first from where does it arise? And then in the present time where does it dwell? And at the end, where does it go? Does it have colour, shape, and so on?" When you look, it is primordially empty, grasping-less. Un-abandoned, anger is mirror wisdom.

Bring to mind in detail and mull over the ways in which you so badly want a beautiful woman, want meat and other good things to eat, want clothes and other good things to wear, want the wealth of horses and other good possessions. Allow yourself to become desirous and then, looking straight at what it is, ask, "This agent desire, first from where does it arise? And then in the present time where does it dwell? And at the end, where does it go? Does it have colour, shape, and so on?" When you look, it is primordially empty, grasping-less. Un-abandoned desire, is discriminating wisdom.

Allow yourselves to become deluded as you do in sleep, in sinking and dullness, and so on, and then, looking straight at what it is, ask, "This agent delusion, first from where does it arise? And then in the present time where does it dwell? And at the end, where does it go? Does it have colour, shape, and so on?" When you look, it is primordially empty, grasping-less. Un-abandoned, delusion is dharmadhatu wisdom.

Bring to mind in detail the extent of your qualities—the strength of your family line, your very fine form and beautiful tone of voice, your ability at threefold hearing, contemplation, and meditation, and reading and writing, your great knowledge and your ability to perform village rites, and so on. Allow yourself to have the pride of thinking, "I am a little better than others" and then, looking straight at what it is, ask, "This agent pride, first from where does it arise? And then in the present time where does it dwell? And at the end, where does it go? Does it have colour, shape, and so on?" When you look, it is primordially empty, grasping-less. Un-abandoned, pride is equality wisdom.

Allow the jealousy of being concerned that others are higher than you to arise through bringing to mind in detail all the good qualities of others—those whose family strengths are greater than yours, who are filled with good qualities and who have more disciples, who are more knowledgeable, better at reciting aloud, and have a finer voice, who understand dharma, know worldly stories, and so on—and then, looking straight at what it is, ask, "This agent jealousy, first from where does it arise? And then in the present time where does it dwell? And at the end, where does it go? Does it have colour, shape, and so on?" When you look, it is primordially empty, grasping-less. Un-abandoned, jealousy is all-accomplishing wisdom.

If you realize it like that, affliction is wisdom. On the other hand, casting aside the realization of affliction then seeking emptiness and wisdom from there is just ludicrous; I feel pity for anyone who seeks it like that then does not find it! It is this way: after knowing that the five poisons are empty, the five poisons henceforth shine forth as realized five poisons, removing the need for the analysis explained in this introduction of birthplace, dwelling-place, destination, and colour and shape. The five poisons already having been understood to be empty, immediately they shine forth set yourself in not following after them but letting them relax in their own place in the state of mindness; there is no doubt that they will go on to vanish of themselves. This has been both introduction and training[89].

It is like this: if training has been done beforehand, then when the five poisonous afflictions shine forth, the force of already having understood their faults will cause both emptiness and wisdom to shine forth simultaneously, with the result that the afflictions will enter a process of shining forth and being liberated at the same time! Understand this to fit with what has been said in the life stories of the forefather gurus—"Many afflicted thoughts, many chances for dharmakaya!"

For the beginner, when afflicted minds appear intensely, it is good to do analysis then resting—this is my personal instruction, so keep it in mind!

This has been the introduction to the self-liberation of the five poisons.

❁ ❁ ❁

E MA HO
Now, listen once more sons who are like my heart!

Wrap smooth things like clothing, and so on around your body and look at your mind's thought "It is smooth". Wrap rough things like serge, and so on around your body and look at your mind's thought "It is rough". On looking, both are equal taste in being empty.

Look at beautiful forms like golden statues, and so on and look at your mind's thought "It is beautiful". Look at ugly forms like frogs, and so on and look at your mind's thought "It is ugly". On looking, both are equal taste in being empty.

Take good-tasting things into your mouth, like sugar, and so on and look at your mind's thought "It is sweet". Take things into your mouth like ginger, and so on and look at your mind's thought "It is foul". On looking, both are equal taste in being empty.

Smell nice smells like sandalwood incense, and so on and look at your mind's thought "It is nice". Smell bad smells such as asafoetida, garlic, and so on and look at your mind's thought "It is rank". On looking, both are equal taste in being empty.

Listen to the sounds of a bell, vina[90], and flute and look at your own mind's thought "It is pleasant". Listen to the sounds of stones and hands being clapped together and look at your mind's thought "It is unpleasant". On looking, both are equal taste in being empty.

Meditate on being born as a wheel-wielding king who governs a realm of the four continents[91] and is surrounded by a retinue of many queens and ministers and, in a palace made of the five precious substances[92], eats food having one hundred flavours. When this appears in mind, look at your mind's thought "It is pleasant". Meditate on having become poor, without a single helper, with a bed in a broken down shack with earthen walls, the rain coming in from above and moisture coming up from the ground beneath, your body struck by many illnesses, such as leprosy, and the like, and your hands and feet gone. You have so many difficulties that you experience unremitting suffering. When that sort of appearance has been brought to mind, look at your mind's thought "It is suffering". On looking, pleasure and pain are equal taste in being empty.

It is like this: the sixfold group is known to be empty beforehand[93], then after that, however it shines forth, whether good or bad, analysis as explained in this introduction will be unnecessary. Because it is groundless, primordially liberated, empty, just as it shines forth, do not follow after it but set yourself into letting it relax in its own place in the state of mindness; there is no doubt that it will go on to vanish of itself.

This has been the introduction to the sixfold group self-liberating.

❀ ❀ ❀

E MA HO
Now, once more listen well sons of the family!

Set yourselves so that your minds are relaxed, allowed to be themselves, then look at how they are when they abide! Fortunate mind sons, having looked, understand that because this is abiding in rigpa's state, this is the abiding yet empty state of rigpa! That was the introduction to how abiding is an ornament of mind.

For the elaboration of discursive thoughts, look at the way in which they are emitted and then fortunate sons of the family understand that, because there is not so much as the slightest shift away from that state of empty-luminous rigpa, this is the emitting but empty state of rigpa! That is the introduction to emitting, the play of mind.

For example, a wave that appears on an ocean does not shift in the slightest from being the ocean; likewise, mind whether it abides or moves does not shift in the slightest being from rigpa-emptiness.

Thus, whichever way abides, take that as being the state of rigpa; whichever way it shines forth, take that as being the offput of rigpa!

The assertions that mind when abiding is meditation and that mind when emitting is not meditation, with their failure to appreciate the faults inherent in both abiding and movement, signify that threefold abiding, movement, and knowing rigpa have not been merged into one. Therefore, all of you excellent fortunate mind sons, for us there is the state of rigpa in which abiding and movement are equally fine. Thus, with these points absorbed beforehand, practise threefold abiding, moving, and knowing rigpa as one!

This has been the introduction to emitting and abiding being non-dual.

❁ ❁ ❁

E MA HO
Only mind sons, you who are fortunate, listen here with undistracted and attentive ears!

The singer of this song, I, Tshogdrug Rangrol who has abandoned activities, have a melodious song pleasant to hear, so take it into your snow-white minds.

When all phenomena have been determined to be one-taste in being empty, samsara and nirvana are freed of abandonment-adoption, the confusion of grasping at enemies and friends is destroyed, and there are none of the appearances that come with dualistically grasping at self and other, because everything has been realized to be one-taste in being empty.

Here is a summation of the essential points of extensive
explanations:
In the pinnacle of vehicles, Great Completion,

All of samsara and nirvana are free of ground and root;
Primordially buddhahood, they are one taste in the dharmakaya.
In the state of Great Completion, there is no duality of gods and demons;
In the land of Great Completion, there are no buddhas and sentient beings;
In the ground of Great Completion, there is no good and bad;
In the path of Great Completion, there is no near and far;
In the fruition of Great Completion, there is no attained and not attained;
In the dharma of Great Completion, there is no doing and not doing the conduct;
In the fact of Great Completion, there is no meditating and not meditating;
Stay like that, which is the Great Completion king of views.

When you realize that sort of Great Completion view, all of the coarse and subtle thoughts of the three doors are pacified, so you remain, like wool to which water has been applied[94], in a state in which your three doors are pacified and tamed. The samadhis of bliss, luminosity, and no-thought arise and, for all the migrators wandering in samsara who have not realized such, an uncontrived compassion like the love a mother has for an only son is produced. Those are special features of the Great Completion view[95], so know that too!

After you have firmly decided that everything is emptiness, if you develop a conduct in which you abandon virtue and do not avoid evil deeds, that will be the view of the mara of bad action run wild. Keep yourself from falling under the control of the view of that sort of mara! These are the introductions of Great Completion.

These introductions are extremely important: while you have not realized that every one of all the external fictional visible and audible phenomena are emptiness, you might think you are meditating in the view but what meditation is it? Therefore, first you should proceed like this: sometimes look while supplicating the guru and sometimes look carefully while relaxing and tightening. When you look in that way, your mind will be glad and everything will be shining forth while obviously empty. There will definitely be the birth of a deep certainty in which you think "I can touch the objects of external appearances with my hand but there is nothing to apprehend there" and "This is definitely the view." This is the time of discovering certainty of the view. Do not spoil it with grasping; relax into a state without grasping.

Even if you do not practise after having received the introduction[96], at the time of death no matter which fears arise in the bardo, you will know that everything is own appearance, the own forms of emptiness, and will become buddha in the alpha purity ground. To practise without having received the introduction will be like the example of someone who is mistaken on the first day of the month being still being mistaken on the fifteenth day of the month. When you have not realized that all fictional phenomena are truthless, what a huge lie it is to say, "I have realized emptiness."

Thus, this sort of introduction must first be received while sitting in front of the guru so that it is determined based on what is real—then you won't go down a mistaken path. Therefore, fortunate sons keep this advice in your hearts!

❁ ❁ ❁

E MA HO
Now, once more fortunate sons of the family, listen!

When you have taken in that actuality of the view, sever all ties of attachment and aversion to people and homeland. Alone in forest tracks and mountain valleys, give up endeavours of the body and let it be natural; cut talk and other expressions of speech, and stay silent; allow mind to be like space, beyond the realm of thinking. Relax in that state without addition or subtraction[97].

If there is no focus in mind, that is the view[98]. Stay in the state in which there is no meditation to be done! Attain the fruition of attainment-less Great Completion! Moreover, when you set yourself in equipoise on the view, do not catch yourself in nets of thought such as "This is how to rest in the state of rigpa!" or "I am falling under the control of sinking and agitation!" Instead, set yourself relaxed in the state absent of the things of referenced focus, a state clear and open, free of restrictions, a state of transparency, free to be as it pleases[99].

You cannot see the fact beyond rational mind using the stuff of rational mind and you cannot reach the activity-less place with the stuff of activity, so, if you want to attain the beyond rational mind, activity-less fact, instead of engaging in the spoilage of contrivance, set yourself in naked rigpa[100].

That is the supreme, free of all grasped-grasping view.
That is the supreme, absent of abandonment-adoption meditation.
That is the supreme, beyond conceived-endeavour conduct.
That is the supreme, hope-free self-abiding fruition.

It is not seen by looking at a view, so put aside all searching for the view!
It is not discovered by meditation, so cast away the referenced foci of thinking with grasping.
It is not accomplished by conduct, so let go of grasping at illusions.
It is not gained by seeking it, so leave aside hopes of a fruition.

The awareness of the present is un-manufactured and hanging loose, so do not engage in biasses, do not spoil it with grasping!

This rigpa of non-thing which is luminous—just this is the pinnacle of all views. This freedom from rational mind smeared all over with referenced foci—just this is the pinnacle of all meditation. This placement in uncontrived grasping-less looseness—just this is the pinnacle of all conduct. This unsought primordially spontaneously-existing situation—just this is the pinnacle of all fruition.

Look at the heart of the view, empty luminosity without grasping!
Preserve the heart of meditation, self-liberation without grasping!
Set yourself in the heart of conduct, the sixfold group left loose!
The heart of the fruition is the collapse of hope and fear.

If you are free of bounding extremes, that is the supreme king of views. If you are free of vacillatory foci[101], that is the supreme king of meditation. If you are free of accepting and rejecting, that is the supreme king of conduct. If you are free of hope and fear, that is the supreme king of fruition.

Since there is nothing to view, cast off referenced foci of the view. Since there is nothing to meditation on, let whatever arises do as it pleases. Since there is no conduct to be done, release suppression and furtherance[102], abandonment and adoption. Since there is nothing to be attained, leave aside hopes for a fruition.

By letting what it[103] is be, do not engage in grasping on its account. By being without "This is it", do not engage in suppression and furtherance. By being without vacillatory foci, do not engage in biasses.

In primal purity's self-knowing self-illumination, because it is beyond rational mind's objects of thought, there is nothing to view; because its entity is free of a ground, there is nothing to meditate on; because it is self-liberation beyond extremes, there is no conduct to be done; because it is beyond the clinging that goes with conceived endeavours' accomplishment, there is no fruition.

Because the entity is emptiness, there is no abandonment and no attainment. Because the nature is luminosity-emptiness, conceived endeavours' accomplishment has collapsed. Because everything is stoppageless, there are no biasses. No matter which way it shines forth, do not grasp at it being so!

A yogin's awareness is comparable to a bird's path in the sky. As with a bird's trace which is not visible because it has ceased to begin with, thinking and thought are nothing to be seen because they cease to begin with, so do not attempt to continue thinking and though by grasping at following after them! As with a bird's trace which is nothing because of not happening afterwards, do not go out to greet thinking and thought afterwards! As with a bird's trace which in the present has no colour and shape, the thinking and thought of the present in the end goes its own way so do not create the spoilage of contrivance by using an antidote directed at "it".

No matter how it shines forth, do not grasp at it being like that! This is the ultimate heart instruction for bringing it to the path: no matter which way it shines forth, if you do not grasp at it being like that, affliction, vanishing of itself, is great wisdom.

It is a birthless beyond-thought primordially-liberated view,
So if you work hard at it, there will be no view of it.
It is a relaxation-into-being-left-to-be-itself naturally-occurring meditation,
So if you work hard at it, there will be no meditation on it.
It is a non-duality of abandonment-adoption illusory conduct,
So if you work hard at it, there will be no conduct of it.
It is a non-duality-of-hope-and-fear nature of fruition,
So if you work hard at it, there will be no fruition.

This mindness, being free of root of the three times, unmeditated directly appears—what a happy event! Phenomena from beginning to end are by nature pure, primordially liberated, wholly liberated, with all conceived effort-endeavours collapsed—how wondrous!

This common awareness left un-manufactured and hanging loose is the conqueror's mind, extreme-free, a wide-open interior space. Moreover, analysis and meditation done with conceived efforts will not make mindness, actuality, the innate, become visible. In the uncontemplated, unanalysed, common dharmata[104], there is no meditating and not meditating, no being distracted and not distracted—it is through unmeditated looseness that many have been liberated.

Liberation and non-liberation are non-dual in its fact. If you know actuality, whether you make conceived endeavours or not, mind remains at ease. If you are bound by thought that wants to be without thought, discursive thought having risen up, it will try its best to go all over the place. If, on the basis of the innate character which is rigpa without coming and going, you relax into letting it do what it wants, then, having given it the freedom to do as it pleases, it will stay put, unmoving, steady as a mountain. Sons, understand its perverse ways!

The point to be most highly treasured is that, for this, there is no reference to even a speck of meditation to be done, nevertheless, it must be kept in place, without distraction, by mindfulness.

❁ ❁ ❁

E MA HO
Now, listen here once more, fortunate sons!

This own-form of appearance-emptiness without external object, because it is primordially empty, comparable to a moon in water, does not need to be cleansed. The internal thoughts of the thinking process vanish of themselves, without trace, so it is not necessary to apply the antidotes of effort-filled endeavours to them. The appearing mind, which is primordially-liberated hanging-loose wisdom, does not need the superimposition of any abandonment-adoption, hope and fear, at all. For this directly seen, naked, rigpa, do not dress it in the clothes of mental analysis's elaborations[105] but relax yourself into its being just as it is, just what it is, evanescent, and traceless[106], in bias-less great equality.

In that state, whichever ideas of the thought process shine forth, know all of them to be bias-less self-arising rigpa's own offput, and then, instead of following after them, if you let the jingling and jangling, blaring on and off, elusive comings and goings of appearing mind[107] be a vast sameness of the dharmata's shifting events[108], you will have arrived at Samantabhadra's mind space. That is referred to as "Great Completion, the yoga of self-liberation of the whole variety produced in primordially-liberated spontaneous-existence".

You have not gone anywhere, yet have arrived at the level of a buddha. You have not accomplished anything, yet your fruition is spontaneously existing. You have left the afflictions un-abandoned, so that they are now purified in their own place. Your mind is equal to the mind of the holy gurus. You have followed after them and completed all works. There is this key point, so sons, you should know it!

Through the kindness of the old father, Chokyi Gyalpo, I, Tshogdrug Rangrol, the man whose sixfold group is self-liberated, have arrived at the mind of activity-free spontaneous existence.

There is this key point, though some do not understand it.
Everything is already primordially done but they say "I will do it!"
Everything is already primordially liberated but they say "I will liberate it!"
Everything is already primordially in equipoise but they say "I will enter equipoise on it!"
Everything is already primordially in meditation but they say "I will meditate on it!"

Everything is already primordially seen but they say "I will see it!"
Everything is already primordially traversed but they say "I will traverse it!"

Speaking like that, they are people who put their hopes in a mental analysis type of view. They have learning, but being theoretical, dead words only, it is discursive thought; they have realization, but being a result of can-do meditation[109], it is a product of rational mind; they have analysis but being a dualistic accomplishment, it is samsaric.

These people who approach dharmata through mental analysis certainly have no karmic connection to Quintessence Great Completion. Engaging in activity is not necessary; doing so does not achieve it. It is beyond the accounting of acting and not acting. In non-meditation beyond meditation, meditation only ruins it. In non-viewing beyond viewing, what will be viewed? In non-seeking beyond seeking, there is no finding. Rigpa is present with transparency; that's how it is. The person who has that explained but does not listen, has no karmic connection to Great Completion, how ridiculous!

Wherever you look, since it is the mind of alpha purity great space shining forth, samsara and nirvana are without duality. Having put the mind of that sort into song, the conquerors of the three times will be pleased, no doubt!

If you ask, "But, having given confusion's externally appearing objects the freedom to go to their own place, won't one return to being confused again?" An ordinary person grasps at a self in them and so is confused; a yogin, knowing them to be groundless, root-free, does not treat them with contrivance-spoiled adoption and rejection but leaves them to be themselves, without grasping, and so is unconfused. If you then ask, "Is there a point in this where one could deviate?" The answer is no, there is not a single point of deviation nor mistake in it. Points of deviation happen when there is clinging and attachment[110]; if there is no grasping at what shines forth, where could there be a point of deviation to fall into? Still, there is the point that, at the time when rigpa shines forth as an object, the meditation of viewing the entity of the discursive thinking is not what is proclaimed; what is to be preserved is the rigpa of that time's factor of being naked and clearly present. Furthermore, when rigpa is not emitting-withdrawing[111], when it is abiding, it is not the no-thought abiding factor itself that is the actual meditation—at that time, the factor which is the strength of the luminous pure part which at that time is vividly present and clear is what is to be preserved. Hot having understood this key point, if you think "The viewing of both abiding and shining forth is the entity of meditation", then you have become confused, heart sons! Mere abiding is the same as the dhyana of the gods[112] and mere shining forth is the same as ordinary thought. You could meditate in those ways but you would not attain buddhahood. In short, for as long as the rigpa factor being naked, transparent, and comparable to a crystal ball has not become interior space, you must preserve its clear presence! When it has, do not be separated from that state!

The main issue of Thorough Cut's view stated as "Rigpa is to be stripped naked then have its clear presence preserved", is the particular key point that is of the greatest importance—it is the central issue of a hundred statements about the subject because of which you fortunate heart sons must know it!

❁ ❁ ❁

E MA HO
Now, once more fortunate sons listen with respect!

The four great spotlights that unmistakenly illuminate are as follows[113]. The great spotlight of view without mistake is exactly this awareness of the present clearly present; because it illuminates this un-mistakenly it is called “a spotlight”. The great spotlight of meditation without mistake is exactly this awareness of the present clearly present; because it illuminates this un-mistakenly it is called “a spotlight”. The great spotlight of conduct without mistake is exactly this awareness of the present clearly present; because it illuminates this un-mistakenly it is called “a spotlight”. The great spotlight of fruition without mistake is exactly this awareness of the present clearly present; because it illuminates this un-mistakenly it is called “a spotlight”.

The four great nails that make an unchanging situation are as follows. The great nail of changeless view is exactly this awareness of the present clearly present; because it is steady through the three times, it is called “a nail”. The great nail of changeless meditation is exactly this awareness of the present clearly present; because it is steady through the three times, it is called “a nail”. The great nail of changeless conduct is exactly this awareness of the present clearly present; because it is steady through the three times, it is called “a nail”. The great nail of changeless fruition is exactly this awareness of the present clearly present; because it is steady through the three times, it is called “a nail”.

There are a vast number of differing views, but in the self-knowing rigpa self-arising wisdom of the present there is no duality of view and viewer. Do not look at the view but seek the viewing agent. If the viewing agent having been sought is not found, at that time, the view is reaching the exhaustion point. This view in which there is nothing at all to be viewed does not go into the primordial absence of a cut-off emptiness, a blankness—this awareness of the present, uncontrived and clearly present, is Great Completion’s view exactly.

There are a vast number of differing meditations, but in transparent common awareness of the present there is no duality of meditated on and meditator. Do not meditate but seek the agent of meditation. Having been sought, if the agent of meditation is not found, at that time, meditation is reaching the exhaustion point. This meditation in which there is no meditation at all to be done does not fall under the control of agitation, dullness, and absence of knowing—uncontrived equipoise on the awareness of the present, uncontrived and self-luminous, is the meditation.

There are a vast number of differing conducts, but in the single unique sphere of self-knowing wisdom there is no duality of conduct to be done and doer of it. Do not engage in conduct but seek the agent of the conduct. Having been sought, if the agent of the conduct is not found, at that time, conduct is reaching the exhaustion point. This conduct in which there is no conduct at all to be done does not fall under the control of latencies' confusion—in the awareness of the present, uncontrived and self-luminous, not engaging at all in contrivance-spoiled adopting and rejecting exactly is the conduct of complete purity[114].

There are a vast number of differing fruitions, but in the self-knowing three kayas, conceived endeavour-less spontaneous-existence, there is no duality of accomplishment and accomplisher. Do not engage in accomplishment of a fruition but seek the agent of the accomplishing. Having been sought, if the agent of accomplishing the fruition is not found, at that time, fruition is reaching the exhaustion point. This fruition in which there is no accomplishment at all to be made does not fall under the control of adoption-rejection, hope and fear—the awareness of the present, self-luminous spontaneous existence, the manifest three kaya self-illuminating emptiness is itself the fruition of primordial buddhahood.

❁ ❁ ❁

E MA HO
Now, once more sons of the family listen well!

If like that, first you have preserved being without distraction, then later, even if you allow everything without inhibition, based on the factual state it all will be left normal but there will be no coming and going.

When both appearance and emptiness are inseparable,
At that time the view has become internalized.
When both dream and day times are without difference,
At that time the meditation has become internalized.
When both happiness and suffering are without difference,
At that time the conduct has become internalized.
When both this and the next life are without difference,
At that time the actuality has become internalized.
When both mind and space are without difference,
At that time dharmakaya has become internalized.
When your mind and buddha are without difference,
At that time the fruition has become internalized.

❁ ❁ ❁

E MA HO
Still, sons of the family, please listen to me!

View this material body as a moon in water! Let your verbal expressions of speech be as echoes! Allow mind's mass of thoughts to be cleared out in their own place!

Seeing all visible, audible, and mental phenomena as though they were illusions, mirages, dreams, reflections, moons in water, gandharva's cities, visual distortions, apparitions, bubbles, or echoes, do your conduct without grasping; do all types of behaviour within that state! Conduct yourself like that day and night around the clock without cutting it up into sessions and breaks. Stay in a state without the spoilage of contrivance of the thought process, where everything is left to be itself; there, self-complexion self-liberated without grasping is luminous and empty[115]—stay in truthless, meditation-less, conceived endeavour-less, tracelessness. Treat all discursive thinking that goes by as the traceless flight of a bird in the sky. With the awareness of the present like a dustless space and future thoughts like a mill with its water cut off, in tranquil relaxation without manufacturing or altering, set yourself loose in the state where thought is left to be itself, free of all restriction.

Leave alone coarse and subtle thoughts, the three poisons, five poisons, and so on treating them like a thief who has arrived in an empty house. Leave all appearing objects of the sixfold group to be traceless, treating them as a city of illusion which has collapsed.

In short, threefold birth, cessation, and dwelling, ground, path, and fruition, view, meditation, and conduct, fruition, time, place, and words expressed, that to be placed and placer of it, that to be liberated and liberator of it, and so on are in self-illumination biasless, without the grasped endeavours of abandoning and adopting. Like streamlets merging with a great ocean, all phenomena are, in mind's expanse, alpha purity; having developed assurance in this, cross over into being without grasping.

At the time of meditating like that, many thoughts will be elaborated, but there is no need for the suffering that comes from thinking "Meditation is not happening!" Mind elaborates but is empty and abides but is empty. Whichever way it shines forth, it is rigpa's state, so, not engaging in suppression and furtherance, adoption and rejection at all, put yourself into relaxation in the state of the uncontrived innate. By doing so, it is certain that discursive thought will be liberated in its own place.

If you are a person of lesser ability, unable to stay in the state, you should alternate analysis and resting as described earlier in the introductions. Alternatively, you can force the issue to a resolution with discursive thought like this: provoke discursive thoughts needed or otherwise till all sorts of thoughts are being produced, one after another, and keep it up until mind becomes tired of the process. Then, when mind has become tired of it, enter relaxation. Alternatively, meditate on the genuine guru in the centre of your heart; keep your mind on him for a long time, then, after that, set yourself in the state of grasping-less rigpa. Alternatively, meditate on a sphere in the centre of your heart and imagine that it descends down until reaching the place of Great Indra; doing so will definitely sever agitation. When the agitation has been cut, put yourself in the state of rigpa.

If there is a greater level of dullness, intensify your gaze then, having stripped rigpa naked, preserve its clear presence. Alternatively, with your own mindness visualized as a sphere, exclaim the sound of PHAṬ and immediately expel it from the Brahma aperture as though shot by a mighty archer; think that it has thoroughly merged with space, then make your mind into the characteristic of space. It is impossible that doing so will not clear away the sinking. When the sinking has been cleared, put yourself into the grasping-less state. These are my personal oral instructions, so understand them!

Not being bound by thoughts of wanting to be without thought, make your rigpa vast, let go into an infinite reach of elevated scope, then remain at ease and happy, open and unhindered.

First discursive thought is like water rushing through a ravine, in the middle, it is like the slow-flowing Ganges, in the end, like all rivers having become one taste with the ocean, abide in the state of mother and child luminosities having met.

In particular, whatever trickery of sickness and dons[116] arises, do not try to solve the problem using various rituals[117]; instead, take the upper hand using equalization of taste. Go to frightening, anxiety-inducing places such as forests, charnel grounds, islands, productive groves[118], rock caves, deserted houses, the foot of a single tree[119], and so on, transform your body and containers and contents, appearance and existence, into nectar and offer it to all of the conquerors together with their sons in the ten directions. Having been pleased, they show a loving appearance. You visualize that they melt into light and the whole of samsara and nirvana, all of it, is totally filled with luminosity nectar. Then the ones of good qualities who have become guests, the samaya'd dharma protectors[120], the excellent field of compassion—the six classes of sentient beings, those with retribution to make[121]—all the dons, obstructors, and elementals[122], all of the migrators equal to the limits of space are satisfied by this nectar which liberates on being tasted. Then, having firmly decided that samsara and nirvana are of one taste, from the state of mindness, uncontrived dharmakaya, engage in the conducts of going, staying, jumping, running, talking, laughing, crying, singing, and being alternately subdued and agitated, the behaviour of a madman. At the end, stay in a peaceful and happy state.

At night-time, sleep peacefully remaining just as you are, free of all the discursive thoughts that come from the emitting and withdrawing of the thought process. Sleep in the state of the birthless, complete as you remember it, innate.

If you do that, sickness and dons will be pacified of themselves, then view and meditation will be enhanced, you will have a realization like space, meditation will be self-illumining, and conduct will be like that of a small boy. Through the state free of all vacillatory foci, you will be like a madman. Without the duality of self and other, you will be like a noble person. Whatever you say, being without grasping, will be like a melodious echo. With no attachment to anything, you will be like a garuda. You will be like a lion who has no anxiety or concern. Everything being primordially liberated, you will be the sky cleared of clouds.

That sort of yogin is a real sugata vidyadhara worthy of the prostrations that come with placed above the crowns of hundreds of faithful beings, superior in greatness to even a wish-fulfilling jewel.

❁ ❁ ❁

E MA HO
Now, listen once more fortunate ones to this song of one who has abandoned activities!

Vairochana does not exist outside, he exists within. Mindness free of elaboration, dharmadhatu wisdom, the very entity of delusion purified in its own place is the actual bhagavat Vairochana.

Vajrasatva does not exist outside, he exists within. Rigpa liveliness's unstopped basis of shining forth, mirror-like wisdom, the very entity of anger purified in its own place, is the actual bhagavat Vajrasatva[123].

Ratnasambhava does not exist outside, he exists within. Without adoption-rejection, stoppage-furtherance, equality wisdom, the entity of pride purified in its own place, is the actual bhagavat Ratnasambhava.

Amitabha does not exist outside, he exists within. Discriminating wisdom, subsidence into the bliss-empty expanse, the entity of desire purified in its own place, is the actual bhagavat Amitabha.

Amogasiddhi does not exist outside, he exists within. Rigpa unimpededly-occurring self-liberated, all-accomplishing wisdom the entity of jealousy purified in its own place is the actual bhagavat Amogasiddhi.

❁ ❁ ❁

E MA HO

Now, listen once more fortunate only mind sons, glad and thankful, to this vajra song!

When you have realized it that way, the whole of appearance and existence, all of it, is a mandala showing the meaning of the books of oral instruction. On papers of the various red and white appearances[124], the pen of self-arising wisdom, rigpa, writes groundless, primordially liberated, grasping-less letters. Having looked at these books in the state of non-dual appearance-emptiness, all of the third-order thousand worlds are a spontaneous-existence mandala. Their rain sprinkles the mandala with the water of things left to be themselves, their straight roads have the nature of the baselines laid out, their foot marks are the coloured sand drawing. Your body is the apparent-empty body of the yidam deity, your verbal expressions are the empty sounds of vajra recitation and your thoughts grasping-less self-liberated are the deity's mind. Your limbs' movements all are prostrations, your food and drink are dharmata offerings. Everything apparent in form is the deity's body. All sounds and expressions you make are music. This is the without keeping, without corruption, left-to-be-itself samaya.

For that sort of yogin, no matter what he does oral instructions together with development stage and samaya are completed in the state of luminosity dharmata and that being so, he does not need to rely on the cause-and-effect conceived-endeavour dharma.

Fortunate heart sons, the attainment of wondrous and marvellous siddhis quickly and without application of conceptual efforts is one of the special features of Great Completion!

If your practice turns into that kind of certainty, samsara-nirvana's masses of thoughts will have been purified in the primal ground like clouds having vanished in the state of the sky and self-knowing luminosity, the dharmakaya, will have been manifested like the sun's disk which is luminous without obscuration. Then you will be able to revive the dead and understand the secret[125], and will tame migrators by showing various miracles.

Having perfected all good qualities of the levels and paths without exception, those of you with the best of faculties will be liberated in this life, those with intermediate ones at the point of death, and those with inferior ones in the bardo. Having been liberated in the alpha purity ground, you will be perpetually seated in the inner expanse without disconnection from the wisdom three kayas. Then you will distribute the taming emanations and they will enact benefit for migrators uninterruptedly.

Hold the meaning of these words in your minds and the sun of happiness will surely shine from within!

The singer of this song of the understanding expressed here is Activities Abandoned Sixfold Group Self-Liberated[126]. By its virtue, may many fortunate ones to be tamed quickly purify all the stains of ignorance's afflicted thoughts into alpha purity's primal expanse, then attain the fruition in this very life!

◆◆◆

This "Song of the View of the Thorough Cut of Luminosity Great Completion Called 'Flight of the Garuda Capable of Quickly Traversing All the Levels and Paths'" is based on many Great Completion treasures—"Introduction which Brings Naked Sight of Rigpa" by Orgyan Rinpoche, All-Knowing's "Seven Treasuries" and "Three Chariots" and his support dharmas for Great Completion "The Space Trilogy" and

"Billowing Clouds of An Ocean of Profound Meaning", his "Great Completion Dakini Quintessence", "Buddha in the Palm of the Hand", and so on—and ornamented with notes from my guru's foremost instructions and my own experience. It was spoken to benefit the many faithful disciples by [7]Activities Abandoned Tshogdrug Rangdrol[127] . May it also become a cause that holds unfathomable benefit for the teaching and for sentient beings.

This vajra song was roused in order to benefit all the fortunate ones who seek emancipation, so the time to sing it is when yogins are preserving the view. The way to sing it is contained in the words of the eminent vidyadhara Saraha[128] who said,

> *Buddhas' enlightened mind is pervasively present;*
> *Sentient beings' rigpa is partially present;*
> *Making it as vast as space is the great way to enhance it.*

According to that, making your rigpa vast as space, let go into an infinite reach of elevated scope, then bring this vajra song forth from the state of mindness wide open and pervasively spread, and that will enhance view and meditation.

A Summary of the Guidebook to the Thorough Cut View, Flight of the Garuda, Called "A Key to Unravel the Treasury of the Three Lineages' Instructions"

by Ontrul Tenpa'i Wangchug

Zhabkar Rinpoche's *Song of the View of the Thorough Cut of Luminosity Great Completion Called "Flight of the Garuda Capable of Quickly Traversing All the Levels and Paths"* will be explained to have three parts:

1. Prefatory section of being virtuous at the beginning,
2. Main part of being virtuous in the middle,
3. Concluding part of being virtuous at the end.

1. The Prefatory Section

1. In order to understand the meaning contained in the text, the title of the text is given, in "Song of the View of the Thorough Cut of Luminosity Great Completion ..."
2. In order to remove obstacles, there is an expression of worship for the actual lineage gurus, in three verses beginning with "Namo guruvyaḥ ..."
3. Advice is given, through showing the source of the foremost instructions that will be presented, to the fortunate disciples of the need to trust this text, in two verses beginning with "The warm rays of potent blessings radiated from these three seven-horsed disks of knowledge and love ..."

4. The greatness of the text itself is shown; a commitment is made to complete the composition and in order to do that, the ones to be tamed are urged to listen, in one verse beginning with "E MA HO ..."
5. Words of amazement are used to show the essence of what is to be expressed, in four verses beginning with "The loud sound "buddha" is, like the roar of thunder, heard everywhere throughout both samsara and nirvana ..."

2. The Main Part

1. Determination done through the view

1. Resolving the root of mind
    1. Giving the history
        1. The way in which the meaning of all phenomena of sutra and tantra is contained in the key points in three verses and two lines, "E MA HO Fortunate sons of the family listen undistractedly ..."
        2. Showing that the innate character of mind is freedom from stains in two verses "The pure brilliance which is the nature of the sun's essence ..."
        3. Nonetheless, if experience is not gained, the way of no liberation in one verse "For example, like milk is the cause of butter but ..."
        4. Showing that all will realize it regardless of sharpness or dullness of faculty in four verses "If they do practice it, all of them will be liberated ..."
    2. Elimination by severing the root
        1. Showing that, if mind's root is not eliminated, there will be not going to the authentic point in two verses and three lines "E MA HO Now listen once more, all you excellent fortunate sons ..."
        2. Resolving the root by threefold arising, dwelling, and going in eleven verses and three lines "Thus, those who are going to resolve the root of mind ..."

   3. Finding the actuality which is the absence of mind in six verses "E MA HO Now listen here once more, you fortunate sons …"
   4. Extensively explaining the ways of samsara and nirvana's liberation and confusion in ten verses "E MA HO Now, listen once more you fortunate mind sons …"
   5. The way of expressing the names of the tenets in five verses "E MA HO Now listen once more, you fortunate heart sons …"

2. Rigpa introduced
   1. Synopsis in four verses and three lines "Set yourselves in mindness relaxed in its own place …"
   2. Extensive Explanation
      1. Introduction to rigpa as three kayas and five wisdoms going from "E MA HO Now, once more, listen well sons of the family … In this self-knowing self-illumination of the present …" down to "How can you complain that you do not know it?"
      2. The empty luminous inexpressible rigpa factor nakedly introduced, and the whole appearing factor having been recognized as its liveliness and play, all of view, meditation, conduct, and fruition are introduced as being rigpa alone in "E MA HO Now, once more, fortunate sons listen with respect … One's own mind is like the non-thing empty space…" down to "Sever the confusion of clinging and attachment, heart sons!"
      3. A synopsis the method for introducing appearances as mind in "E MA HO Excellent mind sons of good fortune … A horse not struck with a whip …" down to "Similarly, appearance, however it occurs, is empty".
      4. Everything not in accord with that to be viewed of the six classes of sentient beings being made by one's own mind and the method for introducing all of what appears as mind extensively explained in "E MA HO Only sons of mind … All appearances are indefinite …" down to "This

has been the introduction to the discursive thought as mind".

5. Introduction to that mind of agent doing like that also being appearance-emptiness non-dual in "E MA HO Now, listen once more, all you excellent mind sons ... Even the buddhas did not teach that ..." down to "This has been the introduction to non-dual self-liberation".
6. Introduction to ground's rigpa and rigpa at the time of ground appearances both being the three kaya inseparable in "E MA HO Now, listen once more to this song of mine, a man who has abandoned activity ..." down to "And the enactment of benefit for migrators goes on continuously".
7. Introduction to the five poisons being the five wisdoms in "E MA HO Now, listen once more to this song of mine, a man who has abandoned activity ... In the past you have been harmed ..." down to "This has been the introduction to the self-liberation of the five poisons".
8. Introduction to the good and bad objects of the sixfold group being the great equal taste in "E MA HO Now, listen once more sons who are like my heart ..." down to "This has been the introduction to the sixfold group self-liberating".
9. Introduction to threefold abiding, movement, and rigpa being one in "E MA HO Now, once more listen well sons of the family ... Set yourselves so that your minds are relaxed ..." down to "This has been the introduction to emitting and abiding being non-dual".

2. *How to gain experience, through meditation, in the ground view which has just been determined*

1. Explaining the uncontrived, left-as-it-is-primordially meditation
    1. Actual
        1. Showing the meditation of realizing in one taste of all phenomena of samsara in the great rigpa-empty

primordial equality in three verses and one line in "E MA HO Only mind sons, you who are fortunate ..."

2. Showing the meditation of non-meditation which is free of all elaboration's concept tokens hope and fear, good and bad, in the state of the Great Completion view in two verses in "In the state of Great Completion, there is no duality of gods and demons ..."

2. Ancillary
   1. Assessing the extent of signs of the path of authentic meditation in two verses and one line in "When you realize that sort of Great Completion view ..."
   2. Stopping wrong concepts which mislead into a wrong path of meditation in one verse and one line in "After you have firmly decided that everything is emptiness ..."
   3. Showing the faults and good qualities of coming down and not right on the key points of introduction and showing the extent of having produced certainty of the view in seven verses in "These introductions are extremely important ..."

2. Showing the way to preserve using meditation in which the birthplaces of dhyana are view, meditation, conduct, and fruition that are not kept distinct from each other
   1. Showing the birth places of dhyana in one verse in "E MA HO Now, once more fortunate sons of the family, listen ... When you have taken in that actuality of the view ..."
   2. Explaining the left-to-be-itself method of placement for relaxing the three doors in three verses and one line in "Give up endeavours of the body and let it be natural ..."
   3. Showing the need for freedom from rational mind-made grasping at concept tokens in one verse in "You cannot see the fact beyond rational mind using the stuff of rational mind ..."
   4. Connecting to the conventions such as supreme, and pinnacle, and essence, and king of all view, meditation, conduct, and fruition in six verses and two lines in "That is the supreme, free of all grasped-grasping view ..."

5. Showing that in fact there is not separate, individual view, meditation, conduct, and fruition apart from elaboration-free, directly seen rigpa alone in four verses in "Since there is nothing to view, cast off referenced foci of the view …"
6. Showing that the masses of thoughts of the three times are like the traceless flight of a bird in three verses and one line in "A yogin's awareness is comparable to a bird's path in the sky …"
7. Showing the key point that for all of view, meditation, conduct, and fruition there is no accomplishment through assiduous effort and that it is a liberation through un-meditated, left-to-be-itself, loose placement in seven verses and three lines in "No matter how it shines forth, do not grasp at it being like that …"

3. Showing the meditation of uncontrived left-to-be-itself innate character in freed of adoption-rejection, suppression and furtherance
   1. Having understood that external appearances are primordially empty and internal grasping is primordially liberated, there is the meditation of having placed oneself by leaving it as it is in the state of the naked rigpa factor without adoption-rejection in two verses and three lines in "E MA HO Now, listen here once more, fortunate sons … This own-form of appearance-emptiness without external object …"
   2. Manifesting the extent of assurance over the appearing mind being taken into the internal space of primordially liberated dharmakaya in two verses and one line in "In that state, whichever ideas of the thought process shine forth …"
   3. Showing that the author of the text has himself produced that measure of assurance in two verses and one line in "You have not gone anywhere, but have arrived at the level of a buddha …"
   4. Explaining the way that the dharmata cannot be fathomed by mental analysis in five verses and one line in "There is this key point though some do not understand it …"

5. The features of the yoga of realizing what arises as dharmakaya in one verse in "Wherever you look, the mind of alpha purity great space ..."
6. Removing obstructors and difficult places of meditation in seven verses in "If you ask, "Having given confusion's externally appearing objects ..."
7. Explaining how that the innate character free of misdirection sits in two verses and one line in "In short, for as long as the rigpa factor ..."

4. In the context of meditation, the baseline of non-mistaken view, meditation, conduct, and fruition and driving the nails of changelessness
   1. The four great dots of non-mistakenness in three verses and two lines in "E MA HO Now, once more fortunate sons listen with respect ... The four great spotlights that unmistakenly illuminate are as follows ..."
   2. The four great nails of changelessness in three verses and one line in "The four great nails that make an unchanging situation as follows ..."
   3. The way of view, meditation, conduct, and fruition reaching the exhaustion point in ten verses and two lines "There are a vast number of differing views but ..."
5. Showing the signs of reaching the measure of ultimate meditation, the way that view, meditation, conduct, and fruition become the inner space in four verses in "E MA HO Now, once more sons of the family listen well ... If like that, first you have preserved being without distraction, then ..."

3. *Training up through conduct*

1. First, the conduct of the three doors is put into uncontrivance, left to being itself in one verse in "E MA HO Still, sons of the family, please listen to me ..."
2. All sights and sounds are identified as being like the ten analogies of illusion then for all types of conduct that state is preserved in six verses and two lines in "Seeing all visible, audible, and mental ..."

3. Showing the conduct of a variety of methods so that the beginner's discursive thoughts, elaboration and agitation of all types, goes on to self-dissolution in five verses and two lines in "At the time of meditating like that, many thoughts will be elaborated but …"
4. Showing the conduct which has threefold sinking, dullness, and darkness go on to self-dissolution in four verses and one line in "If there is a greater level of dullness, intensify your gaze and then …"
5. The way in which, no matter what appearing circumstances shine forth, obstructors are dispelled through reliance on conduct of equal taste taking the upper hand in five verses and two lines in "In particular, whatever trickery of sickness and dons arises …"
6. The way that dreams are mixed with luminosity in three verses in "At night-time, sleep peacefully being just as you are …"
7. Explaining the features of the conduct of the three doors of a person who has gained the full measure of assurance of realization in three lines in "That sort of yogin is a real sugata vidyadhara …"

4. *The mode of the manifested fruition*

1. Showing that the fruition phenomena of kayas and wisdoms and so forth are inherently present in rigpa itself in five verses and one line in "E MA HO Now, listen once more fortunate ones to this song of the one who has abandoned activities … Vairochana does not exist outside, it exists within …"
2. The mode of the appearance and existence as universal purity, as it actually is, manifested
   1. The way that all of whatever liveliness and play of rigpa shines forth is an ornament of the expanse and only the universal purity in six verses and three lines in "E MA HO Now, listen once more fortunate only mind sons, Glad and thankful, to this vajra song …"

2. The way that threefold birth, death, and bardo are suitable to be liberated in three verses in "If your practice turns into that kind of certainty ..."
3. Having been liberated, the way that the aims of migrator sentient beings are enacted in one verse and two lines in "Then you will distribute the taming emanations and they ..."

I. The Conclusion

1. Dedication of the virtue for the sake of others in one verse in "By its virtue, may many fortunate ones to be tamed ..."
2. The colophon which begins "*This "Song of the View of the Thorough Cut of Luminosity Great Completion ...*"

With the thought to benefit oneself and others, this was written by the one with the name Tenpa at The Sanctuary of Elaboration-Free Alpha Purity[129].

ENDNOTES

1. This is the Sanskrit in the text for "I prostrate to the guru". It should be "namo gurave" but this mistake is common in Tibetan texts. This initial prostration is usually given in Sanskrit as a way of retaining the blessings of the original language of the teaching.

2. The principal theme in this prefatory section headed by these verses is enlightened being and its qualities. Enlightened being is wisdom at root. Its qualities can be summed up into three: knowledge, love, and capability. The example for wisdom is the sun and its rays, the sun being wisdom with its qualities of knowledge and love and its rays being the wisdom's capacity to help sentient beings at work in the form of radiated energy. In the verses here "seven-horsed disk" is an ancient Indian name for the sun, given that the sun's disk was thought to be drawn by seven horses. Compassionate activity is the special name used for the capability aspect as it is understood in the Great Completion teaching. For compassionate activity and migrators, see the glossary. The first three verses pay homage to the author's three principal gurus mentioned in the introduction.

3. For fortunate, see the glossary.

4. The special wish is the name for the aspect of enlightenment mind, bodhicitta, that wishes above all else that sentient beings could be taken to enlightenment.

5. For kaya and three kayas, see the glossary.

6. One who has abandoned activities means a dharma practitioner who has let go of all worldly types of activity. In Quintessential Great Completion, it is taught that it is necessary to abandon all activities of body, speech, and mind in order to gain any significant level of accomplishment. The author often refers to himself in this text as having this quality. Despite the wording in other translations, these words do not mean "vagabond" or "vagrant", though it is true that the author was a wandering yogi.

7. For rigpa, see the glossary.

8. For mindness, see the glossary.

9. Primal and primordial both are used extensively in these explanations. Primal is (Skt. adi, Tib. gdod ma) meaning something in the very first position, the situation that comes before and is the head of all others, for example, as in "prime minister". Primordial has a very similar meaning, referring to the original situation, a situation that has and does prevail from the outset. Thus primordially liberated means something which, from the very beginning has been liberated, that is its original situation and it will always remain that way. Thus, "primally pure" means that the situation to begin with is one of purity and "primordially liberated" means that the content of that situation has been, from the outset, liberated.

10. The Tibetan text says "sons" exactly and not anything else. Some Westerners feel that it should be changed but this is a translation and as such it is not appropriate to change its wording because of the whims expressed by some people in other cultures. Those who would continue to insist on it demonstrate a lack of knowledge of the subtleties of the language used in these texts. For example, "sons" here denotes those who have strength, capacity, and intelligence; it is a very positive statement where the use of "children" or "child" in this class of literature indicates the opposite. This is a text of another culture, one whose norms even now are very different from that of present-day Western culture; we should respect that and use the wording to understand the text as it was written, rather than attempting to sanitize it according to our own ideas.

11. "Of the family" means who karmically belong to the family or line of those who can be involved with this particular level of teaching.

12. The current buddha Shakyamuni's teaching, characterized as a mass of eighty-four thousand teachings, is used as an example of buddhas' spoken teachings in general.

13. For grasped-grasping, see the glossary.

14. For luminosity, see the glossary.

15. For confusion, see the glossary.

16. For sugatagarbha, see the glossary.

17. A cowherd in Tibet in the past has no education at all.

18. Sugar here and elsewhere in the text is the Tibetan word "bu ram" which originally meant the sweet juice of sugar-cane, a drink very popular in India. In Tibet over time it came to refer to all degrees of unrefined sugar, starting with the juice itself, going to various forms of molasses and treacle, and ending up with raw sugar.

19. The distance between the sky and the earth is very great according to Tibetan culture because the sky and earth are regarded as two different things that never come into contact with each other, anywhere.

20. "The authentic" is one of many names for reality. Reality is none other than one's own, innate mindness which is characterized here as luminosity.

21. For key point, see the glossary.

22. Tibetan medicine considers that a human comes from the union of the subtle elements of the parents, the white vitality of the father and the red blood vitality of the mother. The sperm and egg are outer manifestations of these more subtle substances.

23. Object faculties are the faculties for each of the six senses.

24. For discursive thought, see the glossary.

25. "Cleared-out empty state" is a practitioner's approach to emptiness; it means a state of being empty which has had all the thought-stuff of dualistic mind cleared out from it.

26. "Identification of things" refers to the process of samsaric mind in which phenomena are known through a process of identifying them with labels. The labelled phenomena are then solidified as "things".

27. Any explanation given to you, the practitioner, by someone else that says your mind is empty is dry because it comes without your own experience. That is not helpful; what is needed is your own direct experience of mind being empty.

28. Again, identified refers to the process of samsaric mind in which a phenomenon is picked out using concept.

29. Note that, since emptiness is being emphasized here, it is empty movement and empty appearance. The first member of these types of pairs always indicates which member of the pair is the most important in the discussion at hand. This is true throughout the book.

30. Having investigated mind and found that it has no source, dwelling place, or final destination, there is the supreme discovery of its not being findable and, with that, it is understood that the coming and going called "mind" in fact is empty appearance. With that, one has gone past mind and arrived at mind's nature, also called mindness. The qualities of "this mindness" which you have just discovered through personal experience will now be described.

31. For shine forth, see the glossary.

32. For without stoppage, unstopped, and stoppage less, all of whih have the same meaning, see the glossary.

33. Tib. sa ler gnas. The term "sa le" or "clearly" is unique to Mahamudra and Great Completion presentations of the nature of mind. It means that the mindness, the nature of mind, from its own side, sits there presenting itself fully and clearly just as it is. If we are obscured, we might not see it clearly but this term is specifically indicating how it sits from its own side and is also indicating that there

is no increase or decrease of this from its own side—it is always presenting itself fully and clearly, just as it is.

34. For actuality, see the glossary.

35. In ancient cultures it was thought that a clear crystal, for example a quartz prism, possessed internal lights of the five colours that were made evident externally when the rays of the sun struck the crystal. This understanding is key to understanding this example, an example used consistently in these teachings.

36. For wisdom, see the glossary. Rigpa can come out either as wisdom or ignorance. The name "rigpa wisdom" is used to indicate rigpa of the wisdom side. "Life wind" is an unusual term here, normally this process is simply described using the term "wind". The explanation of its use is that this is the very force of rigpa wisdom, like the life-wind that keeps sentient beings alive.

37. For field realms, see the glossary.

38. For own appearance, see the glossary.

39. For alpha purity, see the glossary.

40. For offput, see the glossary.

41. Tib. thom me ba. In colloquial usage, this term is used to indicate those moments when one has lost track of what one is doing, one "loses it" for a period and just blanks out, not knowing what one is doing.

42. For awareness, see the glossary.

43. This is the second level of ignorance. Once the fundamental co-emergent ignorance (which actually is co-emergent no-rigpa) is in place, it is fortified by the production of a mind that only deals in concepts. This is known with the name given here in the text. As the next line says, we are now firmly entrenched in the dualistic mind of samsara.

44. For latencies, see the glossary.

45. The *Illuminator Tibetan-English Dictionary* gives: "water wheel: a device from ancient India that was used to carry water to a higher level; the equivalent of a modern-day pump. One form of the device was used for raising water from a well and had buckets strung along a rope, these buckets would be driven around and around up and down, swinging all over the place, during the operation of the device. This was then used as a metaphor for sentient beings being pushed around helplessly all over cyclic existence by karma. A water wheel is for example, the wheel of a mill driven by water; it just goes around and around and cannot do anything else."

46. All-Knowing in this text always refers to All-Knowing Longchen Rabjam. The text mentioned is one of his seven Treasuries.

47. Tīrthika is a name coined by the Buddha for followers of other religions in his time. Although the name is usually translated as "non-buddhist", there is more meaning to it than that. The term means "those who, because they have undertaken a spiritual journey even if it is not a true journey, have arrived at the beginning of the journey across the ocean of samsara". It has a lot of kindness to it. The point here is that people such as the Hindus called the mind "the atman" meaning the eternal self.

48. For dharmadhatu, see the glossary.

49. For alaya, see the glossary.

50. For common awareness, see the glossary.

51. In this section he has gone through many levels of view, starting with the lowest—that of common, worldly people who think of mind as "I"—and going all the way up to the view of innermost unsurpassed Great Completion, which he, beginning with this line, will now explicitly show.

52. Clearly present here and in the next line is the Tibetan term "sal le" described in a previous note.

53. Tib. hrig ge ba. This and the term clearly present are very similar. This term has the sense that it is, from its own side, vividly present, as

though the rigpa is standing up and showing itself to you.

54. For third order world, see the glossary.

55. Meaning it will be impossible for him to find so much as the name buddha apart from his own mindness which has just been pointed out.

56. Factual introduction means an introduction which leads the disciples directly to the fact of one's own mind beyond dualistic understanding. We are now past the point of the preliminary introductions and have reached the main part in which the state of actuality beyond dualistic mind is entered directly.

57. For shining forth, see the glossary.

58. Luminosity in the case of mind refers to its ability to know. In the example of the mirror, it is the mirror's fundamental quality of being able to make things visible.

59. Where Vairochana means "appearing in all different ways", Akshobyavajra means "immutable", Amitabha means "boundless light", Ratnasambhava means "jewel source of all", and Amoghasiddhi means "all-accomplishing acts". Kaya in each case means the collective aspect of self-arising rigpa which behaves in that way.

60. For liveliness, see the glossary.

61. "Setting yourself just so" in Tibetan is called the Chogzhag approach; for Chogzhag, see the glossary.

62. Here again, "thing" means a conceived of thing, so this is referring to space free of concepts.

63. Note that luminosity is a metaphor for knowing.

64. For transparency, see the glossary.

65. There are a number of phrases like abandonment-adoption and rejection-acceptance which in English sound as though they refer to the same thing. However, each of these pairs has its own specific use and meaning and because of that, they are translated in a consistent way throughout the text so that the reader can gain the full meaning

intended. Abandonment-adoption (Tib. spangs blang) is a standard phrase that refers specifically to following the proscriptions and prescriptions of the Buddha's formal dharma teaching which are often summed up in the form of vowed behaviour. Rejection and acceptance has a more general meaning of giving up on whatever is generally bad for oneself as a human and taking up whatever is good. The common thread is that concepts of "this is good" and "this is bad" have been set in place in either case, concepts which enforce a dualistic approach to the path to enlightenment in particular and to human living in general. This Great Completion teaching deals only in unification in which these approaches that belong to and enforce a dualistic approach have been set aside.

66. Appearance and existence, meaning all of the appearing container worlds and all of the contained being existing in them, is one of several standard phrases used to sum up the entirety of samsara and nirvana.

67. For elaboration, see the glossary.

68. Tib cho 'phrul. This term has several connotations. It means something which has been produced using some sort of magic or trickery and which in itself creates a false sense of existence in mind. It could equally be translated as "conjury", "trickery", "gadgetry". I have translated it as trickery throughout this book because that fits best with its usage here.

69. For floaters, see the glossary.

70. For fictional, see the glossary.

71. Here nature means "a solid, self-existing nature".

72. Devaputra was one of Shakyamuni Buddha's disciples. This conversation is recorded in the sutras. Throughout the remainder of this section there are a number of statements marked with "It was taught" or the like. These are extracts from various sutras and in one case from a tantra. He uses them here to lend the weight of the Buddha's own statements to what he is presenting.

73. For Capable One, see the glossary.

74. The beings of the transient hells have a birth for a day or so of our time in which they believe that they are trapped in a door, pillar, etcetera, and suffer greatly for it. The door, pillar, or what have you is their own projection and is sufficiently strong that it is seen as such by the humans of our world.

75. The third order world system in which we humans reside was given the name Endurance by Shakyamuni Buddha because, he explained, the beings in it have the quality of enduring suffering. The Buddha also spoke of its cosmic location, for example, in the quote from the sutras mentioned here.

76. Samantabhadra, in the innermost unsurpassed Great Completion tantras, explained the good qualities of a person who has reached the third—Rigpa Reaching it Measure—of the four appearances, which are the states of Direct Crossing practice.

77. The meaning of assurance is not the same as confidence. Assurance in these teachings means that one knows, through personal and direct experience born of practice, that it is so, and because of that, one is assured of one's capabilities because of it, just as a bird is not merely confident of flying but is assured of flying because of the capabilities it has developed with its bird-type body.

78. When speaking of all appearances, they are often characterized, as they are here, by visual sights and audible sounds. Of course, appearance includes the appearances of all senses—which for humans and animals number six. The reason then for mentioning only visible and audible phenomena is that these are the ones primarily known by humans. If you examine your own experience you will see that you are mainly occupied with sights and sounds and the smells, tastes, touches, and mentally known phenomena make up less of your sensed appearance. Thus, on reading phrases like "sights and sounds" or "visible and audible phenomena" understand that it in fact means all phenomena of the senses.

79. For preserve, see the glossary.

80. The bad migrations are the hell, preta, and animal realms.

81. For mara, see the glossary.

82. For concept tokens, see the glossary.

83. For rational mind, see the glossary.

84. A cut off emptiness is one which is empty only and has no relation to any other quality such as knowing or appearance. Blankness (Tib. had po) specifically refers to a mistaken state of meditation in which the meditator, in trying to achieve emptiness, falls into a blank state of dualistic mind in which the luminous or knowing factor is absent. Blankness has not even transcended dualistic mind and is a very serious mistake in meditation.

85. According to most learned people that I have spoken with, this topic is one of the most difficult to comprehend topics of Great Completion. Longchenpa explains it at length in the first vajra topic of his *Meaning of the Words Treasury* but it remains conceptually very difficult to fathom.

86. Never any meeting and parting it is always exactly that way without any change of degree. In other words, it is a ground situation in which things are primordially so, rather than a path situation.

87. Where it is the ground. A unique feature of this Great Completion teaching is that ground and ground appearances are two distinct phases.

88. "This agent" mentioned at this point in all of these verses means the mind as opposed to the object at which the delusion has been directed which is what he discusses first in each case.

89. Thorough Cut is practised in three steps: introduction, training, and finalization.

90. A vina is a stringed instrument of ancient India, similar to a lute but with a very long neck.

91. In ancient Indian cosmology there were not only kings who controlled areas on this earth but kings who controlled cosmic domains. These kings were called Chakravartins, meaning that they hold

a wheel which is a sign of their governance. There are four levels of these kings. The lowest level controls a first order thousand world domain, which is comprised of one Mt. Meru system and four continents. This sort of king, even though he is the lowest of the four, has fantastic, in the true sense of the word, enjoyments, far beyond the enjoyments of our world.

92. The five precious substances are gold, silver, pearl, coral, and mumen. Mumen is a semi-precious stone of the same chemical family as sapphire. Sometimes it is used to mean sapphire, as is the case here.

93. The sixfold group is the set of sense consciousnesses of humans as a whole.

94. Applying water to wool makes it manageable.

95. One's being is tamed simply by realizing the view. This leads to the meditation—which is generally characterized as having the three qualities mentioned—being aroused. With that, compassion and love for all migrators is effortlessly produced, and the conduct has been gained. Thus, through the view, the meditation and conduct are automatically produced. All of this is part of the special character of Great Completion.

96. Here, introduction does not mean "these introductions ..." referred to a little bit above. Here, it means the introduction to the nature of mind, which is the necessary feature of entering into this path. The introduction to the nature of mind was covered in one of the earlier songs.

97. "Without subtraction or addition" means that there is no need to change anything—no need to remove something seen to be unnecessary and no need to add something seen to be missing.

98. "A focus" is a concept which dualistic mind is taking as its reference point.

99. For referenced, see referencing in the glossary. The state of Great Completion is an open state because the pollution of concepts has been removed. This is carefree, not subject to the usual controls that come

with the biasses of conceptual mind. Moreover, it is a state of transparency, meaning that the totality of the view is seen because there are no obscuring concepts; such a state of transparency is allowed to do as it wishes, because there is not need to control it.

100. For contrivance's spoilage, see the glossary. Dualistic mind is always a contrived situation and that contrivance causes spoilage of the innate wisdom.

101. For vacillatory foci, see the glossary.

102. For suppression and furtherance, see the glossary.

103. Where it continues to refer to the naked state of rigpa mentioned a little above.

104. For dharmata, see the glossary.

105. Mental analysis refers to the process of dualistic mental investigation, examination, and so on. It always involves elaboration, so it is always the opposite of rigpa.

106. This line is composed of what are called "experiential terms" whose use evokes direct experience of what is being discussed. In this line it is something like "freely moving and dancing and staying without inhibition, sitting there as itself without anything interrupting that view of it, an evanescent uncatchable experience, which is there like that but which leaves no trace as it goes about being itself. There are several lines like this in the text. All of them are very beautiful and evoke a precise experience at the same time; unfortunately there are simply no English equivalents. The next line points out that this rigpa being itself like that is the great state evenness in which all phenomena appear without any conceptual biasses whatsoever but are equal in being empty.

107. These two lines likewise are filled with experiential terms. The image being painted is very similar to the idea of cosmic noise. The stuff of the thinking process, if not covered over with dualistic grasping, is like blaring cosmic static and the way to approach that is to

understand that all of rigpa's offput or output is nothing other than the shifting events of the dharmata.

108. For shifting events, see the glossary.

109. Can-do meditation is meditation done by someone who is convinced that they personally can push through and do the meditation.

110. Existence here means samsaric existence.

111. Emitting and withdrawing refers to the process of thinking—thoughts are first emitted and then withdrawn again. Rigpa can either be producing thoughts or not producing them and these two situations are dealt with here in that order. The second situation is called abiding.

112. For dhyana see the glossary. The dhyana of the gods refers to the deep states of absorption that sustain the god-like existences of the form and formless realms.

113. The actual term translated by spotlight is "thig". This referred in ancient Indian culture to a round and luminous sphere. The closest thing in current Western culture is a spotlight that shows up the matter under scrutiny, illuminating it so fully that it is unmistakably and clearly seen. These are four spot lights that highlight four specific issues, illuminating them so thoroughly that there can be no mistake over the meaning.

114. For complete purity, see the glossary.

115. For complexion, see the glossary.

116. For dons, see the glossary. Obstructors are anything that gets in the way of practice. Elementals are spirits who are strongly attached to the elements, for example, a spirit that prefers to live near water; unless appeased they can get in the way of practice.

117. It is very common in Tibet for people each day to send some money to the afternoon assembly of monks with a request that certain mantras or sutras, etcetera, be recited in order to remove whatever

problem is ailing them that day. This is saying not to take such a cheap approach.

118. Productive grove is a general name for all areas where the vegetation produces something useful.

119. Making one's dwelling at the foot of a single tree in a forest and not moving to another location then staying seated in meditation is one of the twelve ascetic acts of Buddhist monks.

120. This line refers to the upper beings who are the guests of a feast.

121. These are other beings with whom you have a karmic debt that will result in harm or death to you when it ripens.

122. For dons, see the glossary. Obstructors are anything that gets in the way of practice. Elementals are spirits who are strongly attached to the elements, for example, a spirit that prefers to live near water; unless appeased they can get in the way of practice.

123. For the spelling of Vajrasatva, see sattva and satva in the glossary.

124. Red and white appearances are the two kinds of appearances that occur based on the red and white elements of the subtle body.

125. Where the secret is the teachings of the Vajra Vehicle.

126. The name of Tshogdrug Rangdrol.

127. The numeral seven is not a mistake. This is a sign used in Tibetan literature to indicate the greatness of someone. It means that the person is considered to have the Seven Noble One's Riches, a set of good qualities of a noble being which were set forth by the Buddha in the teachings of the sutras.

128. Saraha is generally put as one of the great Mahamudra yogins of ancient India. However, he is regarded as the greatest of the eighty-four siddhas and so is also counted as a vidyadhara in this system.

129. This was written by Tenpa'i Wangchug one of his two monasteries.

GLOSSARY

Actuality, Tib. gnas lugs: A key term in both sutra and tantra and one of a pair of terms, the other being "apparent reality" (Tib. snang lugs). The two terms are used when determining the reality of a situation. The actuality of any given situation is how (lugs) the situation actuality sits or is present (gnas); the apparent reality is how (lugs) any given situation appears (snang) to an observer. Something could appear in many different ways, depending on the circumstances at the time and on the being perceiving it but, regardless of those circumstances, it will always have its own actuality of how it really is. The term actuality is frequently used in Mahamudra and Great Completion teachings to mean the fundamental reality of any given phenomenon or situation before any deluded mind alters it and makes it appear differently.

Affliction, Skt. kleśha, Tib. nyon mongs: This term is usually translated as emotion or disturbing emotion, etcetera, but the Buddha was very specific about the meaning of this word. When the Buddha referred to the emotions, meaning a movement of mind, he did not refer to them as such but called them "kleśha" in Sanskrit, meaning exactly "affliction". It is a basic part of the Buddhist teaching that emotions afflict beings, giving them problems at the time and causing more problems in the future.

Alaya, Skt. ālaya, Tib. kun gzhi: This term, if translated, is usually translated as all-base or thereabouts. It is a Sanskrit term that means a range that underlies and forms a basis for something else. In Buddhist teaching, it means a particular level of mind that sits beneath all other levels of mind. However, it is used in several different ways in the Buddhist teaching and changes to a different meaning in each case. In the Great Completion teachings, an important distinction is made between alaya alone and alaya consciousness.

All-Knowing One, Tib. kun mkhyen: Every century in Tibet, there were just a few people who seemed to know everything so were given the title "All-Knowing One". One of them was Longchen Rabjam and throughout this text All-Knowing One always refers to him. Moreover, of all the All-Knowing ones, Longchenpa was regarded as the greatest, therefore, he is also frequently referred to as the "great" or "greatest" All-Knowing One. Note that "All-Knowing" does not mean "omniscient one" even though it is often translated that way.

Alpha purity, Tib. ka dag: A Great Completion term meaning purity that is there from the first, that is, primordial purity. There are many terms in Buddhism that express the notion of "primordial purity" but this one is unique to the Great Completion teaching. The term "alpha purity" matches the Tibetan term both literally and in meaning.

Alteration, altered: Same as contrivance *q.v.*

Assurance, Tib. gdeng: Although often translated as confidence, this term means assurance with all of the extra meaning conveyed by that term. A bird might be confident of its ability to fly but more than that, it has the assurance that it will not fall to the ground because of knowing that it has wings and the training to use them. Similarly, a person might be confident that he could liberate the afflictions but not be assured of doing so because of lack of training or other causes. However, a person who has accumulated the causes to be able to liberate afflictions is assured of the ability to do so.

Awareness, Skt. jñā, Tib. shes pa. "Awareness" is always used in our translations to mean the basic knower of mind or, as Buddhist teaching itself defines it, "a general term for any registering mind", whether dualistic or non-dualistic. Hence, it is used for both samsaric and nirvanic situations; for example, consciousness

(Tib. "rnam par shes pa") is a dualistic form of awareness, whereas rigpa, wisdom (Tib. "ye shes"), and so on are non-dualistic forms of awareness. See rigpa in the glossary for more.

It is noteworthy that the key term "rigpa" is often mistakenly translated as "awareness", even though it is not merely an awareness; this creates considerable confusion amongst practitioners of the higher tantras who are misled by it.

Bardo, Tib. bar do: Literally, "interval" or "in-between place". The general teachings of Buddhism teach this as the interval between one life and the next. However, Nature Great Completion teaches that the cycle of samsaric life consists of four intervals, with the interval between lives consisting of two of the four.

Becoming, Skt. bhāvanā, Tib. srid pa: This is another name for samsaric existence. Beings in samsara have a samsaric existence but, more than that, they are constantly in a state of becoming—becoming this type of being or that type of being in this abode or that, as they are driven along without choice by the karmic process that drives samsaric existence.

Bodhisatva: A bodhisatva is a person who has engendered the bodhichitta, enlightenment mind, and, with that as a basis, has undertaken the path to the enlightenment of a truly complete buddha specifically for the welfare of other beings. Note that, despite the common appearance of "bodhisattva" in Western books on Buddhism, the Tibetan tradition has steadfastly maintained since the time of the earliest translations that the correct spelling is bodhisatva; see under satva and sattva.

Capable One, Skt. muni, Tib. thub pa: The term "muni" as for example in "Shakyamuni" has long been thought to mean "sage" because of an entry in Monier-Williams excellent Sanskrit-English dictionary. In fact, it has been used by many Indian religions since the times of ancient India to mean in general, a religious practitioner "one who could do it", one who has made progress on a spiritual path and thereby become able to restrain his three doors away from non-virtue and affliction.

Chog Zhag, Tib. cog bzhag: The teaching on four Chog Zhag is part of the Thorough Cut teaching of Great Completion. The four Chog

Zhag are four ways of being in which the practitioner has put himself "chog zhag", meaning "set just so". The four are mountain, ocean, appearances, and rigpa. They show the way of being that is taught in the Thorough Cut practice; they can be used as an introduction to that practice but also to give profound instruction on the details of the practice.

Clarity or Illumination, Skt. vara, Tib. gsal ba: This term should be understood as an abbreviation of the Tibetan term, "'od gsal ba", which is translated with luminosity *q.v.* Clarity is not another factor of mind distinct from luminosity but merely a convenient abbreviation in both Indian and Tibetan dharma language for luminosity.

Clinging, Tib. zhen pa: In Buddhism, this term refers specifically to the twofold process of dualistic mind mis-taking things that are not true, not pure, as true, pure, etcetera and then, because of seeing them as highly desirable even though they are not, attaching itself to or clinging to those things. This type of clinging acts as a kind of glue that keeps a person joined to the unsatisfactory things of cyclic existence because of mistakenly seeing them as desirable.

Common awareness, Tib. tha mal gyi shes pa: One of several path terms used to indicate mind's essence. It is equivalent to "mindness" and "rigpa". These terms are used by practitioners as a code word for their own, personal experience of the essence of mind. These words are secret because of the power they are connected with and should be kept that way.

This term is often referred to as "ordinary mind", a term that was established by Chogyam Trungpa Rinpoche for his students. However, there are two problems with that word. Firstly, "tha mal" does not mean "ordinary". It means the awareness which is common to all parts of samsaric mind and also which is common to all beings. It is glossed in writings on Mahamudra to mean "nature". In other words, it refers to that part of mind which, being common to all events of mind, is its nature. This is well attested to in the writings of the Kagyu forefathers. Secondly, this is not "mind", given that mind is used to mean the dualistic mind of beings in cyclic existence. Rather this is "shes pa", the most general term for all kinds of awareness.

Compassionate activity, Tib. thugs rje: This does not mean compassionate activity in general. Rather, it is a specific term of the most profound level of teachings of Mahamudra and Great Completion. These teachings describe innate wisdom as having three characteristics. The third characteristic is this compassionate activity. It refers to the fact that wisdom spontaneously does whatever needs to be done, throughout all reaches of time and space, for all beings. Although it includes the word "compassion" in its name, it is more primordial than that. It is the dynamic quality of enlightenment which choicelessly, ceaselessly, spontaneously, and pervasively acts to benefit others. The term is often used in discussions of Great Completion and essence Mahamudra.

Complete purity, rnam dag: This term refers to the quality of a buddha's mind, which is completely pure compared to a sentient being's mind. The mind of a being in samsara has its primordially pure nature covered over by the muck of dualistic mind. If the being practises correctly, the impurity can be removed and mind can be returned to its original state of complete purity.

Complexion, Tib. mdangs: In both Mahamudra and Great Completion there is the general term "gdangs" meaning what is given off or emitted by something in general, for example the sound given off by a loudspeaker or what the empty factor of mind emits. The Mahamudra teaching does not distinguish between "gdangs" and "mdangs" but the Great Completion teaching does. In Great Completion, this term has the more refined meaning of the "complexion" or "lustre" of thing. In this teaching, there is the "gdangs" offput or output of the empty aspect of mind in general, but there is also the more subtle "mdangs" complexion or lustre which is an aspect of the offput or output of that emptiness.

Conceived effort, conceived endeavour, Tib. rtsol ba: In Buddhism, this term usually does not merely mean effort but has the specific connotation of effort of dualistic mind. In that case, it is effort that is produced by and functions specifically within the context of dualistic concept. For example, the term "mindfulness with effort" specifically means "a type of mindfulness that is occurring within the context of dualistic mind and its various operations". The term "effortless" is often used in Mahamudra and Great Completion to mean a way of being in which dualistic mind has been abandoned and, therefore, in which there is none of the striving of ordinary people.

Concept tokens, Tib. mtshan ma: This is the technical name for the structures or concepts which function as the words of conceptual mind's language. For example, a table seen in Adirect visual perception will have no concept tokens involved with knowing it. However, when thought becomes involved and there is the thought "table" in an inferential or conceptual perception of the table, the name-tag "table" will be used to reference the table and that name tag is the concept token.

Although we usually reference phenomena via these concepts, the phenomena are not the dualistically referenced things we think of them as being. The actual fact of the phenomena is quite different from the concept tokens used to discursively think about them and is known by wisdom rather than concept-based mind. Therefore, this term is often used in Buddhist literature to signify that samsaric mind is involved rather than non-dualistic wisdom.

Confusion, Tib. 'khrul pa: In Buddhism, this term mostly refers to the fundamental confusion of taking things the wrong way that happens because of fundamental ignorance, although it can also have the more general meaning of having lots of thoughts and being confused about it. In the first case, it is defined like this "Confusion is the appearance to rational mind of something being present when it is not" and refers, for example, to seeing an object, such as a table, as being truly present, when in fact it is present only as mere, interdependent appearance.

Contrivance, contrived, Tib. bcos pa: A term meaning that something has been altered from its native state.

Cyclic existence: See under samsara.

Dharmadhatu, Skt. dharmadhātu, Tib. chos kyi dbyings: This is the name for the range or basic space in which all dharmas, meaning all phenomena, come into being. If a flower bed is the place where flowers grow and are found, the dharmadhatu is the dharma or phenomena bed in which all phenomena come into being and are found. The term is used in all levels of Buddhist teaching with that basis meaning but the explanation of it becomes more profound as the teaching becomes more profound. In Great Completion and Mahamudra, it is the all-pervading sphere of luminosity-wisdom, given that luminosity is where phenomena arise and that the luminosity is none other than wisdom.

Dharmakaya, Skt. dharmakāya, Tib. chos sku: In the general teachings of Buddhism, this refers to the mind of a buddha, with "dharma" meaning reality and "kaya" meaning body. In the Thorough Cut practice of Great Completion it additionally has the special meaning of being the means by which one rapidly imposes liberation on oneself.

Dharmata, Skt. dharmatā, Tib. chos nyid: This is a general term meaning the way that something is, and can be applied to anything at all; it is similar in meaning to "actuality" *q.v.* For example, the dharmata of water is wetness and the dharmata of the becoming bardo is a place where beings are in a samsaric, or becoming mode, prior to entering a nature bardo. It is used frequently in Tibetan Buddhism to mean "the dharmata of reality" but that is a specific case of the much larger meaning of the term. To read texts which use this term successfully, one has to understand that the term has a general meaning and then see how that applies in context.

Dhyana, Skt. dhyāna, Tib. bsam gtan: A Sanskrit term technically meaning all types of mental absorption. Mental absorptions cultivated in the human realm generally result in births in the form realms which are deep forms of concentration in themselves. The practices of mental absorption done in the human realm and the godly existences of the form realm that result from them both are named "dhyāna". The Buddha repeatedly pointed out that the dhyānas were a side-track to emancipation from cyclic existence.

In a more general way, the term also means meditation in general where one is concentrating on something as a way of developing oneself spiritually. Texts on Great Completion often use the word in this sense when making the point that attempts to meditate on anything are the very opposite of the Great Completion practice and will inevitably keep the practitioner within samsara.

Direct Crossing, Tib. thod rgal: The name of one of the two main practices of the innermost level of Great Completion. The other one is Thorough Cut *q.v.*

Discursive thought, Skt. vikalpa, Tib. rnam rtog: This means more than just the superficial thought that is heard as a voice in the head. It includes the entirety of conceptual process that arises due to mind contacting any object of any of the senses. The Sanskrit and Tibetan literally mean "(dualistic) thought (that arises from the mind wandering among the) various (superficies *q.v.* perceived in the doors of the senses)".

Don(s), Tib. gdon: A general term for any kind of negative force that hits a person and brings trouble. It could be any external or internal thing that causes trouble. A good way to think of it is "negative influence" or "negative force".

Effort, Conceived effort, Tib. rtsol ba: In Buddhism, this term usually does not merely mean effort but has the specific connotation of effort of dualistic mind. In that case, it is effort that is produced by and functions specifically within the context of dualistic concept. For example, the term "mindfulness with effort" specifically means "a type of mindfulness that is occurring within the context of dualistic mind and its various operations". The term "effortless" is often used in Mahamudra and Great Completion to mean a way of being in which dualistic mind has been abandoned and, therefore, has with it none of the effort of dualistic mind.

Elaboration, Tib. spro ba: This is a general name for what is given off by dualistic mind as it goes about its conceptual process. In general, elaborations prevent a person from seeing emptiness directly. Freedom from elaborations implies direct sight of emptiness.

Entity, Tib. ngo bo: The entity of something is just exactly what that thing is. In English we would often simply say "thing" rather than entity. However, in Buddhism, "thing" has a very specific meaning rather than the general meaning that it has in English. It has become common to translate this term as "essence". However, in most cases "entity", meaning what a thing is rather than an essence of that thing, is the correct translation for this term.

Equipoise and post-attainment, Tib. mnyam bzhag and rjes thob: Although often called "meditation and post-meditation", the actual term is "equipoise and post-attainment". There is great meaning in the actual wording which is lost by the looser translation.

Expressions, Tib. brjod pa: According to Sanskrit and Tibetan grammar following it, expressions refers to mental and verbal expressions. Thus, for example, the phrase seen in translation of "word, thought, and expression" is mistaken. The phrase is actually "expressions mental and verbal".

Expanse, Skt. dhātu, Tib. dbyings: A Sanskrit term with over twenty meanings. Many of those meanings are also present in the Tibetan equivalent. In the Vajra Vehicle teachings it is used as a replacement for the term emptiness that conveys a non-theoretical sense of the experience of emptiness. When used this way, it has the sense "expanse" because emptiness is experienced as an expanse in which all phenomena appear.

Fact, Skt. artha, Tib. don: "Fact" is that knowledge of an object that occurs to the surface of mind. It is not the object but what the mind understands as the object.

Fictional, Skt. saṃvṛti, Tib. kun rdzob: This term is paired with the term "superfactual" *q.v.* Until now these two terms have been translated as "relative" and "absolute" but these translations are nothing like the original terms. These terms are extremely important in the Buddhist teaching so it is very important that they be corrected, but more than that, if the actual meaning of these terms is not presented, then the teaching connected with them cannot be understood.

The Sanskrit term samvṛti means a deliberate invention, a fiction, a hoax. It refers to the mind of ignorance which, because of being obscured and so not seeing suchness, is not true but a fiction. The things that appear to that ignorance are therefore fictional. Nonetheless, the beings who live in this ignorance believe that the things that appear to them through the filter of ignorance are true, are real. Therefore, these beings live in fictional truth.

Fictional and superfactual: Fictional and superfactual are our greatly improved translations for "relative" and "absolute" respectively.

Briefly, the original Sanskrit word for fiction means a deliberately produced *fiction* and refers to the world projected by a mind controlled by ignorance. The original word for superfact means "that *super*ior *fact* that appears on the surface of the mind of a noble one who has transcended samsara" and refers to reality seen as it actually is. Relative and absolute do not convey this meaning at all and, when they are used, the meaning being presented is simply lost.

Field, Field realm, Tib. zhing, zhing khams: This term is often translated "buddha field" though there is no "buddha" in the term. There are many different types of "fields" in both samsara and nirvana. Thus there are fields that belong to enlightenment and ones that belong to ignorance. Moreover, just as there are "realms" of samsara—desire, form, and formless—so there are realms of nirvana—the fields dharmakaya, sambhogakaya, and nirmanakaya and these are therefore called "field realms".

Finality obtained, Tib. gtan pa thob ba: the path of a the Thorough Cut practitioner proceeds in a three step process of introduction, followed by training, followed by attaining finality. This term is sometimes translated as stability but that does not capture the full meaning. The original term means that one has gone to the point where the whole training is finalized; it has been taken to the definitive point.

Five kayas: See under kaya.

Five paths, Tib. lam lnga: In the Prajñaparamita teachings of the Great Vehicle, the Buddha explained the entire Buddhist journey as a set of five paths called the paths of accumulation, connection, seeing, cultivation, and no more training. The first four paths are part of journeying to enlightenment; the fifth path is that one has actually arrived and has no more training to undergo. There are a set of five paths that describe the journey of the Lesser Vehicle and a set of five paths that describe the journey of the Greater Vehicle. The names are the same in each case but the details of what is accomplished at each stage are different.

Floaters, Tib. rab rib: This term has usually been mistakenly translated as "cataracts". It is the medical term for eyes with a disease known as *Muscaria volante* in Western ophthalmology. The disease is common to a large portion of the world's population and has the common term "floaters" given to it by the medical profession. Almost anyone who looks out at a clear source of light will see grey threads, sometimes twisted, sometimes straight, floating in the field of vision. When an eye is moved, because the gel of the eye shifts, the floaters can seem to be like hairs falling through the field of vision and so are sometimes called "falling hairs". They seem to be "out there" when in fact they are shadows being cast on the retina by fissures in the gel inside the eye. The point is that they seem real when in fact they are an aberration produced by an illness of the eye.

Focus, foci, Tib. gtad so: A focus is a particular issue that rational mind is focussing on. Sometimes this term is used to infer the presence of dualistic mind.

Foremost instruction, Skt. upadeśha, Tib. man ngag: There are several types of instruction mentioned in Buddhist literature: there is the general level of instruction which is the meaning contained in the words of the texts of the tradition; on a more personal and direct level there is oral instruction which has been passed down from teacher to student from the time of the buddha; and on the most profound level there are foremost instructions which are not only oral instructions provided by one's guru but are special, core instructions that come out of personal experience and which convey the teaching concisely and with the full weight of personal experience. Foremost instructions or upadesha are crucial to the Vajra Vehicle because these are the special way of passing on the profound instructions needed for the student's realization.

Fortune, fortunate person, Tib. skal ldan: To meet with any given dharma teaching, a person must have accumulated the karmic fortune needed for such a rare opportunity, and this kind of person is then called "a fortunate one" or "fortunate person". This term is especially used in the Vajra Vehicle, whose teachings and practices are generally very hard to meet with.

Grasped-grasping, Tib. gzung 'dzin: When mind is turned outwardly as it is in the normal operation of dualistic mind, it has developed two faces that appear simultaneously. Special names are given to these two faces: mind appearing in the form of the external object being referenced is called "that which is grasped" and mind appearing in the form of the consciousness that is registering it is called the "grasper" or "grasping" of it. Thus, there is the pair of terms "grasped-grasper" or "grasped-grasping". When these two terms are used, it alerts one to the fact that a Mind Only style of presentation is being discussed. This pair of terms pervades Mind Only, Middle Way, and tantric writings and is exceptionally important in all of them.

Note that one could substitute the word "apprehended" for "grasped" and "apprehender" for "grasper" or "grasping" and that would reflect one connotation of the original Indian terminology. The solidified duality of grasped and grasper is nothing but an invention of dualistic thought; it has that kind of character or characteristic.

Ground, Tib. gzhi: This is the first member of the formulation of ground, path, and fruition. Ground, path, and fruition is the way that the teachings of the path of oral instruction belonging to the Vajra Vehicle are presented to students. Ground refers to the basic situation as it is.

Ignorance, Skt. avidya, Tib. ma rig pa: Rigpa *q.v.* is a key term in these discussions. It refers to the enlightened kind of knowing. Its opposite, not-rigpa, which refers to the unenlightened way of knowing, is equally important. As it says in the *Abhidharmakosha*, "not-rigpa is not merely a discordance with rigpa but is its very opposite". Not-rigpa is usually translated as ignorance though this has the great fault in Great Completion discussions that it masks the all-important relationship between rigpa and not-rigpa.

Innate, Tib. gnyug ma: This is a standard term of the higher tantras used to mean the inner situation of samsaric mind, which is its indwelling or innate wisdom.

Introduction and To Introduce, Tib. ngos sprad and ngos sprod pa respectively: This pair of terms is usually translated today as "pointing out" and "to point out" but this is a mistake that has, unfortunately, become entrenched. The terms are the standard terms used in day to day life for the situation in which one person introduces another person to someone or something. They are the exact same words as our English "introduction" and "to introduce".

In the Vajra Vehicle, these terms are specifically used for the situation in which one person introduces another person to the nature of his own mind. There is a term in Tibetan for "pointing out", but that term is never used for this purpose because in this case no one points out anything. Rather, a person is introduced by another person to a part of himself that he has forgotten about.

Kagyu, Tib. bka' brgyud: There are four main schools of Buddhism in Tibet—Nyingma, Kagyu, Sakya, and Gelug. Nyingma is the oldest school dating from about 800 C.E. Kagyu and Sakya both appeared in the 12th century C.E. Each of these three schools came directly from India. The Gelug school came later and did not come directly from India but came from the other three. The Nyingma school holds the tantric teachings called Great Completion (Dzogchen); the other three schools hold the tantric teachings called Mahamudra. Kagyu practitioners often join Nyingma practice with their Kagyu practice and Kagyu teachers often teach both, so it is common to hear about Kagyu and Nyingma together.

Kaya, Skt. kāya, Tib. sku: The Sanskrit term means a functional or coherent collection of parts, similar to the French "corps", and hence also comes to mean "a body". It is used in Tibetan Buddhist texts specifically to distinguish bodies belonging to the enlightened side from ones belonging to the samsaric side.

Enlightened being in Buddhism is said to be comprised of one or more kayas. It is most commonly explained to consist of one, two, three, four, or five kayas, though it is pointed out that there are infinite aspects to enlightened being and therefore it can also be said to consist of an infinite number of kayas. In fact, these descriptions of enlightened being consisting of one or more kayas are given for the sake of understanding what is beyond conceptual understanding so should not be taken as absolute statements.

The most common description of enlightened being is that it is comprised of three kayas: dharma, sambhoga, and nirmanakayas. Briefly stated, the dharmakaya is the body of truth, the sambhogakaya is the body replete with the good qualities of enlightenment, and the nirmanakaya is the body manifested into the worlds of samsara and nirvana to benefit beings.

Dharmakaya refers to that aspect of enlightened being in which the being sees the truth for himself and, in doing so, fulfils his own needs for enlightenment. The dharmakaya is purely mind, without form. The remaining two bodies are summed up under the heading of rupakayas or form bodies manifested specifically to fulfil the needs of all un-enlightened beings. "Sambhogakaya" has been mostly translated as "body of enjoyment" or "body of rapture" but it is clearly stated in Buddhist texts on the subject that the name refers to a situation replete with what is useful, that is, to the fact that the sambhogakaya contains all of the good qualities of enlightenment as needed to benefit sentient beings. The sambhogakaya is extremely subtle and not accessible by most sentient beings; the nirmanakaya is a coarser manifestation which can reach sentient beings in many ways. Nirmanakaya should not be thought of as a physical body but as the capability to express enlightened being in whatever way is needed throughout all the different worlds of sentient beings. Thus, as much as it appears as a supreme buddha who shows the dharma to beings, it also appears as anything needed within sentient beings worlds to give them assistance.

The three kayas of enlightened being is taught in all levels of Buddhist teaching. It is especially important in Great Completion and is taught there in a unique and very profound way.

Key points, Tib. gnad: Key points are those places in one's being that one works, like pressing buttons, in order to get some desired effect. For example, in meditation, there are key points of the body; by adjusting those key points, the mind is brought closer to reality and the meditation is thus assisted.

In general, this term is used in Buddhist meditation instruction but it is, in particular, part of the special vocabulary of the Great Completion teachings. Overall, the Great Completion teachings are given as a series of key points that must be attended to in order to bring forth the various realizations of the path.

Knower, Tib. ha go ba: "Knower" is a generic term for that which knows. There are many types of knower, with each having its own qualities and name, too. For example, *wisdom* is a non-dualistic knower, *mind* is the dualistic samsaric version of it, *consciousness* refers to the individual "registers" of samsaric mind, and so on. Sometimes a term is needed which simply says "that which knows" without further implication of what kind of knowing it might be. *Knower* is one of a few terms of that sort.

Latency, Skt. vāsanā, Tib. bag chags: The original Sanskrit has the meaning exactly of "latency". The Tibetan term translates that inexactly with "something sitting there (Tib. chags) within the environment of mind (Tib. bag)". Although it has become popular to translate this term into English with "habitual pattern", that is not its meaning. The term refers to a karmic seed that has been imprinted on the mindstream and is present there as a latency, ready and waiting to come into manifestation.

Left to be itself, Tib. rang babs bzhag: An important term in Mahamudra and Great Completion which refers to the basic style of meditation in these systems. It has the same meaning as uncontrived resting but instead of saying "without contrivance" it says "left as it naturally is". It means that the resting is not made up, forced or produced but allowed to happen of itself.

Liveliness, Tib. rtsal: A key term in both Mahāmudrā and Great Completion. The term is sometimes translated as "display" or "expression" but neither are correct. The primary meaning is the ability of something to express itself but in use, the actual expression of that ability is also included. Thus, in English it would not be "expression" but "expressivity" but that is too dry. This term is not at all dry; it is talking about the life of something and how that life comes into expression; "liveliness" fits the meaning of the original term very well.

Luminosity or illumination, Skt. prabhāsvara, Tib. 'od gsal ba: The core of mind has two aspects: an emptiness factor and a knowing factor. The Buddha and many Indian religious teachers used "luminosity" as a metaphor for the knowing quality of the core of mind. If in English we would say "Mind has a knowing quality", the teachers of ancient India would say, "Mind has an illuminative quality; it is like a source of light which illuminates what it knows".

This term been translated as "clear light" but that is a mistake that comes from not understanding the etymology of the word. It does not refer to a light that has the quality of clearness (something that makes no sense, actually!) but to the illuminative property which is the nature of the empty mind.

Note also that in both Sanskrit and Tibetan Buddhist literature, this term is frequently abbreviated just to Skt. "vara" and Tib. "gsal ba" with no change of meaning. Unfortunately, this has been thought to be another word and it has then been translated with "clarity", when in fact it is just this term in abbreviation.

Maha Atí, Skt. mahāti, Tib. shin tu chen po: Mahā Ati or Ati Yoga is the name of the ninth and last of the nine vehicles taught in the Nyingma system of nine vehicles. The name "ati" literally means that it is the vehicle at the end of the sequence of all other vehicles. It is not only the final vehicle at the end of the sequence but the peak of all vehicles given that it presents reality more directly than any of the vehicles below it. It is therefore also called the king of vehicles.

"Mahāsaṅdhi"—"Dzogpa Chenpo" in the Tibetan language and "Great Completion" in the English language—is the name of the teachings on reality contained in the Maha Ati vehicle and also of the reality itself. Great Completion and Maha Ati are often used interchangeably even through their references are slightly different. See Great Completion in the glossary for more.

Mahamudra, Skt. mahāmudrā, Tib. phyag rgya chen po: Mahamudra is the name of a set of ultimate teachings on reality and also of the reality itself. This is explained at length in the book *Gampopa's Mahamudra: The Five-Part Mahamudra of the Kagyus* by Tony Duff, published by Padma Karpo Translation Committee, 2008, ISBN: 978-9937-2-0607-5.

Mara, Skt. māra, Tib. bdud: A Sanskrit term closely related to the word "death". Buddha spoke of four classes of extremely negative influences that have the capacity to drag a sentient being deep into samsara. They are the "maras" or "kiss of death": of having a samsaric set of five skandhas; of having afflictions; of death itself; and of the son of gods, which means being seduced and taken in totally by sensuality.

Migrator, Tib. 'gro ba: Migrator is one of several terms that were commonly used by the Buddha to mean "sentient being". It shows sentient beings from the perspective of their constantly being forced to go here and there from one rebirth to another by the power of karma. They are like flies caught in a jar, constantly buzzing back and forth. The term is often translated using "beings" which is another general term for sentient beings but doing so loses the meaning entirely: Buddhist authors who know the tradition do not use the word loosely but use it specifically to give the sense of beings who are constantly and helplessly going from one birth to another, and that is how the term should be read. The term "six migrators refers to the six types of migrators within samsaric existence—hell-beings, pretas, animals, humans, demi-gods, and gods.

Mind, Skt. chitta, Tib. sems: There are several terms for mind in the Buddhist tradition, each with its own, specific meaning. This term is the most general term for the samsaric type of mind. It refers to the type of mind that is produced because of fundamental ignorance of enlightened mind. Whereas the wisdom of enlightened mind lacks all complexity and knows in a non-dualistic way, this mind of un-enlightenment is a very complicated apparatus that only ever knows in a dualistic way.

The Mahamudra and Great Completion teachings use the terms "entity of mind" and "mind's entity" to refer to what this complicated, samsaric mind is at core—the enlightened form of mind.

Mindfulness, Skt. smṛiti, Tib. dran pa: A particular mental event, one that has the ability to keep mind on its object. Together with alertness, it is one of the two causes of developing shamatha. See under alertness for an explanation.

Mindness, Skt. chittatā, Tib. sems nyid: Mindness is a specific term of the tantras. It is one of many terms meaning the essence of mind or the nature of mind. It conveys the sense of "what mind is at its very core". It has sometimes been translated as "mind itself" but that is a misunderstanding of the Tibetan word "nyid". The term does not mean "that thing mind" where mind refers to dualistic mind. Rather, it means the very core of dualistic mind, what mind is at root, without all of the dualistic baggage.

Mindness is a path term. It refers to exactly the same thing as "actuality" or "actuality of mind" which is a ground term but does so from the practitioner's perspective. It conveys the sense to a practitioner that he has baggage of dualistic mind that has not yet been purified but that there is a core to that mind that he can work with.

Muni: See under capable one.

Nail, Tib. gzer: Nail is used to mean an instruction or a procedure by which a particular point of understanding or realization is "pegged" or "pinned" down so that it does not leave the practitioner's experience.

Nature Great Completion, Tib. rang bzhin rdzogs pa chen po: This is one of several names for Great Completion that emphasizes the path aspect of Great Completion. It is not "natural great completion" nor is it "the true nature Great Completion" as commonly seen. In terms of grammar, the first term is the noun "nature" not the adjective "natural". In terms of meaning, the noun nature is used because it refers to the nature aspect in particular of the three characteristics of the essence of mind—entity, nature, and unstopped compassionate activity—used to describe Great Completion as experienced by the practitioner. Thus, this name refers to the approach taken by Great Completion and does not refer at all to Great Completion being a "natural" practice or its being connected with a "natural reality" or any of the many other, incorrect meanings that arise from the mistaken translation "natural Great Completion".

Noble one, Skt. ārya, Tib. 'phags pa: In Buddhism, a noble one is a being who has become spiritually advanced to the point that he has passed beyond cyclic existence. According to the Buddha, the beings in cyclic existence were ordinary beings, spiritual commoners, and the beings who had passed beyond it were special, the nobility.

Not stopped, Tib. ma 'gags pa: An important path term in the teaching of both Mahamudra and Great Completion. There are two ways to explain this term: theoretically and from a practice perspective. The following explanation is of the latter type. The core of mind has two parts—emptiness and luminosity—which are in fact unified so must come that way in practice. However, a practitioner who is still on the path will fall into one extreme or the other and that results in "stoppage" of the expression of the luminosity. When emptiness and luminosity are unified in practice, there is no stoppage of the expression of the luminosity that comes from having fallen into one extreme or the other. Thus "non-stopped luminosity" is a term that indicates that there is the luminosity with all of its appearance yet that luminosity, for the practitioner, is not mistaken, is not stopped off. "Stopped luminosity" is an experience like luminosity but in which the appearances have, at least to some extent, not been mixed with emptiness.

Offput, Tib. gdangs: Offput is a general term for that which is given off by something, for example, the sound that comes from a loudspeaker. In Mahamudra and Great Completion, it refers to what is given off by the emptiness factor of the essence of mind. Emptiness is the empty condition of the essence of mind, like space. However, that emptiness has liveliness which comes off the emptiness as compassion and all the other qualities of enlightened mind, and, equally, all the apparatus of dualistic mind. All of this is called its offput. Note that the Great Completion teachings have a special word that is a more refined version of this term; see under complexion for that.

Own Appearance, Tib. rang snang: This is regarded as one of the more difficult terms to explain within Buddhist philosophy. It does not mean "self-appearance" in the sense of something coming into appearance of itself. Suffice it to say that it refers to a situation that is making its own appearances in accord with its own situation.

Poisons, Tib. dug: In Buddhism, poison is a general term for the afflictions. For samsaric beings, the afflictions are poisonous things which harm them. The Buddha most commonly spoke of the three poisons, which are the principal afflictions of desire, aggression, and ignorance. He also spoke of "the five poisons" which is a slightly longer enumeration of the principal afflictions: desire, aggression, delusion, pride, and jealousy.

Preserve, Tib. skyong ba: An important term in both Mahamudra and Great Completion. In general, it means to defend, protect, nurture, maintain. In the higher tantras it means to keep something just as it is, to nurture that something so that it stays and is not lost. Also, in the higher tantras, it is often used in reference to preserving the state where the state is some particular state of being. Because of this, the phrase "preserve the state" is an important instruction in the higher tantras.

Primal Guardian, Skt. ādinātha, Tib. gdod ma'i mgon po: Primal Guardian protector is one of many names for the *primal* state of enlightenment innate to each person personified as the *guardian* who in Nyingma tradition is Samantabhadra and in new translation schools is Great Vajradhara.

Rational mind, Tib. blo: Rational mind is one of several terms for mind in Buddhist terminology. It specifically refers to a mind that judges this against that. With rare exception it is used to refer to samsaric mind, given that samsaric mind only works in the dualistic mode of comparing this versus that. Because of this, the term is mostly used in a pejorative sense to point out samsaric mind as opposed to an enlightened type of mind.

The Gelugpa tradition does have a positive use for this mind and their documents will sometimes use this term in a positive sense; they claim that a buddha has an enlightened type of this mind. That is not wrong; one could refer to the ability of a buddha's wisdom to make a distinction between this and that with the term "rational mind". However, the Kagyu and Nyingma traditions in their Mahamudra and Great Completion teachings, reserve this term for the dualistic mind. In their teachings, it is the villain, so to speak, which needs to be removed from the practitioner's being in order to obtain enlightenment.

This term has been commonly translated simply as "mind" but that fails to identify this term properly and leaves it confused with the many other words that are also translated simply as "mind".

It is not just another mind but is specifically the sort of mind that creates the situation of this and that (*ratio* in Latin) and hence, at least in the teachings of Kagyu and Nyingma, upholds the duality of samsara. In that case, it is the very opposite of the essence of mind. Thus, this is a key term which should be noted and not just glossed over as "mind".

Realization, Tib. rtogs pa: Realization has a very specific meaning: it refers to correct knowledge that has been gained in such a way that the knowledge does not abate. There are two important points here. Firstly, realization is not absolute. It refers to the removal of obscurations, one at a time. Each time that a practitioner removes an obscuration, he gains a realization because of it. Therefore, there are as many levels of realization as there are obscurations. Maitreya, in the *Ornament of Manifest Realizations*, shows how the removal of the various obscurations that go with each of the three realms of samsaric existence produces realization.

Secondly, realization is stable or, as the Tibetan wording says, "unchanging". As Guru Rinpoche pointed out, "Intellectual knowledge is like a patch, it drops away; experiences on the path are temporary, they evaporate like mist; realization is unchanging".

A special usage of "realization" is found in the Essence Mahamudra and Great Completion teachings. There, realization is the term used to describe what happens at the moment when mindness is actually met during either introduction to or self-recognition of mindness. It is called realization because, in that glimpse, one actually directly sees the innate wisdom mind. The realization has not been stabilized but it is realization.

Referencing, Tib. dmigs pa: This is the name for the process in which dualistic mind references an actual object by using a conceptual token instead of the actual object. The term referencing implies the presence of dualistic mind and the term non-referencing or without reference implies the presence of non-dualistic wisdom.

Rigpa, Tib. rig pa: This is the singularly most important term in the whole of Great Completion and Mahamudra. In particular, it is the key word of all words in the Great Completion system of the

Thorough Cut. Rigpa literally means to know in the sense of "I see!" It is used at all levels of meaning from the coarsest everyday sense of knowing something to the deepest sense of knowing something as presented in the system of Thorough Cut. The system of Thorough Cut uses this term in a very special sense, though it still retains its basic meaning of "to know". To translate it as "awareness", which is common practice today, is a poor practice; there are many kinds of awareness but there is only one rigpa and besides, rigpa is substantially more than just awareness. Since this is such an important term and since it lacks an equivalent in English, I choose not to translate it.

This is the term used to indicate enlightened mind as experienced by the practitioner on the path of these practices. The term itself specifically refers to the dynamic knowing quality of mind. It absolutely does not mean a simple registering, as implied by the word "awareness" which unfortunately is often used to translate this term. There is no word in English that exactly matches it, though the idea of "seeing" or "insight on the spot" is very close. Proof of this is found in the fact that the original Sanskrit term "vidyā" is actually the root of all words in English that start with "vid" and mean "to see", for example, "video", "vision", and so on. Chogyam Trungpa Rinpoche, who was particular skilled at getting Tibetan words into English, also stated that this term rigpa really did not have a good equivalent in English, though he thought that "insight" was the closest. My own conclusion after hearing extensive teaching on it is that rigpa is best left untranslated. Note that rigpa has both noun and verb forms.

Samsara, Skt. saṃsāra, Tib. 'khor ba: This is the most general name for the type of existence in which sentient beings live. It refers to the fact that they continue on from one existence to another, always within the enclosure of births that are produced by ignorance and experienced as unsatisfactory. The original Sanskrit means to be constantly going about, here and there. The Tibetan term literally means "cycling", because of which it is frequently translated into English with "cyclic existence" though that is not quite the meaning of the term.

Satva and sattva: According to the Tibetan tradition established at the time of the great translation work done at Samye under the watch of Padmasambhava not to mention the one hundred and sixty-three of the greatest Buddhist scholars of Sanskrit-speaking India, there is a difference of meaning between the Sanskrit terms "satva" and "sativa", with satva meaning "an heroic kind of being" and "sattva" meaning simply "a being". According to the Tibetan tradition established under the advice of the Indian scholars mentioned above, satva is correct for the words Vajrasatva and bodhisatva, whereas sattva is correct for the words samayasattva, samadhisattva, and jñanasattva, and is also used alone to refer to any or all of these three satvas.

Shifting events, Tib. yo lang: This refers to the events of a practitioner's life being seen as the shifting events of the dharmakāya. The dharmakaya has an outpouring of display which comes out not as a nice, rationally-ordered experience but as the random and higgledy-piggledy events experienced by the practitioner of that state.

Shine forth, shining forth, Tib. shar ba: This term means "to dawn" or "to come forth into visibility" either in the outer physical world or in the inner world of mind.

It is heavily used in texts on meditation to indicate the process of something coming forth into mind. There are other terms with this specific meaning but most of them also imply the process of dawning within a samsaric mind. "Shine forth" is special because it does not have that restricted meaning; it refers to the process of something dawning in any type of mind, un-enlightened and enlightened. It is an important term for the higher tantras of Mahamudra and Great Completion texts where there is a great need to refer to the simple fact of something dawning in mind especially in enlightened mind but also in un-enlightened mind.

In the Tibetan language, this term stands out and immediately conveys the meaning explained above. There are words in English like "to appear" that might seem easier to read than "shine forth", but they do not stand out and catch the attention sufficiently. Moreover, terms such as "appear" accurately translate other Tibetan terms which specifically indicate an un-enlightened context or a certain type of sensory appearance, so they do not convey the meaning of this term. There will be many times where this term's specific meaning of something occurring in any type of mind is crucial to a full understanding of the expression under consideration. For example, "shining-forth liberation" means that some content of mind, such as a thought, comes forth in either unenlightened or enlightened mind, and that, on coming forth, is liberated there in that mind.

State, Tib. ngang: This is a key term in Mahāmudrā and Great Completion. Unfortunately it is often not translated and in so doing much meaning is lost. Alternatively, it is often translated as "within" which is incorrect. The term means a "state". A state is a certain, ongoing situation. In Buddhist meditation in general, there are various states that a practitioner has to enter and remain in as part of developing the meditation.

Stoppageless, Tib. 'gag pa med pa: This is a key term in Mahamudra and Great Completion. It is usually translated as "unceasing" but this is a different verb. It refers to the situation in which one thing is not being stopped by another thing. It means "not stopped", "without stoppage", "not blocked and prevented by something else" that is, stoppageless. The verb form associated with it is "not stopped" *q.v.* It is used in relation to the practice of luminosity. A stoppageless luminosity is the actual state of reality and what the practitioner has to aim for. At the beginning of the practice, a practitioner's experience of luminosity will usually not be stoppageless but with stoppages.

Stopped, Tib. 'gags pa: See under not-stopped and stoppageless.

Sugatagarbha, Tib. bde war gshegs pa'i snying po: This is a Sanskrit term literally meaning "the birthplace of those who go to bliss" and used as a name for the buddha nature. The buddha nature is the potential that we all have which allows us to go to the state of enlightenment, the blissful state beyond all the unsatisfactoriness of normal existence. Sugatagarbha has the same basic meaning as tathagatagarbha though its use indicates a more practical way of talking whereas tathagatagarbha is more theoretical. A discussion which uses the term sugatagarbha is one that is talking about the practical realities of an essence that can be or is being developed into enlightened being.

Suppression and furtherance, Tib. dgag sgrub: Suppression and furtherance is the term used to express the way that dualistic mind approaches the path to enlightenment. In that case, some states of mind are regarded as ones to be discarded, so the practitioner takes the approach of attempting to suppress or stop them, and some are regarded as ones to be developed, so the practitioner takes the approach of trying to go further with and develop them. These two poles represent the way that dualistic mind always works with itself. Thorough Cut practice goes beyond that duality.

The nature, Tib. rang bzhin: The nature is one of the three characteristics—entity, nature, and un-stopped compassionate activity—of the core of mind. Using this term emphasizes that the empty entity does have a nature. In other words, its use explicitly shows that the core of mind is not merely empty. If you ask "Well, what is that nature like?" The answer is that it is luminosity, it is wisdom.

Third-order thousandfold world system, Tib. stong gsum 'jig rten: Indian cosmology has for its smallest cosmic unit a single Mt. Meru with four continents type of world system; an analogy might be a single planetary system like our solar system. One thousand of those makes a first order thousandfold world system; an analogy might be a galaxy. One thousand of those makes a second order thousandfold world system; an analogy might be a region of space with many galaxies. One thousand of those makes a third-order thousandfold world system (1000 raised to the power 3); an analogy would be one whole universe like ours. The Buddha said that there were countless numbers of third-order thousandfold world systems, each of which would be roughly equivalent to a universe like ours.

Thorough Cut, Tib. khregs chod: The innermost level of Great Completion has two main practices, the first called Thregcho which literally translates as Thorough Cut and the second called Thogal which translates as Direct Crossing. The meaning of Thorough

Cut has been misunderstood. The meaning is clearly explained in the *Illuminator Tibetan-English Dictionary*:

> Thorough Cut is a practice that slices through the solidification produced by rational mind as it grasps at a perceived object and perceiving subject. It is done in order to get to the underlying reality which is always present in the core of mind and which is called Alpha Purity in this system of teachings. For this reason, Thorough Cut is also known as Alpha Purity Thorough Cut.

The etymology of the word is explained in the Great Completion teachings either as ཁྲེགས་སུ་ཆོད་པ་ or ཁྲེགས་གེ་ཆོད་པ. In either case, the term ཆོད་པ་ is "a cut"; there are all sorts of different "cuts" and this is one of them. Then, in the case of ཁྲེགས་སུ་ཆོད་པ་, ཁྲེགས་སུ་ is an adverb modifying the verb "to cut" and has the meaning of making the cut fully, completely. It is traditionally explained with the example of slicing off a finger. A finger could be sliced with a sharp knife such that the cut was not quite complete and the cut off portion was left hanging. Alternatively, it could be sliced through in one, decisive movement such that the finger was completely and definitely severed. That kind of thorough cut is what is meant here. In the case of ཁྲེགས་གེ་ཆོད་པ་, the term ཁྲེགས་གེ་ is as an adverb that has the meaning of something that is doubtless, of something that is unquestionably so. A translation based on the first explanation would be "Thorough Cut" and on the second would be "Decisive Cut".

Other translations that have been put forward for this term are: "Cutting Resistance" and "Cutting Solidity". Both are grammatically incorrect. Further, the name "Cutting Resistance" is made on the basis of students expressing resistance to practice and the like, but that is not the meaning intended. Similarly, the name Cutting Solidity comes from not understanding that the term ཁྲེགས་ (khregs) has both old and new meanings; the newer meaning of "solid", "solidity" does not apply because the term Thorough Cut was put into use in the time of Padmasambhava when only the old meaning of ཁྲེགས་ was in use. The term means that the practitioner of this system cuts *decisively* through rational mind, regardless of its degree of solidity, so as to arrive directly at the essence of mind.

Three kayas; See under kaya.

Transparency, Tib. zang thal: This term belongs to the unique vocabulary of Great Completion. It has two connotations: that something is seen directly, in direct perception; and that it is seen with full visibility because there is no agent obscuring the view of it. The term is used to indicate that rigpa is truly present for the practitioner. Luminosity when it is the rigpa of the enlightened side and not the not-rigpa, usually translated as ignorance, of the samsaric side, has transparency or, we could say, full visibility, as one of its qualities precisely because it has none of the factors of mind as such in it, which would obscure it. Transparency means that the rigpa is in full view: it really is rigpa seen in direct perception and it is without rational mind so it is seen without any of the obscuring factors that would make it less than immediately and fully visible.

Unaltered or uncontrived, Tib. ma bcos pa: This term is the opposite of altered and contrived. It refers to something which has not been altered from its native state; something which has been left just as it is.

Vacillatory foci, Tib. gza' gtad: This term is twice pejorative. The word "vacillatory" refers to a process of hovering around a subject, seeing it from this angle and that angle because of vacillating over how it really is. "Focus" means that rational mind takes one of the possible angles and settles on that. For example, in the process of resting in the essence of mind, there can be the fault of not leaving rational mind but staying within in it and thinking, "Yes, this is the essence of mind" or "No, this is not it. It is that". Each of those is a vacillatory focus. Any vacillatory focus implies that the practitioner has not left rational mind and so is not in rigpa.

Wisdom, Skt. jñāna, Tib. ye shes: This is a fruition term that refers to the kind of mind, the kind of knower possessed by a buddha. Sentient beings do have this kind of knower but it is covered over by a very complex apparatus for knowing, dualistic mind. If they practise the path to buddhahood, they will leave behind their obscuration and return to having this kind of knower.

The Sanskrit term has the sense of knowing in the most simple and immediate way. This sort of knowing is present at the core of every being's mind. Therefore, the Tibetans called it "the particular type of awareness which is there primordially". Because of the Tibetan wording it has often been called "primordial wisdom" in English translations, but that goes too far; it is just "wisdom" in the sense of the most fundamental knowing possible.

SUPPORTS FOR STUDY

I have been encouraged over the years by all of my teachers to pass on the knowledge I have accumulated in a lifetime dedicated to study and practice, primarily in the Tibetan tradition of Buddhism. On the one hand, they have encouraged me to teach. On the other, they are concerned that, while many general books on Buddhism have been and are being published, there are few books that present the actual texts of the tradition. Therefore they, together with a number of major figures in the Buddhist book publishing world, have also encouraged me to translate and publish high quality translations of individual texts of the tradition.

My teachers always remark with great appreciation on the extraordinary amount of teaching that I have heard in this life. It allows for highly informed, accurate translations of a sort not usually seen. Briefly, I spent the 1970's studying, practising, then teaching the Gelugpa system at Chenrezig Institute, Australia, where I was a founding member and also the first Australian to be ordained as a monk in the Tibetan Buddhist tradition. In 1980, I moved to the United States to study at the feet of the Vidyadhara Chogyam Trungpa Rinpoche. I stayed in his Vajradhatu community, now called Shambhala, where I studied and practised all the Karma Kagyu, Nyingma, and Shambhala teachings being presented there and was a senior member of the Nalanda Translation Committee. After the vidyadhara's nirvana, I moved in 1992 to Nepal, where I have been continuously involved with the study, practise, translation, and teaching of the Kagyu system and especially of the Nyingma system of Great Completion. In recent years, I have spent extended times in Tibet with the greatest living Tibetan masters of Great Completion, receiving very pure transmissions of the ultimate levels of this teaching directly in Tibetan and practising them there in retreat. In that way, I have studied and practised extensively not in one Tibetan tradition as is usually done, but in three of the four Tibetan traditions—Gelug, Kagyu, and Nyingma—and also in the Theravada tradition, too.

With that as a basis, I have taken a comprehensive and long term approach to the work of translation. For any language, one first must have the lettering needed to write the language. Therefore, as a member of the Nalanda Translation Committee, I spent some years in the 1980's making Tibetan word-processing software and high-quality Tibetan fonts. After that, reliable lexical works are needed. Therefore, during the 1990's I spent some years writing the *Illuminator Tibetan-English Dictionary* and a set of treatises on Tibetan grammar, preparing a variety of key Tibetan reference works needed for the study and translation of Tibetan Buddhist texts, and giving our Tibetan software the tools needed to translate and research Tibetan texts. During this time, I also translated full-time for various Tibetan gurus and ran the Drukpa Kagyu Heritage Project—at the time the largest project in Asia for the preservation of Tibetan Buddhist texts. With the dictionaries, grammar texts, and specialized software in place, and a wealth of knowledge, I turned my attention in the year 2000 to the translation and publication of important texts of Tibetan Buddhist literature.

Padma Karpo Translation Committee (PKTC) was set up to provide a home for the translation and publication work. The committee focusses on producing books containing the best of Tibetan literature, and, especially, books that meet the needs of practitioners. At the time of writing, PKTC has published a wide range of books that, collectively, make a complete program of study for those practising Tibetan Buddhism, and especially for those interested in the higher tantras. All in all, you will find many books both free and for sale on the PKTC web-site. Most are available both as paper editions and e-books.

It would take up too much space here to present an extensive guide to our books and how they can be used as the basis for a study program. However, a guide of that sort is available on the PKTC web-site, whose address is on the copyright page of this book and we recommend that you read it to see how this book fits into the overall scheme of PKTC publications. In short, the author of the text presented in this book is one of the important figures in the transmission of the Quintessential Great Completion teachings in Tibet; the importance of his text for those studying the Thorough Cut aspect of thatteaching has been explained in the introduction. We have published many texts on the Thorough Cut teaching, each one carefully selected for its particular treatment of the subject. When studying the Thorough Cut teaching, the texts on the Three Lines teaching originally from Garab Dorje will be essential reading:

- *The Feature of the Expert, Glorious King* by Dza Patrul
- *About the Three Lines* by Dodrupchen III
- *Relics of the Dharmakaya* by Ontrul Tenpa'i Wangchug

A few of the many other texts published by PKTC that deal with Thorough Cut and add further ornamentation are:

- *Empowerment and AtiYoga* by Tony Duff
- *Peak Doorways to Emancipation* by Shakya Shri
- *Alchemy of Accomplishment* by Dudjom Rinpoche
- *The Way of the Realized Old Dogs* by Ju Mipham
- *The Method of Preserving the Face of Rigpa* by Ju Mipham
- *Essential Points of Practice* by Zhechen Gyaltshab
- *Words of the Old Dog Vijay* by Zhechen Gyaltshab
- *Hinting at Dzogchen* by Tony Duff

The other main practice of Quintessential Dzogchen is Direct Crossing; other PKTC publications on Direct Crossing are:

- *Key Points of Direct Crossing called Nectar of the Pure Part* by Khenchen Padma Namgyal
- Jigmey Lingpa's most important text *Guidebook called "Highest Wisdom" (Triyig Yeshe Lama)*

We make a point of including, where possible, the relevant Tibetan texts in Tibetan script in our books. We also make them available in electronic editions that can be downloaded free from our web-site, as discussed below. The Tibetan text for this book is included at the back of the book and is available for download from the PKTC web-site.

Electronic Resources

PKTC has developed a complete range of electronic tools to facilitate the study and translation of Tibetan texts. For many years now, this software has been a prime resource for Tibetan Buddhist centres throughout the world, including in Tibet itself. It is available through the PKTC web-site.

The wordprocessor TibetDoc has the only complete set of tools for creating, correcting, and formatting Tibetan text according to the norms of the Tibetan language. It can also be used to make texts with mixed Tibetan and English or other languages. Extremely high quality Tibetan fonts, based on the forms of Tibetan calligraphy learned from old masters from pre-Communist Chinese Tibet, are also available. Because of their excellence, these typefaces have achieved a legendary status amongst Tibetans.

TibetDoc is used to prepare electronic editions of Tibetan texts in the PKTC text input office in Asia. Tibetan texts are often corrupt so the input texts are carefully corrected prior to distribution. After that, they are made available through the PKTC web-site. These electronic texts are not careless productions like so many of the Tibetan texts found on the web, but are highly reliable editions useful to non-scholars and scholars alike. Some of the larger collections of these texts are for purchase, but most are available for free download.

The electronic texts can be read, searched, and even made into an electronic library using either TibetDoc or our other software, TibetD Reader. Like TibetDoc, TibetD Reader is advanced software with many capabilities made specifically to meet the needs of reading and researching Tibetan texts. PKTC software is for purchase but we make a free version of TibetD Reader available for free download on the PKTC web-site.

A key feature of TibetDoc and Tibet Reader is that Tibetan terms in texts can be looked up on the spot using PKTC's electronic dictionaries. PKTC also has several electronic dictionaries—some Tibetan-Tibetan and some Tibetan-English—and a number of other reference works. The *Illuminator Tibetan-English Dictionary* is renowned for its completeness and accuracy.

This combination of software, texts, reference works, and dictionaries that work together seamlessly has become famous over the years. It has been the basis of many, large publishing projects within the Tibetan Buddhist community around the world for over thirty years and is popular amongst all those needing to work with Tibetan language or deepen their understanding of Buddhism through Tibetan texts.

TIBETAN TEXTS

༄༅། །འོད་གསལ་རྫོགས་པ་ཆེན་པོའི་ཁྲེགས་ཆོད་ལྟ་བའི་གླུ་དབྱངས་ས་
ལམ་མ་ལུས་མྱུར་དུ་བགྲོད་པའི་རྩལ་ལྡན་མཁའ་ལྡིང་གཤོག་རླབས་ཞེས་བྱ་བ་
བཞུགས་སོ།།

༄༅། །ན་མོ་གུ་རུ་བྷྱཿ ཀུན་གསལ་མཁྱེན་བརྩེའི་ཧྲ་བདུན་དཀྱིལ་འཁོར་ལས། །ཚད་མེད་ཐུགས་རྗེའི་འོད་ཟེར་རབ་སྤྲོས་ནས། །ཁམས་གསུམ་འགྲོ་བའི་མ་རིག་མུན་པ་ཀུན། །དུས་གཅིག་སེལ་མཛད་ཆོས་ཀྱི་རྒྱལ་པོར་འདུད། །སྟོང་གསལ་ཆོས་སྐུའི་ལྟ་ལམ་ཡངས་པའི་ངོས། །བྱམས་དང་བརྩེ་བའི་རྒྱུ་འཛིན་རབ་འཁྲིགས་ནས། སྐལ་བར་ལྡན་པའི་གདུལ་བྱའི་འཛིན་མ་ལ། །ཆོས་ཆར་འབེབས་མཁས་ཐུགས་འཆང་རྡོ་རྗེར་འདུད། །ལྟ་བའི་གྲུ་དབུས་ལྷུག་བསམ་དར་ཆེན་འཕྱུར། །བརྩོན་འགྲུས་རླུང་གིས་བསྐྱོད་ནས་སྲིད་མཚོ་རུ། །བྱིངས་པའི་འགྲོ་རྣམས་སྐུ་གསུམ་ནོར་བུའི་གླིང་། །འགོད་མཛད་དེད་དཔོན་འཇམ་དབྱངས་རྒྱ་མཚོར་འདུད། །དེ་གསུམ་མཁྱེན་བརྩེ་ཧྲ་བདུན་དཀྱིལ་འཁོར་ལས། །འཕྲོས་པའི་བྱིན་རླབས་ནུས་མཐུའི་ཚ་བའི་ཟེར། །སྐལ་ལྡན་བྱ་བཏང་པད་དཀར་བདག་ལ་ཕོག །རིག་པའི་ཁ་ཕྱེ་ཉམས་རྟོགས་འདབ་སྟོང་བཞད། །བདག་བློའི་གེ་སར་ལྟོ་བར་ལེགས་འཁྱིལ་བའི། །ལྟ་བའི་གླུ་དབྱངས་སྦྱོང་གྲོལ་བདུད་རྩིའི་བཅུད། །

སྐལ་ལྡན་སློབ་མ་རྐང་དྲུག་ཚོགས་ལ་འབུལ། །ངོམས་པ་མེད་པར་གསུས་པའི་ཡིད་ཀྱིས་རོལ།། ༄ ཨེ་མ་ཧོ། བྱ་བཏང་གུ་ཡངས་ཡན་པ་བློ་བདེ་ངས། །ས་ལམ་མ་ལུས་མྱུར་དུ་བགྲོད་བྱེད་པའི། །ལྟ་བའི་གླུ་དབྱངས་མཁའ་ལྡིང་གཤོག་རླབས་ལེན། །སྐལ་ལྡན་སེམས་ཀྱི་བུ་རྣམས་ལྷན་ནེར་ཉོན། །འཁོར་འདས་གཉིས་ལ་འབྲུག་གི་སྒྲ་བཞིན་དུ། །ཡོངས་གྲགས་སངས་རྒྱས་ཟེར་བའི་སྒྲ་བོ་ཆེ། །འགྲོ་དྲུག་སེམས་ཅན་རྒྱུད་ལ་རྟག་བཞུགས་ནས། །སྐད་ཅིག་ཙམ་ཡང་གཡེལ་མེད་འགྲོགས་འདི་མཚར། །སངས་རྒྱས་རང་ལ་ཡོད་པར་མ་ཤེས་པར། །ཕྱི་རོལ་གཞན་དུ་སངས་རྒྱས་བཙལ་བ་མཚར། །གསལ་དྭངས་ཉི་མའི་སྙིང་པོ་ཇི་བཞིན་དུ། །མངོན་སུམ་གསལ་ཀྱང་མཐོང་མཁན་ཉུང་བ་མཚར། །ཕ་མ་མེད་པའི་རང་སེམས་སངས་རྒྱས་ཉིད། །སྐྱེ་མ་མྱོང་ཞིང་འཆི་རྒྱུ་མེད་པ་མཚར། །བདེ་སྡུག་སྣ་ཚོགས་ཇི་ལྟར་མྱོང་ན་ཡང་། །བཟང་དང་ངན་དུ་ཅུང་ཟད་མི་འགྲོ་མཚར། །མ་སྐྱེས་གདོད་ནས་དག་པའི་སེམས་ཉིད་འདི། །མ་བཅོས་ཡེ་ནས་ལྷུན་གྱིས་གྲུབ་པ་མཚར། །རང་བཞིན་ཡེ་ནས་གྲོལ་བའི་རང་རིག་ཉིད། །གང་བྱུང་གང་བདེར་བཞག་པས་གྲོལ་བ་མཚར།། ༄ །།ཨེ་མ་ཧོ། སྐལ་ལྡན་རིགས་ཀྱི་བུ་རྣམས་ལ་མ་ཡེངས་ཉོན། །དུས་གསུམ་རྒྱལ་བ་མ་ལུས་ཐམས་ཅད་ཀྱིས། །ཆོས་ཕུང་བརྒྱད་ཁྲི་བཞི་སྟོང་ལ་སོགས་པའི། །གསུང་རབ་ནམ་མཁའི་མཐའ་མཉམ་དཔག་མེད་ཀྱང་། །དོན་ལ་རང་སེམས་རྟོགས་ཕྱིར་གསུངས་པ་ལས། །གཞན་དུ་ཅི་ཡང་རྒྱལ་བས་གསུངས་པ་མེད། །དཔེར་ན་སྡོང་པོའི་རྩ་བ་གཅིག་བཅད་ན། །ཡལ་ག་ལོ་མ་ཁྲི་འབུམ་དུས་གཅིག་བསྐམས། །དེ་བཞིན་སེམས་ཀྱི་རྩ་བ་གཅིག་བཅད་ན། །གཟུང་འཛིན་ལ་སོགས་འཁོར་བའི་ལོ་འདབ་བསྐམས། །ཁང་སྟོང་མུན་པ་ལོ་སྟོང་ལོན་པ་ཡང་། །སྒྲོན་མེས་སྐད་ཅིག་ཉིད་ལ་སེལ་བ་བཞིན། །རང་སེམས་འོད་གསལ་རྟོགས་པའི་སྐད་ཅིག་ལ། །བསྐལ་པ་གྲངས་མེད་བསགས་པའི་སྡིག་སྒྲིབ་འདགས། །གསལ་དྭངས་ཉི་མའི་སྙིང་པོའི་རང་བཞིན་དེ། །བསྐལ་པ་སྟོང་གི་མུན་པས་སྒྲིབ་མི་ནུས། །དེ་བཞིན་རང་

སེམས་སྙིང་པོའི་འོད་གསལ་དེ། །བསྐལ་པར་འཁྲུལ་པས་སྒྲིབ་པར་མི་ནུས་སོ། །ནམ་མཁའི་རང་བཞིན་མདོག་དབྱིབས་ཚད་ལས་འདས། །དཀར་ནག་སྤྲིན་གྱིས་གོས་པར་མི་འགྱུར་ལྟར། །སེམས་ཀྱི་རང་བཞིན་མདོག་དབྱིབས་ཚད་ལས་འདས། །དགེ་སྡིག་དཀར་ནག་ཆོས་ཀྱིས་གོས་མི་འགྱུར། །དཔེར་ན་འོ་མ་མར་གྱི་རྒྱུ་ཡིན་ཀྱང་། །མ་སྦྲོག་པར་དུ་མར་ནི་མི་འབྱུང་ལྟར། །འགྲོ་ཀུན་བདེར་གཤེགས་སྙིང་པོའི་རྒྱུ་ཡིན་ཀྱང་། །ཉམས་སུ་མ་བླངས་སེམས་ཅན་སངས་མ་རྒྱས། །འདི་ཉིད་ཉམས་སུ་བླངས་ན་ཀུན་གྲོལ་ཏེ། །དབང་པོ་རྣམས་ལ་རྣོ་བརྟུལ་ཁྱད་པར་མེད། །ཉམས་སུ་བླངས་ན་བ་གླང་རྫི་ཡང་གྲོལ། །མངོན་སུམ་རང་སེམས་འོད་གསལ་དོན་རྟོགས་ན། །ཁ་བཤད་མཁས་པ་འདི་ལ་མི་དགོས་ཏེ། །བུ་རམ་རང་གི་ཁ་རུ་ཟོས་པའི་ཚེ། །བུ་རམ་རོ་བཤད་མི་དགོས་ཇི་བཞིན་ནོ། །འདི་ཉིད་མ་རྟོགས་པཎྜི་ཏ་ཡང་འཁྲུལ། །ཐེག་དགུའི་བཤད་པ་ཡོངས་ལ་མཁས་གྱུར་ཀྱང་། །མ་མཐོང་རྒྱང་གི་གཏམ་རྒྱུད་བཤད་པ་བཞིན། །སངས་རྒྱས་ས་ལ་གནམ་ས་བས་ཀྱང་རིང་། །ཡང་དག་རང་སེམས་འོད་གསལ་མ་རྟོགས་ན། །བསྐལ་པའི་བར་དུ་ཚུལ་ཁྲིམས་བསྲུངས་བ་དང་། །ཡུན་རིང་བར་དུ་བཟོད་པ་བསྒོམས་བྱས་ཀྱང་། །ཁམས་གསུམ་འཁོར་བའི་གནས་ནས་མི་འཕགས་པས། །དེའི་ཕྱིར་འབད་པས་སེམས་ཀྱི་རྩད་གཅོད་ཀྱིས།། ༄ །།ཨེ་མ་ཧོ། ད་ཡང་སྐལ་ལྡན་བུ་མཆོག་ཀུན་གྱིས་ཉོན། །རང་གི་སེམས་ཀྱི་རྩ་བརྡར་མ་ཆོད་ན། །དགེ་སྦྱོར་གང་བྱས་གནད་དུ་མི་འགྲོ་སྟེ། །དཔེར་ན་འབེན་ནི་དྲུང་དུ་བཞག་ནས་ཀྱང་། །མདའ་ནི་ཐག་རིང་ཕྱོགས་སུ་འཕེན་དང་མཚུངས། །རྐུན་མ་རང་གི་ཁྱིམ་དུ་བཞག་ནས་ཀྱང་། །རྩད་གཅོད་དྲག་པོ་ཕྱི་རུ་བྱེད་དང་མཚུངས། །འདྲེ་ནི་ཤར་སྒོའི་ཕྱོགས་སུ་བཞག་ནས་ཀྱང་། །གླུད་ནི་ནུབ་ཀྱི་ཕྱོགས་སུ་གཏོང་དང་མཚུངས། །དབུལ་པོའི་སྦྱིད་རྡོ་གསེར་དུ་མ་ཤེས་པར། །གཞན་ནས་སློང་མོ་བྱེད་པ་ཇི་བཞིན་ནོ། །དེས་ན་རང་གི་སེམས་ཀྱི་རྩད་བརྡར་རྣམས། །འདི་བཞིན་ཚོད་ཅིག་སྐལ་ལྡན་སྙིང་གི་བུ། །སེམས་ཞེས་བྱ་བའི་རིག་རིག་འགྱུ་འགྱུ་པོ། །

བདས་ན་མི་ཟིན་ཡལ་ཡལ་བན་བུན་པོ། །བཞག་ན་མི་སྡོད་ཚུབ་ཚུབ་ཡེར་ཡེར་པོ། །འདི་ཞེས་མཚོན་མེད་སྟོང་པ་ཕྱང་ཆད་པོ། །བདེ་སྡུག་སྣ་ཚོགས་སྐྱོང་མཁན་རང་གི་སེམས། །དང་པོ་འདི་ནི་བྱུང་ས་གང་ནས་བྱུང་། །ཕྱི་ཡི་སྣང་བ་རི་བྲག་ཤིང་དང་། །ནམ་མཁའི་རླུང་སོགས་རྟེན་བཅས་རྟེན་མེད་པ། །གང་ལས་བྱུང་ངམ་འདྲི་ཞིང་རྩད་བཅར་ཆོད། །ཡང་ན་ཕ་མ་གཉིས་ཀྱི་ཁུ་ཁྲག་ལས། །བྱུང་ངམ་སྙམ་ན་ཇི་ལྟར་བྱུང་ཚུལ་དཔྱོད། །དེ་ལྟར་དཔྱད་པས་བྱུང་ས་མ་རྙེད་ཚེ། །བར་དུ་ད་ལྟ་རང་ལུས་སྡོད་སྐབས་དང་། །དབང་པོ་དོན་སྙིང་ལ་སོགས་གང་ལ་གནས། །སྙིང་ལ་གནས་ན་མགོ་འཇུག་གང་ན་གནས། །དབྱིབས་དང་ཁ་དོག་ལ་སོགས་ཇི་ལྟར་འདུག །ལེགས་པར་དཔྱོད་ལ་གནས་ས་མ་རྙེད་ཚེ། །ཐ་མར་འགྲོ་དུས་ཡུལ་གྱི་དབང་པོའི་སྒོ། །གང་ནས་འགྲོ་དང་ཕྱི་རོལ་ཡུལ་རྣམས་སུ། །ཡུད་ཙམ་ཉིད་ལ་སླེབ་པའི་དུས་དེ་རུ། །ལུས་ཀྱིས་ཕྱིན་ནམ་སེམས་ཉིད་ཁོ་ནས་ཕྱིན། །ལུས་སེམས་ཚོགས་པས་ཕྱིན་སོགས་རྩད་བཅར་ཆོད། །དེ་ཡང་ཉོན་མོངས་རྣམ་རྟོག་སྐྱེ་བའི་ཚེ། །དང་པོ་གང་ནས་སྐྱེས་དང་ད་ལྟའི་དུས། །གང་ལ་གནས་དང་མདོག་དབྱིབས་ཇི་འདུག་ལྟོས། །ཐ་མར་རང་སར་ཞི་ནས་ཡལ་བའི་ཚེ། །གང་དུ་ཡལ་ནས་འགྲོ་སོགས་རྩད་བཅར་ཆོད། །འཆི་བའི་ཚེ་ན་ཇི་ལྟར་བྱས་ནས་འགྲོ། །ཞིབ་ཏུ་དཔྱོད་ལ་སྐྱེ་འཆི་འགྲོ་འོང་དང་། །དངོས་བཟུང་བྲལ་བའི་སྟོང་སངས་བརྗོད་མེད་དུ། །ངེས་པར་གཏན་ལ་མ་ཕེབས་བར་དུ་དཔྱོད། །གཞན་གྱིས་དཔེ་དང་ཁ་བཤད་སྐམ་པོ་ཡིས། །སྟོང་པ་ཉིད་ཡིན་ཟེར་བས་མི་ཕན་ཏེ། །དཔེར་ན་སྟག་ཡོད་ཟེར་བའི་ས་ཆ་རུ། །གཞན་གྱིས་སྟག་ནི་མེད་པར་བརྗོད་ན་ཡང་། །རང་ཉིད་དེ་ལ་ཡིད་ཆེས་མི་སྐྱེ་བར། །ཡིད་གཉིས་ཐེ་ཚོམ་ཟ་བ་ཇི་བཞིན་ནོ། །རང་གི་སེམས་ཀྱི་རྩ་བ་རང་ཉིད་ཀྱིས། །ཞིབ་ཏུ་བཙད་ནས་གཏན་ལ་ཕབ་པའི་ཚེ། །དཔེར་ན་སྟག་ཡོད་ཟེར་བའི་ལུང་པ་དེར། །རང་ཉིད་སོང་ནས་ཕུ་མདོ་ཐམས་ཅད་དུ། །སྟག་ནི་ཨེ་ཡོད་བརྩད་བཅར་བཅད་གྱུར་ན། །མ་རྙེད་ཚེ་ན་རང་ཉིད་ཡིད་ཆེས་ཏེ། །ཕྱིན་ཆད་ས་དེར་སྟག་ཡོད་

སླམ་པ་ཡི། །ཡིད་གཉིས་ཐེ་ཚོམ་མེད་པ་ཧཱི་བཞིན་ནོ།། ༈ །།ཨེ་མ་ཧོ།
ད་ཡང་སྐལ་ལྡན་བུ་རྣམས་ཚུར་ཉོན་དང་། །ཁྱེད་རྣམས་དེ་ལྟར་བརྟགས་ཤིང་དཔྱད་
པའི་ཚེ། །སེམས་ཞེས་མཛུབ་མོ་བཙུགས་ནས་འདི་ཡིན་ཞེས། །དངོས་པོར་
གྲུབ་པ་རྡུལ་ཙམ་མ་རྙེད་ཚེ། །མ་རྙེད་པ་དེ་རྙེད་པའི་མཆོག་ཡིན་ནོ། །འོ་སྐལ་
སེམས་ལ་དང་པོ་བྱུང་ས་མེད། །ཡེ་ནས་སྟོང་པས་ངོ་བོ་ངོས་བཟུང་མེད། །བར་
དུ་གནས་ས་དབྱིབས་དང་ཁ་དོག་མེད། །ཐ་མར་འགྲོར་མེད་འདིར་སོང་རྗེས་མེད་
དེ། །འགྱུ་བ་སྟོང་འགྱུ་སྟོང་པ་སྟོང་སྣང་ཡིན། །སེམས་ཉིད་འདི་ནི་དང་པོ་རྒྱུས་
མ་བསྐྱེད། །ཐ་མ་ཕྱི་རོལ་རྐྱེན་གྱིས་འདི་མི་འཇིག །འཕེལ་དང་འགྲིབ་དང་གང་
སྟོང་འདི་ལ་མེད། །འཁོར་འདས་ཡོངས་ལ་ཁྱབ་པས་ཕྱོགས་རིས་མེད། །འདི་
ཞེས་མི་མཚོན་ཅིར་ཡང་འགག་མེད་འཆར། །ཅིར་ཡང་མ་གྲུབ་ཡོད་མེད་མཐའ་
ལས་འདས། །འགྲོ་འོང་མེད་ཅིང་སྐྱེ་འཆི་གསལ་འགྲིབ་མེད། །སེམས་ཀྱི་རང་
བཞིན་དྲི་མེད་ཞལ་གོང་བཞིན། །ངོ་བོ་སྟོང་པ་རང་བཞིན་གསལ་བ་དང་། །
ཐུགས་རྗེ་འགག་པ་མེད་པར་ས་ལེར་གནས། །འཁོར་བའི་སྐྱོན་གྱིས་ཅི་ཡང་མ་
གོས་ཏེ། །སེམས་ཉིད་ཡེ་ནས་སངས་རྒྱས་ཡིན་པར་ངེས། །འདི་ནི་གཞི་ཡི་
སེམས་ཉིད་གནས་ལུགས་ཀྱི། །རང་བཞིན་གཏན་ལ་ཕབ་པའི་ངོ་སྤྲོས་དོ།། ༈
།།ཨེ་མ་ཧོ། ད་ཡང་སྐལ་ལྡན་སེམས་ཀྱི་བུ་རྣམས་ཉོན། །དང་པོ་ཆོས་སྐུ་ཀུན་ཏུ་
བཟང་པོ་ཡིས། །བསྒོམ་པ་རྡུལ་ཙམ་མ་བྱས་གྲོལ་ཚུལ་དང་། །འགྲོ་བ་དྲུག
གྱིས་མི་དགེ་སྡིག་པའི་ལས། །སྤྱུ་ཙམ་མ་བྱས་འཁོར་བར་འཁྱམས་ཚུལ་ནི། །
ཡེ་ཐོག་དང་པོ་ཀུན་གྱི་སྔོན་རོལ་ཏུ། །འཁོར་འདས་མིང་མེད་གདོད་མའི་གཞི་ལ་
གནས། །དེ་དུས་རིག་པ་གཞི་ནས་འཕགས་ཚུལ་ནི། །ཤེལ་ལ་ཉི་ཕོག་རང་འོད་
ཕྱིར་གསལ་ལྟར། །རིག་པའི་ཡེ་ཤེས་སྒྲོག་རླུང་གིས་བསྐྱོད་ནས། །གཞོན་ནུ་
བུམ་པ་སྐུ་ཡི་རྒྱ་རལ་ཏེ། །ལྷུན་གྲུབ་འོད་གསལ་སྐུ་ད་ཡེ་ཤེས་ཀྱི། །ཞིང་ཁམས་
མཁའ་ལ་ཉི་ཤར་བཞིན་དུ་གསལ། །དེ་དུས་ཆོས་སྐུ་ཀུན་ཏུ་བཟང་པོ་ཡིས། །
རང་སྣང་ཡིན་པར་ཤེས་པས་སྐད་ཅིག་ལ། །ཕྱིར་གསལ་སྐུ་དང་ཡེ་ཤེས་ནང་དུ་

ཐིམ། །ཀ་དག་གདོད་མའི་གཞི་ལ་སངས་རྒྱས་སོ། །འོ་སྐོལ་རྣམས་ཀྱིས་རང་
བཞིན་ལྷུན་གྲུབ་ཀྱི། །སྣང་བ་རང་གདངས་ཡིན་པར་མ་ཤེས་པས། །ཤེས་པ་དྲན་
མེད་ཐོམ་མེ་བ་དེ་ཉིད། །དེ་ལ་ལྷན་ཅིག་སྐྱེས་པའི་མ་རིག་ཟེར། །དེ་ནས་གཞི་
སྣང་འོད་གསལ་དེ་ཉིད་ལ། །གཉིས་སུ་འཛིན་པའི་ཤེས་པ་སྐྱེས་པ་དེ། །ཀུན་ཏུ་
བརྟགས་པའི་མ་རིག་པ་ཞེས་ཟེར། །མ་རིག་གཉིས་འཛིན་སྦྲུབས་སུ་དེ་དུས་
ཚུད། །དེ་ནས་བག་ཆགས་རིམ་བཞིན་རྒྱས་ནས་ཀྱང་། །འཁོར་བའི་བྱ་བ་འདི་
རྣམས་ཐམས་ཅད་བྱུང་། །དེ་ནས་ཉོན་མོངས་དུག་གསུམ་དུག་ལྔ་དང་། །བརྒྱད་
ཁྲི་བཞི་སྟོང་ལ་སོགས་རྒྱས་ནས་ཀྱང་། །འཁོར་བའི་གནས་སུ་ཟོ་ཆུའི་འཁྲུད་མོ་
བཞིན། །འཁོར་ཞིང་བདེ་སྡུག་ད་ལྟའི་བར་དུ་མྱོངས། །རྒྱས་པར་འདོད་ན་ཀུན་
མཁྱེན་ཐེག་མཆོག་མཛོད། །ཟབ་དོན་རྒྱ་མཚོའི་སྤྲིན་ཕུང་སོགས་ལ་ལྟོས། །ད་
ནི་བླ་མའི་མན་ངག་ཟབ་མོ་ཡིས། །འཁྲུལ་པའི་རང་མཚང་ཐམས་ཅད་རིག་ནས་
ཀྱང་། །རང་སེམས་སངས་རྒྱས་རང་ངོ་མཐོང་བ་ཡིན། །གདོད་མའི་མགོན་
པོའི་རང་ཞལ་མཇལ་བ་ཡིན། །ཀུན་ཏུ་བཟང་པོར་སྐལ་བ་མཉམ་པ་ཡིན། །སྙིང་
ནས་དགའ་བ་སྒོམས་ཤིག་སེམས་ཀྱི་བུ། །འཁྲུལ་པ་གཏན་ལ་ཕབ་པའི་ངོ་སྤྲོད་དོ༎

༄༅ ༎ཨེ་མ་ཧོ། ད་ཡང་སྐལ་ལྡན་སྙིང་གི་བུ་རྣམས་ཉོན། །སེམས་ཞེས་བྱ་
བའི་ཡོངས་གྲགས་སྒྲ་བོ་ཆེ། །ཡོད་ནི་གཅིག་ཀྱང་ཡོད་པ་མ་ཡིན་ཏེ། །འབྱུང་ནི་
འཁོར་འདས་བདེ་སྡུག་སྣ་ཚོགས་འབྱུང་། །འདོད་ནི་ཐེག་པའི་རྣམ་གྲངས་མང་དུ་
ཡོད། །མིང་ནི་བསམ་གྱིས་མི་ཁྱབ་སོ་སོར་བཏགས། །སོ་སོ་སྐྱེ་བོ་རྣམས་ཀྱིས་
ང་ཡང་ཟེར། །མུ་སྟེགས་ལ་ལས་བདག་ཅེས་མིང་དུ་བཏགས། །ཉན་ཐོས་པ་
ཡིས་གང་ཟག་བདག་མེད་ཟེར། །སེམས་ཙམ་པ་ཡིས་སེམས་ཞེས་མིང་དུ་
བཏགས། །ལ་ལས་ཤེས་རབ་ཕ་རོལ་ཕྱིན་པ་ཟེར། །ལ་ལས་བདེ་གཤེགས་སྙིང་
པོ་མིང་དུ་བཏགས། །ལ་ལས་ཕྱག་རྒྱ་ཆེན་པོ་མིང་དུ་བཏགས། །ལ་ལས་དབུ་མ་
ཞེས་པའི་མིང་དུ་བཏགས། །ལ་ལས་ཐིག་ལེ་ཉག་གཅིག་མིང་དུ་བཏགས། །ལ་
ལས་ཆོས་ཀྱི་དབྱིངས་ཞེས་མིང་དུ་བཏགས། །ལ་ལས་ཀུན་གཞི་ཞེས་པ་མིང་དུ་

བཏགས། །ལ་ལས་ཐ་མལ་ཤེས་པ་མིང་དུ་བཏགས། །མིང་ནི་བསམ་གྱིས་མི་
ཁྱབ་ཙི་བཏགས་ཀྱང་། །དོན་ལ་འདི་ཉིད་ཡིན་པས་ཤེས་པར་གྱིས། །ཁྱེད་རྣམས་
སེམས་ཉིད་རང་སར་གློད་ལ་ཞོག །བཞག་དུ་ཐ་མལ་ཤེས་པ་རྗེན་ནེ་བ། །
བལྟས་པས་མཐོང་རྒྱུ་མེད་པའི་ས་ལེ་བ། །རིག་པ་མངོན་སུམ་ས་ལེ་ཧྲིག་གེ་
བ། །ཅིར་ཡང་མ་གྲུབ་སྟོང་ཞིང་སེང་ངེ་བ། །གསལ་སྟོང་གཉིས་སུ་མེད་པའི་
ཡེ་རེ་བ། །རྟག་པ་མ་ཡིན་ཅིར་ཡང་གྲུབ་པ་མེད། །ཆད་པ་མ་ཡིན་ས་ལེ་ཧྲིག་གེ་
བ། །གཅིག་པུ་མ་ཡིན་དུ་མ་རིག་ཅིང་གསལ། །དུ་མ་མ་ཡིན་དབྱེར་མེད་རོ་
གཅིག་པ། །གཞན་ན་མེད་དེ་རང་རིག་འདི་ཉིད་དོ། །སྙིང་དབུགས་བཞུགས་
པའི་གདོད་མའི་མགོན་པོའི་ཞལ། །མངོན་སུམ་ད་ལྟའི་དུས་འདིར་མཐོང་བ་
ཡིན། །འདི་དང་འབྲལ་མེད་གྱིས་ཤིག་སྙིང་གི་བུ། །འདི་མིན་གཞན་ལས་ལྟག་
པས་སུ་འདོད་པ། །གླང་པོ་རྙེད་ཀྱང་རྗེས་འཚོལ་ཇི་བཞིན། །སྟོང་གསུམ་ཐམས་
ཅད་ཐགས་སུ་བཏགས་ན་ཡང་། །སངས་རྒྱས་མིང་ཙམ་རྙེད་པ་མི་སྲིད་དོ། །
དངོས་གཞིའི་གནས་ལུགས་དོན་གྱི་ངོ་སྤྲོས་དོ།། ༄ ཨེ་མ་ཧོ། ད་ཡང་
རིགས་ཀྱི་བུ་རྣམས་ལེགས་པར་ཉོན། །ད་ལྟའི་རང་རིག་རང་གསལ་འདི་ཉིད་
ལ། །སྐུ་གསུམ་ངོ་བོ་རང་བཞིན་ཐུགས་རྗེ་དང་། །སྐུ་ལྔ་ཡེ་ཤེས་ལྔ་སོགས་
ཐམས་ཅད་ཚང་། །རིག་པའི་ངོ་བོ་ཁ་དོག་དབྱིབས་ལ་སོགས། །ཅིར་ཡང་མ་
གྲུབ་སྟོང་པ་ཆོས་ཀྱི་སྐུ། །སྟོང་པའི་རང་གདངས་གསལ་བ་ལོངས་སྐུའོ། །སྣ་
ཚོགས་འཆར་གཞི་མ་འགགས་སྤྲུལ་པའི་སྐུ། །དེ་རྣམས་མཚོན་པའི་དཔེ་ནི་འདི་
དང་འདྲ། །ཤེལ་གྱི་མེ་ལོང་ཆོས་ཀྱི་སྐུ་དང་མཚུངས། །རང་བཞིན་དྭངས་ཤིང་
གསལ་བ་ལོངས་སྐུའི་མཚོན། །གཟུགས་བརྙན་འཆར་གཞི་མ་འགགས་སྤྲུལ་སྐུའི་
དཔེ། །འགྲོ་རྣམས་སེམས་ཉིད་ཡེ་ནས་སྐུ་གསུམ་དུ། །གནས་པ་ཡིན་ཏེ་རང་ངོ་
ཤེས་ནུས་ན། །འགྲོ་བ་རྣམས་ཀྱིས་སྒོམ་པ་རྩལ་ཙམ་ཡང་། །བྱ་མི་དགོས་ཏེ་
དུས་གཅིག་འཚང་རྒྱའོ། །སྐུ་གསུམ་ངོ་སྤྲོད་ཐ་དད་བསྟན་པ་ནི། །དོན་ལ་
དབྱིངས་གཅིག་མ་གཏོགས་ཐ་དད་དུ། །བཟུང་ནས་འཁྲུལ་པར་མ་འགྲོ་སྙིང་གི་

བུ། །སྐུ་གསུམ་ཡེ་ནས་སྟོང་པ་ཀ་དག་སྟེ། །གསལ་སྟོང་ཟུང་འཇུག་ངོ་བོ་
གཅིག་པ་རུ། །ཤེས་པར་གྱིས་ལ་འཛིན་མེད་ངང་ལ་སྐྱོད། །ངོ་བོ་རང་བཞིན་
ཐུགས་རྗེ་གསུམ་པོ་ཡང་། །ཆོས་སྐུ་ལོངས་སྐུ་སྤྲུལ་སྐུ་ཉིད་དང་མཚུངས། །
གསུམ་ཀ་གསལ་སྟོང་ཟུང་འཇུག་ཆེན་པོ་རུ། །ཤེས་པར་གྱིས་ལ་འཛིན་མེད་ངང་ལ་
སྐྱོད། །དེ་ཡང་རང་བྱུང་རིག་ཡེ་ཤེས་འདི། །ཅིར་ཡང་སྣང་བས་རྣམ་པར་སྣང་
མཛད་སྐུ། །འགྱུར་བ་མེད་པས་མི་བསྐྱོད་རྡོ་རྗེའི་སྐུ། །མཐའ་དབུས་མེད་པས་
སྣང་བ་མཐའ་ཡས་སྐུ། །མཆོག་དང་ཐུན་མོང་དངོས་གྲུབ་ཀུན་འབྱུང་བའི། །
ནོར་བུ་འདྲ་བས་རིན་ཆེན་འབྱུང་ལྡན་སྐུ། །དོན་ཀུན་འགྲུབ་པས་དོན་ཡོད་གྲུབ་པའི་
སྐུ། །དེ་རྣམས་རིག་པའི་རྩལ་ལས་ལོགས་ན་མེད། །རིག་པའི་ཡེ་ཤེས་ངོ་བོ་མ་
འགགས་པར། །མངོན་སུམ་གསལ་བས་མེ་ལོང་ཡེ་ཤེས་སོ། །ཀུན་ལ་ཁྱབ་
པས་མཉམ་ཉིད་ཡེ་ཤེས་སོ། །རྩལ་ལས་སྣ་ཚོགས་འཆར་བས་སོར་རྟོག་གོ། །
དོན་ཀུན་འགྲུབ་པས་བྱ་གྲུབ་ཡེ་ཤེས་སོ། །དེ་དག་རྣམས་ཀྱི་ངོ་བོ་ཀ་དག་ཏུ། །
འདུས་པས་ཆོས་ཀྱི་དབྱིངས་ཀྱི་ཡེ་ཤེས་སོ། །དེ་རྣམས་ཐམས་ཅད་རང་གི་རིག་
རྩལ་ལས། །ལོགས་ན་གྲུབ་པ་རྡུལ་ཙམ་མེད་པའོ། །སྐུ་གསུམ་ངོ་བོ་རང་བཞིན་
ཐུགས་རྗེ་དང་། །སྐུ་ལྔ་ཡེ་ཤེས་ལྔ་པོ་གཅིག་ཆར་དུ། །མངོན་སུམ་མཛུབ་མོ་
བཙུགས་ནས་ངོ་སྤྲོད་ན། །ད་ལྟའི་ཤེས་པ་བཟོ་བཅོས་མ་བྱས་པ། །རྐྱེན་གྱིས་མ་
བསྒྱུར་འཛིན་པས་མ་བསླད་པའི། །རིག་པ་ས་ལེ་ཧྲིག་གེ་འདི་ཀ་ཡིན། །དུས་
གསུམ་སངས་རྒྱས་ཐམས་ཅད་འདི་ལས་བྱུང་། །འདི་ནི་དུས་གསུམ་སངས་རྒྱས་
ཐུགས་ཡིན་པས། །འདི་དང་འབྲལ་མེད་ཀྱིས་ཤིག་སྐལ་ལྡན་ཀུན། །མ་བཅོས་
རང་གསལ་འདི་ཀ་ཡིན་པ་ལ། །རང་སེམས་སངས་རྒྱས་མ་མཐོང་ཅི་ལ་ཟེར། །
འདི་ལ་བསྒོམ་རྒྱུ་ཅི་ཡང་མེད་པ་ལ། །བསྒོམ་རྒྱུ་མ་བྱུང་བྱ་བ་ཅི་ལ་ཟེར། །རིག་
པ་མངོན་སུམ་འདི་ཀ་ཡིན་པ་ལ། །རང་སེམས་མ་རྙེད་བྱ་བ་ཅི་ལ་ཟེར། །
གསལ་ཧྲིག་རྒྱུན་ཆད་མེད་པ་འདི་ཀ་ཡིན། །སེམས་ངོ་མ་མཐོང་བྱ་བ་ཅི་ལ་
ཟེར། །འདི་ལ་བྱ་རྒྱུ་རྡུལ་ཙམ་མེད་པ་ལ། །བྱས་པས་མ་བྱུང་བྱ་བ་ཅི་ལ་

ཟེར། །གནས་དང་མི་གནས་གཉིས་སུ་མེད་པ་ལ། །གནས་སུ་མ་གཏུབ་བྱ་བ་ཅི་
ལ་ཟེར། །རང་རིག་སྐུ་གསུམ་རྩོལ་མེད་ལྷུན་གྲུབ་ལ། །བསྒྲུབས་པས་མ་འགྲུབ་
བྱ་བ་ཅི་ལ་ཟེར། །བྱར་མེད་ཅོག་གེར་བཞག་པས་ཆོག་པ་ལ། །དེ་ལ་མི་ནུས་བྱ་
བ་ཅི་ལ་ཟེར། །རྟོག་པ་ཤར་གྲོལ་དུས་མཉམ་ཡིན་པ་ལ། །གཉེན་པོས་མ་ཐུབ་བྱ་
བ་ཅི་ལ་ཟེར། །དེ་ལྟའི་ཤེས་པ་འདི་ཀ་ཡིན་པ་ལ། །འདི་ལ་མི་ཤེས་བྱ་བ་ཅི་ལ་
ཟེར།། ༄༅ ཨེ་མ་ཧོ། ད་ཡང་སྐལ་ལྡན་བུ་རྣམས་གུས་པས་གསོན། །
རང་སེམས་དངོས་མེད་ནམ་མཁའ་སྟོང་པ་འདྲ། །འདྲ་འམ་མི་འདྲ་སྐལ་ལྡན་བུ་
རྣམས་ཀུན། །བལྟ་རུ་མེད་པའི་ཚུལ་དུ་རང་སེམས་ལ། །ཅེར་གྱིས་ལྟོས་ལ་
ཐྲུམ་གྱིས་ཞོག་དང་ཤེས། །སྟོང་པ་ཕྱང་ཆད་དག་ཀྱང་མ་ཡིན་པར། །རང་རིག་
ཡེ་ཤེས་ཡེ་ནས་གསལ་བར་ངེས། །རང་བྱུང་རང་གསལ་ཉི་མའི་སྙིང་པོ་འདྲ། །
འདྲ་འམ་མི་འདྲ་རང་གི་སེམས་ཉིད་ལ། །ཅེར་གྱིས་ལྟོས་ལ་ཐྲུམ་གྱིས་ཞོག་དང་
ཤེས། །རྣམ་རྟོག་འགྱུ་དྲན་ངོས་བཟུང་མེད་པར་ངེས། །འགྱུ་བ་ངེས་མེད་བར་
སྣང་བསེར་བུ་འདྲ། །འདྲ་འམ་མི་འདྲ་རང་གི་སེམས་ཉིད་ལ། །ཅེར་གྱིས་ལྟོས་
ལ་ཐྲུམ་གྱིས་ཞོག་དང་ཤེས། །ཅིར་སྣང་ཐམས་ཅད་རང་སྣང་ཡིན་པར་ངེས། །
གང་སྣང་ཐམས་ཅད་མེ་ལོང་གཟུགས་བརྙན་འདྲ། །འདྲ་འམ་མི་འདྲ་རང་གི་སེམས་
ཉིད་ལ། །ཅེར་གྱིས་ལྟོས་ལ་ཐྲུམ་གྱིས་ཞོག་དང་ཤེས། །སེམས་ལས་མ་
གཏོགས་གཞན་ལ་ཆོས་མེད་པས། །ལྟ་བ་བལྟ་རྒྱུ་གཞན་ན་ཆོས་མེད་དོ། །
སེམས་ལས་མ་གཏོགས་གཞན་ན་ཆོས་མེད་པས། །སྒོམ་པ་བསྒོམ་རྒྱུ་གཞན་ཆོས་
མེད་དོ། །སེམས་ལས་མ་གཏོགས་གཞན་ན་ཆོས་མེད་པས། །སྤྱོད་པ་སྤྱོད་རྒྱུ་
གཞན་ཆོས་མེད་དོ། །སེམས་ལས་མ་གཏོགས་གཞན་ན་ཆོས་མེད་པས། །དམ་
ཚིག་བསྲུང་རྒྱུ་གཞན་ན་ཆོས་མེད་དོ། །སེམས་ལས་མ་གཏོགས་གཞན་ན་ཆོས་མེད་
པས། །འབྲས་བུ་བསྒྲུབ་རྒྱུ་གཞན་ན་ཆོས་མེད་དོ། །ཡང་ལྟོས་ཡང་ལྟོས་རང་གི་
སེམས་ལ་ལྟོས། །ཕྱི་རོལ་ནམ་མཁའི་ཁམས་ལ་སེམས་ཐོངས་ལ། །རང་
སེམས་ཉིད་ལ་འགྲོ་འོང་ཨེ་འདུག་ལྟོས། །བལྟས་ཚེ་འགྲོ་འོང་སེམས་ལ་མི་གདའ་

ན། །ནང་གི་རང་གི་སེམས་ལ་ཚུར་ལྟོས་ལ། །རྟོག་པ་འཕྲོ་བའི་འཕྲོ་མཁན་ཨེ་འདུག་ལྟོས། །རྟོག་པ་འཕྲོ་བའི་འཕྲོ་མཁན་མི་གདའ་ན། །སེམས་ལ་ཁ་དོག་དབྱིབས་སོགས་ཨེ་འདུག་ལྟོས། །ཁ་དོག་དབྱིབས་མེད་སྟོང་པར་ཐུག་པའི་ཚེ། །སྟོང་པ་ཉིད་ལ་མཐའ་དབུས་ཨེ་འདུག་ལྟོས། །མཐའ་དབུས་མེད་ཚེ་ཕྱི་ནང་ཨེ་འདུག་ལྟོས། །ཕྱི་དང་ནང་མེད་རིག་པ་མཁའ་ལྟར་ཡངས། །ཟང་ངེ་ཐལ་ལེར་རྒྱ་ཆད་ཕྱོགས་ལྷུང་བྲལ། །རང་རིག་ཁྱབ་གདལ་ཀློང་ཆེན་ཡངས་པའི་ངང་། །འཁོར་འདས་ཆོས་རྣམས་བར་སྣང་འཇའ་ཚོན་བཞིན། །སྣ་ཚོགས་སྣང་ཡང་སེམས་ཀྱི་རོལ་པ་སྟེ། །རང་རིག་གཡོ་མེད་ངང་ལས་ཕར་ལྟོས་དང་། །ཆོས་རྣམས་ཐམས་ཅད་སྒྱུ་མ་ཆུ་ཟླ་བཞིན། །སྣང་སྟོང་སོ་སོར་དབྱེ་བར་མི་ནུས་སོ། །རིག་པའི་ངང་ལ་འཁོར་འདས་གཉིས་སུ་མེད། །རང་རིག་གཡོ་མེད་ངང་ལས་ཕར་ལྟོས་དང་། །འཁོར་འདས་ཆོས་རྣམས་མེ་ལོང་གཟུགས་བརྙན་བཞིན། །ཇི་ལྟར་སྣང་ཡང་གདོད་ནས་ཡོད་མ་མྱོང་། །འཁོར་འདས་མིང་མེད་ཐམས་ཅད་ཆོས་སྐུ་ཡིན། །ཁམས་གསུམ་འཁོར་བར་འཁྱམས་པའི་འགྲོ་ཀུན་གྱིས། །ཡེ་ནས་འཁོར་འདས་ཆོས་ཀུན་མཉམ་ཉིད་དུ། །གནས་པའི་ཡེ་ཤེས་རང་ངོ་མ་རྟོགས་པར། །གཉིས་འཛིན་འཁྲུལ་པའི་དབང་གིས་སོ་སོར་བཟུང་། །གཉིས་མེད་དོན་ལ་གཉིས་འཛིན་ཕྱིར་མ་གྲོལ། །ཀུན་གྱི་རང་སེམས་འཁོར་འདས་དབྱེར་མེད་ལ། །སྤང་བླང་འདོར་ལེན་བྱས་པས་འཁོར་བར་འཁྱམས། །རང་རིག་སྐུ་གསུམ་རྩོལ་མེད་ལྷུན་གྲུབ་ལས། །འདི་མིན་ཐག་རིང་གཞན་དུ་འགྲོ་ཐབས་ཀྱི། །ས་ལམ་བཙལ་ནས་བླུན་རྨོངས་འགྲོ་བ་ཀུན། །སངས་རྒྱས་ས་ལ་སླེབས་པའི་དུས་མ་བྱུང་། །གང་སྣང་ཐམས་ཅད་རང་སྣང་ཡིན་པར་ངེས། །རང་རིག་གཡོ་མེད་ངང་ནས་ཕར་ལྟོས་དང་། །སྣང་ཞིང་སྲིད་པ་ཐམས་ཅད་གཟུགས་བརྙན་འདྲ། །སྣང་སྟོང་གྲགས་སྟོང་རང་བཞིན་ཡེ་ནས་སྟོང་། །དེ་ལྟར་ལྟ་མཁན་སེམས་ལ་ཚུལ་ལྟོས་དང་། །དྲན་རྟོག་རང་ཡལ་སྟོང་པ་ནམ་མཁའ་འདྲ། །སྤྲོས་མེད་སྤྲོས་བྲལ་སྨྲ་བསམ་བརྗོད་ལས་འདས། །གང་སྣང་ཐམས་ཅད་སེམས་ཀྱི་ཆོ་

འཕྲུལ་ཏེ། །ཆོ་འཕྲུལ་ཐམས་ཅད་གཞི་མེད་སྟོང་པ་ཡིན། །ཐམས་ཅད་རང་གི་
སེམས་སུ་རྟོགས་གྱུར་ན། །མཐོང་སྣང་ཐམས་ཅད་སྟོང་པ་ཆོས་སྐུ་ཡིན། །སྣང་
བས་མི་འཆིང་ཞེན་པས་འཆིང་བ་ཡིན། །ཞེན་ཆགས་འཁྲུལ་པ་ཆོད་ཅིག་སླེང་གི་
བུ།། ༄ །།ཨེ་མ་ཧོ། སྐལ་བར་ལྡན་པའི་སེམས་ཀྱི་བུ་མཆོག་རྣམས། །
ལྷུག་གིས་མ་བརྒྱབ་རྩ་ལ་བབ་མི་ལྡང་། །མང་དུ་མ་བསྒྲུབས་འོ་མར་མར་མི་
ཆགས། །ཞིབ་ཏུ་མ་བཤད་གཏན་ལ་མི་ཕེབས་པས། །ཀིག་ཀ་མང་པོའི་གླུ་
དབྱངས་བླངས་པ་ལ། །སྣང་བ་མ་སུན་དགའ་བའི་སེམས་ཀྱིས་ཉོན། །སྣང་བ་
ཐམས་ཅད་སེམས་སུ་མ་ཤེས་ན། །སྟོང་ཉིད་དོན་དེ་ནམ་ཡང་མི་རྟོགས་པར། །
སྣང་བ་འདི་དག་དང་པོ་གང་ལས་བྱུང་། །བར་དུ་གར་གནས་ཐ་མ་གང་དུ་
འགྲོ། །སྐལ་ལྡན་བུ་ཀུན་ལེགས་པར་རྟོག་དཔྱོད་ཐོངས། །བརྟགས་ཆེ་དཔེར་ན་
ནམ་མཁའི་ན་བུན་དེ། །མཁའ་ལས་བྱུང་ཞིང་སླར་ཡང་མཁའ་ལ་འགྲོ། །དེ་
བཞིན་སྣང་བ་སེམས་ཀྱི་ཆོ་འཕྲུལ་ཏེ། །རང་གི་སེམས་སུ་ཤར་ཞིང་སེམས་སུ་
འགྲོ། །དཔེར་ན་མིག་གི་དབང་པོ་བསླད་པའི་མིས། །བར་སྣང་ཁམས་བལྟས་
རབ་རིབ་སྣང་བ་དེ། །ནམ་མཁའ་ཡོད་ཡོད་འདྲ་བར་སྣང་ན་ཡང་། །མཁའ་ལ་
མེད་དེ་མིག་གི་ཆོ་འཕྲུལ་ཡིན། །དེ་བཞིན་དངོས་འཛིན་བག་ཆགས་ངན་པ་
ཡིས། །སེམས་ཀྱི་དབང་པོ་བསླད་པའི་མཐུ་ཡིས་ནི། །ཀུན་རྫོབ་སྣང་གྲགས་
ཆོས་རྣམས་ཐམས་ཅད་ཀུན། །བདེན་པར་ཡོད་ཡོད་འདྲ་བར་སྣང་ན་ཡང་། །
གདོད་ནས་དངོས་པོར་གྲུབ་པ་རྡུལ་ཙམ་ཡང་། །མེད་དེ་རང་གི་སེམས་ཀྱི་ཆོ་འཕྲུལ་
ཡིན། །ཆོ་འཕྲུལ་ཐམས་ཅད་གཞི་མེད་སྟོང་པ་ཡིན། །མེད་པ་གསལ་སྣང་སྒྱུ་མ་
ཆུ་ཟླ་འདྲ། །སྣང་སྟོང་དབྱེར་མེད་དོན་ལ་མཉམ་པར་ཞོག །ད་ལྟ་རང་ཅག་
གཉིད་ཀྱི་རྨི་ལམ་ན། །ཕ་ཡུལ་གནས་ཀྱང་ཉེ་འབྲེལ་ལ་སོགས་པ། །མངོན་
སུམ་སྣང་ནས་བདེ་སྡུག་མྱོང་བའི་ཚེ། །རང་གི་ཉེ་དུ་འབྲེལ་བ་གཅིག་ཀྱང་
མེད། །རང་ཉིད་མལ་ནས་ཙུང་ཟད་མ་གཡོས་ཀྱང་། །ཉིན་པར་ཇི་བཞིན་ཉམས་
སུ་མངོན་སུམ་མྱོང་། །དེ་བཞིན་ཚེ་འདིའི་སྣང་བ་ཐམས་ཅད་ཀུན། །མདང་གི་

རྨི་ལམ་ཉམས་སུ་མྱོང་བ་བཞིན། །རང་གི་སེམས་ཡིས་དེར་བརྟགས་དེར་བཟུང་ནས། །དེ་ལྟར་སྣང་སྟེ་སེམས་ཀྱི་མྱོང་བ་ཡིན། །རྨི་ལམ་གཉིད་ཀྱི་སྐབས་སུའང་རང་བཞིན་མེད། །དེ་བཞིན་ཇི་ལྟར་སྣང་ཡང་སྟོང་པའོ།། ༈ །།ཨེ་མ་ཧོ། སྐལ་པར་ལྡན་པའི་སེམས་ཀྱི་བུ་གཅིག་པོ། །སྣང་བ་ཐམས་ཅད་ངེས་པ་མ་ཡིན་ཏེ། །ལ་ལས་སྣང་བ་ལ་ལས་མུན་པའོ། །དེ་ཡང་སེམས་ཅན་འགའ་ཞིག་ས་གཞི་ལ། །ས་ལ་ས་ཡི་འདུ་ཤེས་སེམས་ཅན་ཡོད། །ས་ལ་མེ་ཡི་འདུ་ཤེས་སེམས་ཅན་ཡོད། །ས་ལ་ལོངས་སྤྱོད་འདུ་ཤེས་སེམས་ཅན་ཡོད། །ས་ལ་སྡུག་བསྔལ་འདུ་ཤེས་སེམས་ཅན་ཡོད། །ཆུ་ལ་ཆུ་ཡི་འདུ་ཤེས་སེམས་ཅན་ཡོད། །ཆུ་ལ་མེ་ཡི་འདུ་ཤེས་སེམས་ཅན་ཡོད། །ཆུ་ལ་བདུད་རྩིར་འདུ་ཤེས་སེམས་ཅན་ཡོད། །ཆུ་ལ་གནས་ཁང་འདུ་ཤེས་སེམས་ཅན་ཡོད། །ཆུ་ལ་ས་རུ་འདུ་ཤེས་སེམས་ཅན་ཡོད། །མེ་ལ་མེ་ཡི་འདུ་ཤེས་སེམས་ཅན་ཡོད། །མེ་ལ་ལོངས་སྤྱོད་འདུ་ཤེས་སེམས་ཅན་ཡོད། །མེ་ལ་གནས་སུ་འདུ་ཤེས་སེམས་ཅན་ཡོད། །མེ་ལ་ཟས་སུ་འདུ་ཤེས་སེམས་ཅན་ཡོད། །ནམ་མཁའ་ནམ་མཁར་འདུ་ཤེས་སེམས་ཅན་ཡོད། །ནམ་མཁའ་གནས་སུ་འདུ་ཤེས་སེམས་ཅན་ཡོད། །ནམ་མཁའ་ས་རུ་འདུ་ཤེས་སེམས་ཅན་ཡོད། །དེས་ན་སྣང་བ་ངེས་པ་མེད་པའི་ཕྱིར། །བག་ཆགས་དབང་གིས་གང་ལྟར་སྣང་བ་ཡིན། །དེ་ལྟར་འབྱུང་བ་བཞི་པོ་རང་རང་དུ། །འདུ་ཤེས་པ་ནི་མི་ཡི་སྣང་ངོ་ཡིན། །འགྲོ་བ་གཞན་གྱིས་ས་གཞི་འདི་ལ་ཡང་། །དམྱལ་བའི་མེ་དང་ཞིང་པའི་ལོངས་སྤྱོད་དང་། །རྒྱུད་ཀྱིས་ནོན་པས་སྡུག་བསྔལ་འདུ་ཤེས་པའོ། །དེ་བཞིན་མེ་ལ་མེ་ལྷའི་ལོངས་སྤྱོད་དང་། །ཡི་དྭགས་མེ་ལུས་ཅན་གྱིས་གནས་ཁང་དང་། །མེ་ཡི་སྲིན་བུས་ཟས་སུ་འདུ་ཤེས་པའོ། །དེ་བཞིན་ཆུ་ལ་དམྱལ་བའི་འགྲོ་བས་མེ། །ཡི་དྭགས་སེམས་ཅན་རྣམས་ལ་རྣམ་ཁྲག་དང་། །ཉ་སྐྱི་སླང་པོས་ས་དང་ལྷས་བདུད་རྩི། །གཞན་འཕྲུལ་དབང་བྱེད་ལྷ་ལ་རིན་ཆེན་དང་། །མེ་ཏོག་ཆར་དང་ཀླུ་ཡི་གནས་ཁང་ངོ་། །ནམ་མཁའ་ལ་ཡང་དེ་ལྟར་བྱུས་ནས་གནས། །ལྷ་རྣམས་ཀུན་གྱིས་ས་ཡི་འདུ་ཤེས

སོ། །དེས་ན་ཐམས་ཅད་རང་གི་གང་ལྟར་དུ། །བརྟགས་པ་དེ་ལྟར་བཞིན་དུ་སྣང་
བའོ། །དེ་ཡང་ལྷ་ཡི་བུ་ཡིས་སངས་རྒྱས་ལ། །རི་རབ་ཉི་ཟླ་ལ་སོགས་སུ་ཡིས་
བྱས། །ཞུས་ཚེ་སངས་རྒྱས་ཉིད་ཀྱི་ཞལ་ནས་ཀྱང་། །འདི་ལ་བྱེད་མཁན་གཞན་
ནི་སུ་ཡང་མེད། །རང་གི་རྟོག་པའི་བག་ཆགས་ཨ་འཐས་ཀྱིས། །དེར་བརྟགས་
དེར་བཟུང་དེ་ལྟར་སྣང་བ་ཡིན། །ཐམས་ཅད་རང་གི་སེམས་ཀྱིས་བྱས་པར་
གསུངས། །ལྷ་ཡི་བུ་ཡིས་སངས་རྒྱས་ཡང་ཞུས་ཏེ། །རང་གི་རྟོག་པ་ཇི་ལྟར་ཨ་
འཐས་ཀྱང་། །རི་རབ་ཉི་མ་ཟླ་བ་ལ་སོགས་པའི། །སྲ་ཞིང་བརྟན་པ་འདི་འདྲ་ག
ན་འོངས། །ཞུས་ཚེ་སངས་རྒྱས་ཉིད་ཀྱི་ཞལ་ནས་ཀྱང་། །ལྷ་ར་ཧུ་སིར་རྒན
མོས་རང་ལུས་ནི། །སྟག་ཏུ་བསྒོམ་པས་གྲོང་ཁྱེར་དེ་ཡིས་ཀྱང་། །སྟག་ཏུ
མཐོང་ནས་གྲོང་ཁྱེར་སྟོངས་པས་ན། །ཡུན་ནི་ཐུང་དུས་དེ་ལྟར་སྣང་ནུས་ན། །
སྐྱེ་བ་ཐོག་མ་མེད་ནས་བག་ཆགས་སེམས། །གོམས་ན་འདི་འདྲ་ལོས་སྣང་ཐུབ
པས་གསུངས། །དེས་ན་ཐམས་ཅད་སེམས་ཀྱི་བྱས་པའོ། །དེ་ཡང་ཕྱི་རོལ་མུ
སྟེགས་ཁ་ཅིག་གིས། །འཇིག་རྟེན་འདུ་འཛིའི་གཡེང་བ་འགོག་པའི་ཕྱིར། །
དབེན་གནས་བསྒོམས་པས་དབེན་གནས་མངོན་སུམ་དུ། །གྲུབ་ནས་གཞན་གྱི་མིས་
ཀྱང་མཐོང་བ་བྱུང་། །གཅིག་གིས་ནམ་མཁའ་བྲག་ཏུ་བསྒོམས་ནས་ཀྱང་། །
བྲག་ཏུ་གྱུར་ནས་ཕུང་པོ་ཐོགས་པ་སྐད། །དེས་ན་ཐམས་ཅད་སེམས་ཀྱི་རྟོག་པ
ཡིས། །བྱས་པ་ཡིན་པས་སེམས་ཀྱི་རང་སྣང་སྟེ། །རང་སྣང་ཐམས་ཅད་དོན་ལ
སྟོང་པའོ། །དེ་ཡང་དམྱལ་བ་ཉི་ཚེའི་སེམས་ཅན་གྱིས། །སྒོ་དང་ཀ་བ་ཐབ་དང་
ཐག་པ་སོགས། །གཟུགས་སུ་འདུ་ཤེས་སྡུག་བསྔལ་མྱོང་བའོ། །དེས་ན་སེམས
ཀྱི་རྟོག་པས་གང་ལྟར་དུ། །བརྟགས་པ་དེ་ལྟར་གཞན་དུ་སྣང་བའོ། །འགྲོ་དྲུག
སེམས་ཅན་བདེ་སྡུག་ཐམས་ཅད་ནི། །རང་གི་སེམས་ཉིད་གཅིག་པུ་བྱས་པའི་
ཕྱིར། །ཐམས་ཅད་རང་གི་སེམས་ཀྱི་ཆོ་འཕྲུལ་གྱིས། །མེད་སྣང་སྟོང་པ་ཉིད་ཀྱི་
རང་གཟུགས་སུ། །ཀློ་ཐག་ཆོད་ཀྱིས་ཆོས་ལ་ཁྲུམ་གྱིས་ཞོག །དེ་ཡང་ཐུབ་པ
གངས་ཆེན་མཚོ་ཡིས་ནི། །ཕྱག་ནི་པདྨའི་རྡུལ་གཅིག་སྟེང་ཉིད་ན། །སྟོང་

གསུམ་མི་མཛེད་འཛིག་རྟེན་ཡོད་པར་གསུངས། །ཐོད་རྒལ་རིག་པ་ཚལ་ལ་ཕེབས་པའི་ཚེ། །རང་ལུས་བ་སྤུའི་ཁུང་བུ་རེ་རེ་ནི། །སངས་རྒྱས་ཞིང་ཁམས་ཚད་མེད་མཐོང་བ་དང་། །འགྲོ་དྲུག་སེམས་ཅན་གནས་ཀྱང་ཚད་མེད་མཐོང་། །དེ་ལ་འགྲོ་འདུལ་སྤྲུལ་པ་བཀྱེ་ནས་ཀྱང་། །རྨི་ལམ་ཇི་བཞིན་འགྲོ་དོན་བྱེད་པར་གསུངས། །དེས་ན་འཁོར་འདས་ཆོས་རྣམས་རང་སྣང་ཡིན། །རང་སྣང་ཐམས་ཅད་གཞི་མེད་སྟོང་པ་ཡིན། །སྟོང་གསལ་འཛིན་མེད་ངང་ལ་བློ་གདེང་འཆོས། ། །གཞན་ཡང་རྡུལ་གཅིག་སྟེང་ན་རྡུལ་སྙེད་ཀྱི། །སངས་རྒྱས་ཞིང་ཁམས་དཔག་ཏུ་མེད་པ་དང་། །འགྲོ་དྲུག་གནས་ཀྱང་གྲངས་མེད་ཡོད་པར་གསུངས། །དེ་རྣམས་ཐམས་ཅད་འདྲེས་མེད་རྙོག་པ་མེད། །གནོད་པར་གྱུར་པ་མེད་པར་རྒྱལ་བས་གསུངས། །གཞན་ཡང་སྲིན་འབུ་རེ་རེའི་ཁོག་ན་ཡང་། །སྲིན་འབུའི་གྲོང་ཁྱེར་དཔག་ཏུ་མེད་ཡོད་པར་གསུངས། །ནམ་མཁའི་ཁམས་ན་གྲོང་ཁྱེར་མང་པོ་ཡིས། །མགོ་བོ་ཐུར་དུ་བསྟན་ནས་ཆགས་པ་དང་། །དེ་བཞིན་འཕྲེད་དང་ཕྱིན་དུ་ཆགས་པ་ཡི། །གྲོང་ཁྱེར་དཔག་ཏུ་མེད་པ་ཡོད་པར་གསུངས། །འདི་འདྲ་འདི་དག་སུ་ཡིས་བྱས་སྙམ་ན། །ཐམས་ཅད་སེམས་ཀྱིས་བྱས་པར་རྒྱལ་བས་གསུངས། །སེམས་ཀྱི་ངར་བཞིན་གདོད་ནས་ནམ་མཁའ་འདྲ། །ཆོས་རྣམས་ཐམས་ཅད་དེ་བཞིན་ཤེས་པར་གྱིས། །ཀུན་རྫོབ་སྣང་གྲགས་ཆོས་རྣམས་ཐམས་ཅད་ཀུན། །རང་གི་སེམས་ཉིད་གཅིག་པུའི་རང་སྣང་སྟེ། །འཆི་ཚེ་རང་གི་སེམས་རྒྱུད་འགྱུར་བས་ན། །ཕྱི་རོལ་འགྱུར་བ་མེད་ཀྱང་རང་སྣང་འགྱུར། །དེས་ན་ཐམས་ཅད་སེམས་ཀྱི་རང་སྣང་སྟེ། །རང་སྣང་ཐམས་ཅད་གཞི་མེད་སྟོང་པ་ཡིན། །མེད་པ་གསལ་སྣང་གཟུགས་བརྙན་ཆུ་ཟླ་འདྲ། །གསལ་སྟོང་གཉིས་མེད་རིག་པའི་ངང་ཉམས་སྐྱོངས། །མཐོང་སྣང་ཐམས་ཅད་སེམས་ཀྱི་རང་སྣང་ཡིན། །སྣོད་ཀྱི་འཛིག་རྟེན་བེམ་པོར་སྣང་བ་སེམས། །བཅུད་ཀྱི་སེམས་ཅན་རིགས་དྲུག་སྣང་བའམ་སེམས། །མཐོ་རིས་ལྷ་མའི་བདེ་བ་སྣང་བའང་སེམས། །ངན་སོང་གསུམ་གྱི་སྡུག་བསྔལ་བའང་སེམས། །མ་རིག་ཉོན་མོངས་

དུག་ལྔར་སྣང་བའང་སེམས། །རང་བྱུང་ཡེ་ཤེས་རིག་པ་སྣང་བའང་སེམས། །ངན་རྟོག་འཁོར་བའི་བག་ཆགས་སྣང་བའང་སེམས། །བཟང་རྟོག་སངས་རྒྱས་ཞིང་ཁམས་སྣང་བའང་སེམས། །བདུད་དང་འདྲེ་ཡིས་བར་ཆད་སྣང་བའང་སེམས། །ལྷ་དང་དངོས་གྲུབ་ལེགས་པར་སྣང་བའང་སེམས། །རྣམ་པར་རྟོག་པ་སྣ་ཚོགས་སྣང་བའང་སེམས། །མི་རྟོག་རྩེ་གཅིག་བསྒོམ་པར་སྣང་བའང་སེམས། །དངོས་པོ་མཚན་མ་ཁ་དོག་སྣང་བའང་སེམས། །མཚན་མ་མེད་ཅིང་སྤྲོས་པ་མེད་པའང་སེམས། །གཅིག་དང་དུ་མ་གཉིས་མེད་སྣང་བའང་སེམས། །ཡོད་མེད་གང་ཡང་མ་གྲུབ་སྣང་བའང་སེམས། །སེམས་ལས་མ་གཏོགས་སྣང་བ་གང་ཡང་མེད། །སེམས་ནི་དཔེར་ན་རི་མོ་མཁན་དང་འདྲ། །རང་གི་ལུས་ཀྱང་སེམས་ཀྱིས་བྱས་པ་སྟེ། །སྟོང་གསུམ་འཇིག་རྟེན་ཁམས་ནི་ཧི་སླེད་པ། །དེ་དག་ཐམས་ཅད་སེམས་ཀྱིས་བྲིས་པ་སྟེ། །རང་གི་རྟོག་པས་བྲིས་པའི་རི་མོ་ཡིས། །བྲིས་པའི་བློ་ཅན་འགྲོ་ཀུན་བསླུས་པ་ཡིན། །དེས་ན་ཐམས་ཅད་སེམས་ཀྱི་ཆོ་འཕྲུལ་དུ། །ཐག་ཆོད་ངེས་ཤེས་བསྐྱེད་པ་གལ་ཆེའོ། །འདི་ནམ་རྣམ་རྟོག་སེམས་སུ་ངོ་སྤྲོད་དོ།།

༈ ཨེ་མ་ཧོ། ད་ཡང་སེམས་ཀྱི་བུ་མཆོག་ཐམས་ཅད་ཉོན། །དེ་ལྟར་བྱེད་མཁན་རང་གིས་སེམས་ཉིད་ལ། །ངོ་བོ་ངོས་བཟུང་དབྱིབས་དང་ཁ་དོག་སོགས། །སངས་རྒྱས་ཀྱིས་ཀྱང་བསྟན་དུ་མེད་པ་སྟེ། །ཡེ་ནས་སྟོང་པ་འཛིན་མེད་ནམ་མཁའ་འདྲ། །སེམས་ཉིད་སྟོང་པ་གཞི་མེད་ཡིན་པར་ངེས། །སེམས་ཉིད་མཚོན་དོན་ནམ་མཁའ་དཔེར་བཞག་ཀྱང་། །རེ་ཞིག་སྟོང་ཕྱོགས་ཙམ་གྱི་མཚོན་དཔེ་སྟེ། །སེམས་ཉིད་རིག་བཅས་སྟོང་པ་ཅིར་ཡང་འཆར། །ནམ་མཁའ་རིག་མེད་སྟོང་ཆད་ཧད་པོ་སྟེ། །དེའི་ཕྱིར་སེམས་དོན་ནམ་མཁས་མཚོན་དུ་མེད། །འདི་ནི་སེམས་ཉིད་སྟོང་པར་ངོ་སྤྲོད་དོ། །སེམས་ཉིད་གསལ་སྟོང་དེ་ཡི་རང་རྩལ་ལས། །སྣང་བ་སྣ་ཚོགས་གང་ཡང་འཆར་བ་ཡིན། །ཤར་ཡང་མེ་ལོང་ནང་གི་གཟུགས་བརྙན་བཞིན། །གཉིས་སུ་མེད་དེ་སྟོང་པའི་ངང་དུ་གཅིག །འདི་ནི་སྟོང་པ་སྣང་བར་ངོ་སྤྲོད་དོ། །ཡེ་ནས་སྣང་སྟོང་

གཉིས་སུ་མེད་པ་སྟེ། །རང་སེམས་སྟོང་པས་སྣང་བ་མི་འགག་ཅིང་། །སྟོང་པའི་ངང་ལས་སྣང་བ་འཛིན་མེད་བཀྲ །སྣང་བ་རྣམས་ཀྱི་སྟོང་པ་མི་འགག་ཅིང་། །སྣང་ཡང་རང་བཞིན་ཡེ་ནས་སྟོང་པའོ། །ནམ་མཁའི་འཇའ་ཚོན་ཆུ་ནང་ཟླ་གཟུགས་ལྟར། །སྣང་སྟོང་གཉིས་མེད་རྟོགས་པའི་རྣལ་འབྱོར་ལ། །འཁོར་འདས་ཆོས་རྣམས་སྒྱུ་མའི་ལྟད་མོ་ཡིན། །སྣང་སྟོང་གཉིས་མེད་ལྟད་མོར་བལྟས་པའི་ཚེ། །བློ་སེམས་འགྱུར་བ་མེད་པའི་རྣལ་འབྱོར་བདེ། །དེ་ལྟར་ཡིན་མིན་སྐལ་ལྡན་བུ་རྣམས་ཀུན། །རང་སེམས་སྟོང་པ་ཉིད་དང་སྣང་བ་གཉིས། །སོ་སོར་དབྱེ་རྒྱུ་ཨེ་ཡོད་ལྟོས་དང་ཤེས། །ཡེ་ནས་སྣང་སྟོང་གཉིས་སུ་མེད་པའོ། །འདི་ནི་སྣང་སྟོང་གཉིས་མེད་ངོ་སྤྲོད་དོ། །དེ་ལྟར་སྣང་སྟོང་གཉིས་མེད་རང་བྱུང་གི །རིག་པ་རང་གསལ་ས་ལེ་ཧྲིག་གེ་བ། །སྐུ་གསུམ་ལྷུན་གྱིས་གྲུབ་པའི་དགོངས་པ་སྟེ། །ཐུན་མཚམས་མེད་པར་ཁོར་ཡུག་ཉམས་ལེན་ལ། །ཉིན་མཚན་མེད་པར་སྐྱོངས་ཤིག་སེམས་ཀྱི་བུ། །འདི་ནི་གཉིས་མེད་རང་གྲོལ་ངོ་སྤྲོད་དོ།།

༄ ཨེ་མ་ཧོ། ད་ཡང་བྱ་བཏང་བདག་གི་སླུ་ལ་ཉོན། །གཞི་ཡི་རིག་པ་སྐུ་གསུམ་ཚང་ཚུལ་དང་། །གཞི་སྣང་དུས་ཀྱི་སྐུ་གསུམ་ཚང་ཚུལ་གྱི། །རྣམ་དབྱེ་འདི་གཉིས་ལེགས་པར་ཤེས་བྱས་ནས། །འཁོར་འདས་སྐུ་གསུམ་ཞིང་དུ་རྟོགས་པར་བྱ། །གཞི་ཡི་རིག་པར་སྐུ་གསུམ་ཚང་ཚུལ་ནི། །སྔོན་དུའང་བཤད་ཀྱང་ད་དུང་འདིར་ཡང་འཆད། །རང་རིག་གཞི་ནི་ཤེལ་གྱི་གོང་བུ་འདྲ། །དེ་ཡི་སྟོང་པ་ཆོས་སྐུའི་རང་བཞིན་དང་། །གསལ་བའི་རང་གདངས་ལོངས་སྤྱོད་རྫོགས་པ་དང་། །འཆར་གཞི་མ་འགགས་སྒྲོ་ནི་སྤྲུལ་པའི་སྐུ། །གཞི་ཡི་རིག་པ་སྐུ་གསུམ་ཚང་ཚུལ་ཡིན། །འདི་ལ་ནམ་ཡང་འདུ་འབྲལ་མེད་པའོ། །དཔེར་ན་ཤེལ་ལས་འོད་ལྔ་ཤར་བ་བཞིན། །དེ་ལས་ཤར་བ་གཞི་སྣང་དུས་ན་ཡང་། །དག་པ་རྒྱལ་བའི་ཞིང་ཁམས་སྣང་བ་དང་། །མ་དག་སྣོད་བཅུད་སྣང་བ་གང་སྣང་ཡང་། །ཐམས་ཅད་ངོ་བོ་སྟོང་པ་ཆོས་ཀྱི་སྐུ། །རང་བཞིན་སྣང་བ་ལོངས་སྤྱོད་རྫོགས་པའི་སྐུ། །སྣ་ཚོགས་མ་འགགས་ཤར་བ་སྤྲུལ་པའི་སྐུ། །གཞི་སྣང་དུས་ཀྱི་སྐུ་གསུམ་

ཚང་ཚུལ་ལོ། །གཞན་དུ་འདི་ཡི་རྣམ་དབྱེ་ཕྱེས་པ་ཙུང་། །གནད་འདི་ལེགས་
པར་རྟོགས་དགོས་པ་ཞིག་ཡིན། །ངས་ཀྱང་ཀུན་མཁྱེན་ལེགས་བཤད་དྲིན་ལས་
ཤེས། །དེ་ལྟར་ཤེས་ན་སྣང་སྲིད་ཐམས་ཅད་ཀྱང་། །སྐུ་གསུམ་ལྷུན་གྲུབ་དཀྱིལ་
འཁོར་ཡེ་ནས་ཡིན། །སྐུ་གསུམ་ཞིང་ཁམས་གཞན་ནས་བཙལ་དུ་མེད། །འགྲོ་
དྲུག་སེམས་ཅན་རྣམས་ཀྱང་སྐུ་གསུམ་དུ། །གནས་པ་ཡིན་ཏེ་རང་ངོ་ཤེས་ནུས་
ན། །འགྲོ་བ་རྣམས་ཀྱིས་སྒོམ་པ་རྩལ་ཙམ་ཡང་། །བྱ་མི་དགོས་པར་ཐམས་ཅད་
འཚང་རྒྱའོ། །དེ་ཡང་དོན་ལ་གཞི་ཡི་སྐུ་གསུམ་ཡང་། །ཆོས་སྐུ་ཡིན་པས་སོ་
སོར་མ་འཛིན་ཞིག །གཞི་སྣང་དུས་ཀྱི་སྐུ་གསུམ་དེ་ཉིད་ཀྱང་། །གཟུགས་སྐུ་
ཡིན་པས་སོ་སོར་མ་འཛིན་ཞིག །ཆོས་གཟུགས་གཉིས་ཀྱང་དོན་ལ་སོ་སོར་
མེད། །སྟོང་པ་ཆོས་སྐུའི་ངང་དུ་རོ་གཅིག་གོ །མཐར་ཐུག་གཞི་སྣང་གཞི་ལ་
རང་ཐིམ་ནས། །གཞི་ཡི་ཆོས་སྐུའི་དགོངས་པ་མངོན་གྱུར་ཚེ། །དོན་གྱི་འབྲས་
བུ་མངོན་དུ་གྱུར་པ་ཡིན། །དེ་ནས་ཆོས་སྐུའི་མཁའ་ལས་མ་གཡོས་བཞིན། །
གཟུགས་སྐུ་རྣམ་གཉིས་འཇའ་ཚོན་ཇི་བཞིན་དུ། །བསྟན་ནས་འགྲོ་དོན་རྒྱུན་མི་
འཆད་པའོ།། ༄ །།ཨེ་མ་ཧོ། ད་ཡང་བྱ་བཏང་བདག་གི་སློབ་ལ་ཉོན། །
ཁྱེད་རང་རྣམས་ལ་སྦྱོན་ལ་གནོད་པ་བསྐྱལ། །སྲུན་ནི་དབྱུང་དང་བརྡུང་བཙོག་བྱས་
པ་དང་། །ངོ་ཚ་གཏད་དང་སེམས་ལ་གནོད་པའི་ལས། །ཇི་ལྟར་གཞན་གྱིས་
བྱས་པའི་ཚུལ་རྣམས་ཀུན། །རང་གི་ཡིད་ལ་ཚུལ་བཞིན་བསམ་བྱས་ནས། །ཞེ་
སྡང་སྐྱེར་ཆུག་སྐྱེས་ཚེ་ངོ་བོ་ལ། །ཅེར་གྱིས་ལྟོས་ལ་ཞེ་སྡང་མཁན་པོ་དེ། །དང་
པོ་གང་ནས་བྱུང་དང་ད་ལྟའི་དུས། །གང་དུ་གནས་དང་ཐ་མ་གང་དུ་འགྲོ
།དབྱིབས་དང་ཁ་དོག་ལ་སོགས་ཨེ་འདུག་ལྟོས། །བལྟས་ཚེ་ཡེ་ནས་སྟོང་པ་འཛིན་
མེད་ཡིན། །ཞེ་སྡང་མ་སྤངས་མེ་ལོང་ཡེ་ཤེས་སོ། །ཁྱེད་རྣམས་སྙིང་ལ་སྡུག་
པའི་བུད་མེད་དང་། །ཤ་སོགས་རང་ཉིད་ཟ་བ་གང་འདོད་དང་། །གོས་སོགས་
རང་གི་གོན་པ་གང་འདོད་དང་། །རྟ་སོགས་རང་གི་ཕྱུགས་རྣམས་གང་འདོད་
རྣམས། །ཚུལ་བཞིན་རང་གི་ཡིད་ལ་བསམ་བྱས་ནས། །འདོད་ཆགས་སྐྱེར་

ཆུག་སྐྱེས་ཚེ་ངོ་བོ་ལ། །ཅེར་གྱིས་ལྟོས་ལ་འདོད་ཆགས་མཁན་པོ་དེ། །དང་པོ་གང་ནས་བྱུང་དང་ད་ལྟའི་དུས། །གང་དུ་གནས་དང་ཐ་མ་གང་དུ་འགྲོ། །དཔྱིབས་དང་ཁ་དོག་ལ་སོགས་ཅི་འདུག་ལྟོས། །བལྟས་ཚེ་ཡེ་ནས་སྟོང་པ་འཛིན་མེད་ཡིན། །འདོད་ཆགས་མ་སྤངས་སོར་རྟོག་ཡེ་ཤེས་སོ། །ཁྱེད་རྣམས་གཉིད་དང་བྱིང་རྨུགས་ལ་སོགས་པའི། །གཏི་མུག་སྐྱེར་ཆུག་སྐྱེས་ཚེ་ངོ་བོ་ལ། །ཅེར་གྱིས་ལྟོས་ལ་གཏི་མུག་མཁན་པོ་དེ། །དང་པོ་གང་ནས་བྱུང་དང་ད་ལྟའི་དུས། །གང་དུ་གནས་དང་ཐ་མ་གང་དུ་འགྲོ། །དཔྱིབས་དང་ཁ་དོག་ལ་སོགས་ཅི་འདུག་ལྟོས། །བལྟས་ཚེ་ཡེ་ནས་སྟོང་པ་འཛིན་མེད་ཡིན། །གཏི་མུག་མ་སྤངས་ཆོས་དབྱིངས་ཡེ་ཤེས་སོ། །ཁྱེད་རྣམས་རང་གི་རིགས་སུ་སྤོབས་འགྱུར་དང་། །གཟུགས་བྱད་ལེགས་དང་ངག་གི་དབྱངས་སྙན་དང་། །ཐོས་བསམ་སྒོམ་གསུམ་ཡི་གེ་འདྲི་ཀློག་དང་། །རིག་གནས་མཁས་དང་གྲོང་ཆོག་གདུལ་བྱ་སོགས། །རང་ལ་ཡོད་ཚད་ཡོན་ཏན་བསམ་བྱས་ནས། །གཞན་ལས་ཅུང་ཟད་ང་བཟང་སྙམ་པ་ཡི། །ང་རྒྱལ་སྐྱེར་ཆུང་སྐྱེས་ཚེ་ངོ་བོ་ལ། །ཅེར་གྱིས་ལྟོས་ལ་ང་རྒྱལ་མཁན་པོ་དེ། །དང་པོ་གང་ནས་བྱུང་དང་ད་ལྟའི་དུས། །གང་དུ་གནས་དང་ཐ་མ་གང་དུ་འགྲོ། །དཔྱིབས་དང་དང་ཁ་དོག་ལ་སོགས་ཅི་འདུག་ལྟོས། །བལྟས་ཚེ་ཡེ་ནས་སྟོང་པ་འཛིན་མེད་ཡིན། །ང་རྒྱལ་མ་སྤངས་མཉམ་ཉིད་ཡེ་ཤེས་སོ། །རང་ལས་ཆེ་བའི་གཞན་གྱི་སྤོབས་འགྱུར་དང་། །ཡོན་ཏན་མཁན་དང་གདུལ་བྱ་མང་བ་དང་། །རིག་གནས་མཁས་དང་འདོན་བཟང་སྐད་བཟང་དང་། །ཆོས་ཀྱི་གོ་བ་འཇིག་རྟེན་གཏམ་ལ་སོགས། །གཞན་གྱི་ཡོན་ཏན་ཐམས་ཅད་བསམ་བྱས་ནས། །རང་ལས་མཐོ་བར་དོགས་པའི་ཕྲག་དོག་སེམས། །སྐྱེར་ཆུག་སྐྱེས་ཚེ་ཕྲག་དོག་ངོ་བོ་ལ། །ཅེར་གྱིས་ལྟོས་ལ་ཕྲག་དོག་མཁན་པོ་དེ། །དང་པོ་གང་ནས་བྱུང་དང་ད་ལྟའི་དུས། །གང་དུ་གནས་དང་ཐ་མ་གང་དུ་འགྲོ། །དཔྱིབས་དང་ཁ་དོག་ལ་སོགས་ཅི་འདུག་ལྟོས། །བལྟས་ཚེ་ཡེ་ནས་སྟོང་པ་འཛིན་མེད་ཡིན། །ཕྲག་དོག་མ་སྤངས་བྱ་གྲུབ་ཡེ་ཤེས་སོ། །དེ་ལྟར་རྟོགས་ན་ཉོན་མོངས་ཡེ་ཤེས་

ཡིན། །ཉོན་མོངས་རྟོགས་པ་སྤྱངས་པའི་ཕ་རོལ་ནས། །སྟོང་ཉིད་ཡེ་ཤེས་འཚོལ་བ་དགོད་རེ་བྲོ། །བཙལ་བས་མ་རྙེད་ཚོ་ན་སྙིང་རེ་རྗེ། །འདི་ལྟར་དུག་ལྔ་སྟོང་པར་ཤེས་ནས་ཀྱང་། །ཕྱིན་ཆད་དུག་ལྔའི་རྟོགས་པ་གང་ཤར་ཡང་། །ངོ་སྤྲོད་འདི་བཞིན་སྐྱེ་ས་གནས་ས་དང་། །འགྲོ་ས་དབྱིབས་དང་ཁ་དོག་དཔྱད་མི་དགོས། །སྟོན་དུ་དུག་ལྔ་སྟོང་པར་ཤེས་པའི་ཕྱིར། །ཤར་མ་ཐག་ཏུ་རྗེས་སུ་མི་འབྲང་བར། །སེམས་ཉིད་དང་དུ་རང་སར་གློད་ལ་ཞོག །རང་ཡལ་ཉིད་དུ་འགྲོ་བར་ཐེ་ཚོམ་མེད། །འདི་ནི་ངོ་སྤྲོད་རྩལ་སྦྱོང་གཉིས་ཀ་ཡིན། །འདི་ལྟར་སྟོན་ལ་རྩལ་སྦྱོང་བྱས་གྱུར་ན། །ཕྱིན་ཆད་ཉོན་མོངས་དུག་ལྔ་ནམ་ཤར་ཚེ། །ཉོན་མོངས་རང་མཚར་སྟོན་ལ་ཤེས་སྟབས་ཀྱིས། །སྟོང་ཉིད་ཡེ་ཤེས་གཉིས་ཀ་མཉམ་ཤར་ནས། །ཤར་གྲོལ་དུས་མཉམ་ཤར་གྲོལ་དུས་མཉམ་མོ། །བླ་མ་གོང་མའི་རྣམ་ཐར་གསུང་རྒྱུན་དུ། །ཉོན་མོངས་རྟོགས་པ་མང་ན་ཆོས་སྐུ་ཡང་། །གསུངས་པ་ཇི་བཞིན་ཡིན་པས་ཤེས་པར་གྱིས། །ལས་ནི་དང་པོ་བ་ལ་ཉོན་མོངས་སེམས། །ཤུགས་དྲག་ཤར་ཚེ་དཔྱད་འཛོག་བྱས་ན་བཟང་། །འདི་ནི་ཞལ་ཤེས་ཡིན་པས་ཐུགས་ལ་ཞོག །འདི་ནི་དུག་ལྔ་རང་གྲོལ་ངོ་སྤྲོད་དོ།།

༄ ཨེ་མ་ཧོ། ད་ཡང་སྙིང་དང་འདྲ་བའི་བུ་རྣམས་ཉོན། །གོས་ལ་སོགས་པའི་འཇམ་པོ་ལུས་ལ་དྲིལ། །འཇམ་མོ་སྙམ་པའི་རང་གི་སེམས་ལ་ལྟོས། །རེ་བ་ལ་སོགས་རྩུབ་མོ་ལུས་ལ་དྲིལ། །རྩུབ་པོ་སྙམ་པའི་རང་གི་སེམས་ལ་ལྟོས། །བལྟས་ཚེ་གཉིས་ཀ་སྟོང་པར་རོ་མཉམ་མོ། །གསེར་སྐུ་ལ་སོགས་མཛེས་པའི་གཟུགས་ལ་ལྟོས། །མཛེས་སོ་སྙམ་པའི་རང་གི་སེམས་ལ་ལྟོས། །སྤྲུལ་པ་ལ་སོགས་མི་མཛེས་གཟུགས་ལ་ལྟོས། །མི་མཛེས་སྙམ་པའི་རང་གི་སེམས་ལ་ལྟོས། །བལྟས་ཚེ་གཉིས་ཀ་སྟོང་པར་རོ་མཉམ་མོ། །བུ་རམ་ལ་སོགས་ཞིམ་པོ་ཁ་རུ་ཟོ། །མངར་རོ་སྙམ་པའི་རང་གི་སེམས་ལ་ལྟོས། །བཙའ་ལྷ་ལ་སོགས་ཁ་རུ་མྱུངས་ནས་ཀྱང་། །ཁ་ཁ་སྙམ་པའི་རང་གི་སེམས་ལ་ལྟོས། །བལྟས་ཚེ་གཉིས་ཀ་སྟོང་པར་རོ་མཉམ་མོ། །ཙན་དན་སྤོས་སོགས་དྲི་ནི་ཞིམ་པོར་སྣོམས། །ཞིམ་མོ་སྙམ་པའི་

རང་གི་སེམས་ལ་ལྟོས། །ཤིང་ཀུན་སྒོག་པ་ལ་སོགས་དྲི་ངན་སྣོམས། །མི་ཞིམ་
སྙམ་པའི་རང་གི་སེམས་ལ་ལྟོས། །བལྟས་ཚེ་གཉིས་ཀ་སྟོང་པར་རོ་མཉམ་
མོ། །དྲིལ་བུ་པི་ཝང་གླིང་བུའི་སྒྲ་ལ་ཉོན། །སྙན་ནོ་སྙམ་པའི་རང་གི་སེམས་ལ་
ལྟོས། །རྔ་དང་ཐལ་མོ་རྡེབ་ལ་སྒྲ་ལ་ཉོན། །མི་སྙན་སྙམ་པའི་རང་གི་སེམས་ལ་
ལྟོས། །བལྟས་ཚེ་གཉིས་ཀ་སྟོང་པར་རོ་མཉམ་མོ། །ཁྱེད་རྣམས་གླིང་བཞིའི་
ཁམས་ལ་དབང་བསྒྱུར་བའི། །འཁོར་ལོས་བསྒྱུར་རྒྱལ་ཞིག་ཏུ་སྐྱེས་ནས་
ཀྱང་། །བཙུན་མོ་བློན་པོ་མང་པོའི་འཁོར་གྱིས་བསྐོར། །རིན་ཆེན་སྣ་ལྔ་ལས་
གྲུབ་ཁང་པ་ན། །རོ་བརྒྱ་ལྡན་པའི་ཁ་ཟས་ཟ་བར་བསྒོམ། །དེ་འདྲའི་སྣང་བ་
སེམས་ལ་ཤར་བའི་ཚེ། །བདེའོ་སྙམ་པའི་རང་གི་སེམས་ལ་ལྟོས། །ཁྱེད་རྣམས་
དབུལ་པོ་འཁོར་གཡོག་གཅིག་ཀྱང་མེད། །གྱང་ར་ཞིག་པོ་ཞིག་ཏུ་མལ་བཅས་
ནས། །སྟེང་ནས་ཆར་བབས་འོག་ནས་སས་བརླན་ཞིང་། །ལུས་ལ་མཛེ་སོགས་
ནད་སྣ་མང་པོས་བཏབ། །རྐང་ལག་ཆད་ནས་སྡུག་བསྔལ་དུ་མ་ཡིས། །མནར་
ནས་སྡུག་བསྔལ་མྱོང་བ་ཞིག་ཏུ་བསྒོམ། །དེ་འདྲའི་སྣང་བ་ཡིད་ལ་ཤར་བའི་
ཚེ། །སྡུག་གོ་སྙམ་པའི་རང་གི་སེམས་ལ་ལྟོས། །བལྟས་ཚེ་བདེ་སྡུག་སྟོང་པར་
རོ་མཉམ་མོ། །འདི་ལྟར་ཚོགས་དྲུག་སྟོང་པར་ཤེས་ནས་ཀྱང་། །ཕྱིན་ཆད་
ཚོགས་དྲུག་བཟང་ངན་གང་ཤར་ཚེ། །ངོ་སྤྲོད་འདི་བཞིན་དཔྱད་པ་མི་དགོས་
ཏེ། །གཞི་མེད་ཡེ་གྲོལ་སྟོང་པ་ཡིན་པའི་ཕྱིར། །ཤར་ཙམ་ཉིད་ནས་རྗེས་སུ་མི་
འབྲེང་བར། །སེམས་ཉིད་ངང་དུ་རང་སར་གློད་ལ་ཞོག །རང་གྲོལ་ཉིད་དུ་འགྲོ་
བར་ཐེ་ཚོམ་མེད། །འདི་ནི་ཚོགས་དྲུག་རང་གྲོལ་ངོ་སྤྲོད་དོ།། ༈ ཨེ་མ་ཧོ།
ད་ཡང་རིགས་ཀྱི་བུ་རྣམས་ལེགས་པར་ཉོན། །ཁྱེད་རྣམས་རང་སེམས་གློད་ལ་རང་
བབས་སུ། །ཞོག་ལ་ཇི་ལྟར་གནས་པའི་ཚུལ་ལ་ལྟོས། །བལྟས་ཚེ་རིག་པའི་
ངང་ལ་གནས་པའི་ཕྱིར། །གནས་ཀྱང་སྟོང་པ་རིག་པའི་ངང་ཡིན་པས། །སྐལ་
ལྡན་སེམས་ཀྱི་བུ་རྣམས་ཤེས་པར་གྱིས། །གནས་པ་སེམས་ཀྱི་རྒྱུན་དུ་ངོ་སྤྲོད་
དོ། །རྣམ་རྟོག་སྤྲོས་ལ་ཇི་ལྟར་འགྲོ་ཚུལ་ལ། །ལྟོས་དང་སྟོང་གསལ་རིག་པའི་

ངང་ཉིད་ལས། །ཙུང་ཟད་ཙམ་ཡང་གཡོ་བ་མེད་པའི་ཕྱིར། །འགྲོ་ཡང་སྟོང་པ་
རིག་པའི་ངང་ཡིན་པས། །སྐལ་ལྡན་རིགས་ཀྱི་བུ་རྣམས་ཤེས་པར་གྱིས། །འགྲོ་
བ་སེམས་ཀྱི་རོལ་པར་ངོ་སྤྲོད་དོ། །དཔེར་ན་རྒྱ་མཚོར་ཐ་རླབས་ཅི་ཤར་ཡང་། །
རྒྱ་མཚོ་ཉིད་ལས་ཙུང་ཟད་མ་གཡོས་ལྟར། །སེམས་ནི་གནས་སམ་འགྱུ་ཡང་རིག་
སྟོང་དང་། ཙུང་ཟད་ཙམ་ཡང་གཡོ་བ་མེད་པའི་ཕྱིར། །གང་ལྟར་གནས་ཀྱང་
རིག་པའི་ངང་ཡིན་ཞོག །གང་ལྟར་ཤར་ཡང་རིག་པའི་གདངས་ཡིན་ཞོག །
སེམས་ནི་གནས་ན་སྒོམ་ནི་ཡིན་པར་འདོད། །འགྲོ་ན་སྒོམ་ནི་མིན་པར་འདོད་པ་
དེ། །གནས་འགྱུ་གཉིས་ཀྱི་རང་མཚང་མ་ཤེས་པར། །གནས་འགྱུ་རིག་གསུམ་
གཅིག་ཏུ་མ་འདྲེས་རྟགས། །དེ་ཕྱིར་སྐལ་ལྡན་སེམས་ཀྱི་བུ་མཆོག་ཀུན། །
གནས་རུང་འགྱུ་རུང་རིག་པའི་ངང་ཡིན་པས། །འདི་རྣམས་སྐྱོན་ལ་ཐུགས་སུ་ཆུད་
ནས་ཀྱང་། །གནས་འགྱུ་རིག་གསུམ་གཅིག་ཏུ་ཉམས་སུ་ལོངས། །འགྲོ་གནས་
གཉིས་སུ་མེད་པར་ངོ་སྤྲོད་དོ།། ༄ ཨེ་མ་ཧོ། སྐལ་བར་ལྡན་པའི་སེམས་ཀྱི་
བུ་གཅིག་པོ། །ཁྱེད་རྣམས་མ་ཡེངས་དལ་ལེ་རྣ་བས་ཉོན། །གླུ་པ་བྱེ་བཏང་
ཚོགས་དྲུག་རང་གྲོལ་ངས། །གླུ་དབྱངས་སྙན་མོས་གདངས་དཀར་སེམས་ལ་
འཛོག །ཆོས་རྣམས་ཐམས་ཅད་རོ་གཅིག་སྟོང་པ་རུ། །གཏན་ལ་ཕེབས་ན་
འཁོར་འདས་སྤང་བླང་བྲལ། །དགྲ་དང་གཉེན་དུ་འཛིན་པའི་འཁྲུལ་པ་འཇིག །
བདག་གཞན་གཉིས་སུ་འཛིན་པའི་སྣང་བ་མེད། །ཐམས་ཅད་རོ་གཅིག་སྟོང་པར་
རྟོགས་ཕྱིར་རོ། །རྒྱས་བཤད་མདོ་འགག་བསྡུ་ན་འདི་ཡིན་ཏེ། །ཐེག་པའི་ཡང་
རྩེ་རྫོགས་པ་ཆེན་པོ་རུ། །འཁོར་བ་མྱང་འདས་ཐམས་ཅད་གཞི་རྩ་བྲལ། །ཡེ་
ནས་སངས་རྒྱས་ཆོས་སྐུར་རོ་གཅིག་གོ། །རྫོགས་ཆེན་ངང་ལ་ལྷ་འདྲེ་གཉིས་སུ་
མེད། །རྫོགས་ཆེན་ཡུལ་ལ་སངས་རྒྱས་སེམས་ཅན་མེད། །རྫོགས་ཆེན་གཞི་ལ་
བཟང་དང་ངན་པ་མེད། །རྫོགས་ཆེན་ལམ་ལ་ཉེ་དང་རིང་བ་མེད། །རྫོགས་ཆེན་
འབྲས་བུར་ཐོབ་དང་མ་ཐོབ་མེད། །རྫོགས་ཆེན་ཆོས་ལ་སྤྱོད་དང་མི་སྤྱོད་
མེད། །རྫོགས་ཆེན་དོན་ལ་སྒོམ་དང་མི་སྒོམ་མེད། །རྫོགས་ཆེན་རྒྱལ་པོའི་ལྟ་བ་

དེ་བཞིན་གནས། །དེ་འདྲའི་རྫོགས་ཆེན་ལྟ་བ་རྟོགས་པའི་ཚེ། །སྒོ་གསུམ་བྲ་རགས་རྟོག་པ་ཀུན་ཞི་ནས། །དཔེར་ན་བལ་ལ་ཆུ་བཏབ་ཇི་བཞིན་དུ། །སྒོ་གསུམ་ཞི་ཞིང་དུལ་བའི་ངང་ལ་གནས། །བདེ་གསལ་མི་རྟོག་ཉིང་འཛིན་སྐྱེ་བ་དང་། །དེ་ལྟར་མ་རྟོགས་འཁོར་འཁྱམས་འགྲོ་ཀུན་ལ། །མ་ཡིས་བུ་གཅིག་དག་ལ་བརྩེ་བ་ལྟར། །བཅོས་མིན་སྙིང་རྗེ་སྐྱེ་བ་རྫོགས་ཆེན་གྱི། །ལྟ་བའི་ཁྱད་ཆོས་ཡིན་པའང་ཤེས་པར་གྱིས། །ཐམས་ཅད་སྟོང་པ་ཉིད་དུ་ཐག་བཅད་ནས། །དགེ་སྤངས་སྡིག་ལ་འཛེམ་མེད་སྤྱོད་གྱུར་ན། །ནག་པོ་ཁ་འབྱམས་བདུད་ཀྱི་ལྟ་བ་སྟེ། །དེ་འདྲའི་བདུད་ལྟའི་དབང་དུ་མ་ཤོར་གཅེས། །འདི་རྣམས་རྫོགས་པ་ཆེན་པོའི་ངོ་སྤྲོད་དོ། །ངོ་སྤྲོད་འདི་རྣམས་ཤིན་ཏུ་གལ་ཆེ་སྟེ། །ཕྱི་རོལ་ཀུན་རྫོབ་སྣང་གྲགས་ཆོས་རྣམས་ཀུན། །ཐམས་ཅད་སྟོང་པ་ཉིད་དུ་མ་རྟོགས་པར། །ལྟ་བ་སྒོམ་ན་སླམ་ཡང་ཅི་ཞིག་བསྒོམ། །དེ་ཡི་ཕྱིར་ན་དང་པོ་འདི་ལྟར་དུ། །རེས་འགའ་བླ་མར་གསོལ་བ་འདེབས་ཀྱིན་ལྟོས། །རེས་འགའ་གློད་ཀྱིན་བསྒྲིམས་ཀྱིན་ལེགས་པར་ལྟོས། །དེ་ལྟར་བལྟས་ཚེ་སེམས་ལ་དགའ་བ་དང་། །ཐམས་ཅད་སྟོང་པ་ཉིད་དུ་ལམ་ལམ་དུ། །ཤར་ནས་ཕྱི་རོལ་སྣང་བའི་ཡུལ་རྣམས་ལ། །ལག་པས་རེག་ཀྱང་འཛིན་རྒྱུ་མེད་སླམ་དང་། །ལྟ་བ་འདི་ཉིད་ངེས་པར་ཡིན་པར་འདུག །སླམ་པའི་ངེས་ཤེས་གཏིང་ཚུགས་སྐྱེ་བར་ངེས། །དེ་དུས་ལྟ་བའི་ངེས་ཤེས་རྙེད་པ་ཡིན། །འཛིན་པས་མ་བསླད་འཛིན་མེད་ངང་ལ་གློད། །ངོ་སྤྲོད་ཐེབས་ནས་ཉམས་སུ་མ་ལོན་ཀྱང་། །འཆི་ཚེ་བར་དོར་འཇིགས་སྐྲག་ཅི་བྱུང་ཡང་། །ཐམས་ཅད་རང་སྣང་སྟོང་པའི་རང་གཟུགས་སུ། །ཤེས་ནས་ཀ་དག་གཞི་ལ་འཚང་རྒྱ་འོ། །ངོ་སྤྲོད་མ་ཐེབས་ཉམས་སུ་ལེན་པ་དེ། །དཔེར་ན་ཆོས་པ་གཅིག་ནས་འཁྱུགས་པ་ན། །བཙོ་ལྷུའི་བར་དུ་འཁྱུགས་པ་ཇི་བཞིན་ནོ། །ཀུན་རྫོབ་ཆོས་རྣམས་ཐམས་ཅད་བདེན་མེད་དུ། །མ་རྟོགས་སྟོང་ཉིད་རྟོགས་ཟེར་རྫུན་ཆེན་ཡིན། །དེས་ན་ངོ་སྤྲོད་འདི་བཞིན་དང་པོའི་དུས། །བླ་མའི་དྲུང་དུ་སྡོད་ལ་གནས་ལུགས་ཀྱི། །སྙིང་དུ་གཏན་ལ་ཕབས་དང་གོལ་ས་མེད། །དེའི་ཕྱིར་སྐལ་

ལྡན་བུ་རྣམས་སྙིང་ལ་ཆོངས༎ ༄ ཨེ་མ་ཧོ། ད་ཡང་སྐལ་ལྡན་རིགས་ཀྱི་བུ་རྣམས་ཉོན་དེ་ལྟར་ལྟ་བའི་གནས་ལུགས་ཁོང་ཆུད་ནས། །འཁོར་ཡུལ་ཆགས་སྡང་འབྲེལ་ཐག་ཐད་ཀྱིས་ཆོད། །གཅིག་པུར་ནགས་ཀྱི་གསེབ་དང་རི་སུལ་དུ། །ལུས་ཀྱི་བྱ་རྩོལ་ཐོངས་ལ་རྣལ་མར་སྡོད། །ངག་གིས་སྨྲ་བརྗོད་ཆོད་ལ་བརྗོད་མེད་ཀྱིས། །སེམས་ནི་ནམ་མཁའ་བསམ་པའི་ཡུལ་ལས་འདས། །དེ་ཡི་ངང་ལ་བཏང་བཞག་མེད་པར་གློད། །སེམས་ལ་གཏད་སོ་མེད་ན་ལྟ་བ་ཡིན། །བསྒོམ་དུ་མེད་པའི་ངང་ལ་གནས་པར་གྱིས། །ཐོབ་མེད་རྫོགས་ཆེན་འབྲས་བུ་འཐོབ་པར་མཛོད། །དེ་ཡང་ལྟ་བར་མཉམ་པར་འཇོག་པའི་ཚེ། །འདི་ལྟར་རིག་པའི་ངང་ལ་འཇོག་སླམ་དང་། །ཁྲིང་ཁོད་དབང་དུ་ཤོར་འགྲོ་སླམ་བྱེད་ཀྱི། །རྟོག་པའི་དྭ་བ་གང་གིས་མི་བཅིངས་པར། །དམིགས་གཏད་ཆོས་མེད་ཧྲར་སང་རྒྱ་ཡན་དང་། །ཟང་ཐལ་ཁ་ཡན་ཉིད་དུ་གློད་ལ་ཞོག །བློ་ཡི་ཆོས་ཀྱིས་བློ་འདས་དོན་མི་མཐོང་། །བྱས་པའི་ཆོས་ཀྱི་བྱར་མེད་སར་མི་སླེབས། །བློ་འདས་བྱར་མེད་དོན་དེ་ཐོབ་འདོད་ན། །བཅོས་བསླད་མ་བྱེད་རིག་པ་གཅེར་བུར་ཞོག །གཟུང་འཛིན་ཀུན་བྲལ་ལྟ་བའི་མཆོག་ཡིན་ནོ། །སྤང་བླང་མེད་པ་བསྒོམ་པའི་མཆོག་ཡིན་ནོ། །བྱ་རྩོལ་ལས་འདས་སྤྱོད་པའི་མཆོག་ཡིན་ནོ། །རེ་མེད་རང་གནས་འབྲས་བུའི་མཆོག་ཡིན་ནོ། །བལྟས་པས་མི་མཐོང་ལྟ་བའི་འཆོལ་འཁྲོ་ཞིག །བསྒོམས་པས་མི་རྙེད་དྲན་འཛིན་དམིགས་གཏད་དོར། །སྤྱོད་པས་མི་འགྲུབ་སྒྲུ་མར་འཛིན་པ་ཐོངས། །བཙལ་བས་མི་རྙེད་འབྲས་བུའི་རེ་བ་བོར། །ད་ལྟའི་ཤེས་བཟོ་མེད་ལྷུག་པ་ལ། །ཕྱོགས་རིས་མ་བྱེད་འཛིན་པས་མ་བསླད་ཅིག །ད་ལྟའི་རིག་པ་དངོས་མེད་གསལ་བ་འདི། །འདི་ཀ་ལྟ་བ་ཀུན་གྱི་ཡང་རྩེ་ཡིན། །དམིགས་གཏད་ཁྱབ་གདལ་བློ་དང་བྲལ་བ་འདི། །འདི་ཀ་སྒོམ་པ་ཀུན་གྱི་ཡང་རྩེ་ཡིན། །མ་བཅོས་འཛིན་མེད་ལྷུག་པར་བཞག་པ་འདི། །འདི་ཀ་སྤྱོད་པ་ཀུན་གྱི་ཡང་རྩེ་ཡིན། །མ་བཙལ་ཡེ་ནས་ལྷུན་གྱིས་གྲུབ་པ་འདི། །འདི་ཀ་འབྲས་བུ་ཀུན་གྱི་ཡང་རྩེ་ཡིན། །ལྟ་བའི་སྙིང་པོ་སྟོང་གསལ་འཛིན་མེད་ལྟོས། །སྒོམ་པའི་སྙིང་པོ་རང་

གྲོལ་འཛིན་མེད་སྐྱོང་། །སྤྱོད་པའི་སྙིང་པོ་ཚོགས་དྲུག་ལྷུག་པར་ཞོག །འབྲས་
བུའི་སྙིང་པོ་རེ་དོགས་ཞིག་པ་ཡིན། །མུ་མཐའ་བྲལ་ན་ལྟ་བའི་རྒྱལ་པོ་མཆོག །
གཟའ་གཏད་བྲལ་ན་སྒོམ་པའི་རྒྱལ་པོ་མཆོག །བླང་དོར་བྲལ་ན་སྤྱོད་པའི་རྒྱལ་པོ་
མཆོག །རེ་དོགས་བྲལ་ན་འབྲས་བུའི་རྒྱལ་པོ་མཆོག །བལྟ་རུ་མེད་ཀྱིས་ལྟ་
བའི་དམིགས་གཏད་དོར། །བསྒོམ་དུ་མེད་ཀྱིས་གང་བྱུང་གང་བདེར་ཐོངས། །
སྤྱོད་དུ་མེད་ཀྱིས་དགག་སྒྲུབ་སྤང་བླང་གྲོལ། །འཐོབ་རྒྱུ་མེད་ཀྱིས་འབྲས་བུའི་རེ་བ་
དོར། གང་ཡིན་ཡིན་གྱིས་ཆེད་འཛིན་མ་བྱེད་ཅིག །འདི་ཡིན་མེད་ཀྱིས་དགག་
སྒྲུབ་མ་བྱེད་ཅིག །གཟའ་གཏད་མེད་ཀྱིས་ཕྱོགས་རིས་མ་བྱེད་ཅིག །གདོད་ནས་
དག་པའི་རང་རིག་རང་གསལ་ལ། །བསམ་ཡུལ་བློ་ལས་འདས་པས་བལྟ་རུ་
མེད། །ངོ་བོ་གཞི་ནས་བྲལ་བས་བསྒོམ་དུ་མེད། །རང་གྲོལ་མཐའ་ལས་འདས་
པས་སྤྱོད་དུ་མེད། །རྩོལ་སྒྲུབ་ཞེན་པ་ལས་འདས་འབྲས་བུ་མེད། །ངོ་བོ་སྟོང་
ཉིད་ཡིན་པས་སྤང་ཐོབ་མེད། །རང་བཞིན་གསལ་སྟོང་ཡིན་པས་རྩོལ་སྒྲུབ་
ཞིག །ཐམས་ཅད་འགག་མེད་ཡིན་པས་ཕྱོགས་རིས་མེད། །གང་ལྟར་ཤར་ཡང་
དེ་ལྟར་མ་འཛིན་ཅིག །རྣལ་འབྱོར་ཤེས་པ་ནམ་མཁའི་བྱ་ལམ་འདྲ། །བྱ་རྗེས་སྣ་
མ་འགགས་ནས་མི་མཐོང་ལྟར། །དྲན་བསམ་སྣ་མ་འགག་ཅིང་མཐོང་བ་
མེད། །དེ་ལ་རྗེས་བསླེགས་འཛིན་པས་མ་མཐུད་ཅིག །བྱ་རྗེས་ཕྱི་མ་འོངས་
དངོས་མེད་ལྟར། །དྲན་བསམ་ཕྱི་མས་བསུ་མ་མ་བྱེད་ཅིག །བྱ་རྗེས་ད་ལྟ་ཁ་
དོག་དབྱིབས་མེད་ལྟར། ད་ལྟའི་དྲན་བསམ་ཐ་མ་ལ་རང་འགྲོས་ལ། །འདི་ཞེས་
གཉེན་པོས་བཅོས་བསླད་མ་བྱེད་ཅིག །ཇི་ལྟར་ཤར་ཡང་དེ་ལྟར་མ་འཛིན་ཅིག །
འདི་ནི་མཐར་ཐུག་སྙིང་པོའི་ལམ་ཁྱེར་ཡིན། །གང་ལྟར་ཤར་ཡང་དེ་ལྟར་མ་བཟུང་
ན། །ཉོན་མོངས་རང་ཡལ་ཡེ་ཤེས་ཆེན་པོ་ཡིན། །སྐྱེ་མེད་བསམ་འདས་ཡེ་གྲོལ་
ལྟ་བ་སྟེ། །ནན་ཏན་བྱས་ན་ལྟ་རྒྱུ་མེད་པ་ལས། །རང་བབས་ལྷོད་ཆགས་རང་
གནས་བསྒོམ་པ་སྟེ། །ནན་ཏན་བྱས་ན་བསྒོམ་རྒྱུ་མེད་པ་ལགས། །སྤང་བླང་
གཉིས་མེད་སྒྱུ་མའི་སྤྱོད་པ་སྟེ། །ནན་ཏན་བྱས་ན་སྤྱོད་རྒྱུ་མེད་པ་ལགས། །རེ་

རྟོགས་གཉིས་མེད་འབྲས་བུའི་རང་བཞིན་སྐྱེ། །ནན་ཏན་བྱས་ན་འབྲས་བུ་མེད་པ་ལགས། །དུས་གསུམ་རྩ་བ་བྲལ་བའི་སེམས་ཉིད་འདི། །མ་བསྒོམ་མངོན་སུམ་སྣང་བ་བློ་རེ་བདེ། །ཐོག་མ་ཐ་མ་རང་བཞིན་དག་པའི་ཆོས། །ཡེ་གྲོལ་ཡོངས་གྲོལ་འབད་རྩོལ་ཞིག་པ་མཚར། །ཐ་མལ་ཤེས་པ་བཟོ་མེད་ལྷུག་པ་འདི། །རྒྱལ་བའི་དགོངས་པ་མཐའ་བྲལ་ཀློང་ཡངས་ཡིན། །དེ་ཡང་འབད་པས་དཔྱད་ཅིང་བསྒོམས་པ་ཡིས། །སེམས་ཉིད་གནས་ལུགས་གཅུག་མ་མཐོང་མི་འགྱུར། །མ་བསམས་མ་དཔྱད་ཐ་མལ་ཆོས་ཉིད་ལ། །བསྒོམ་དང་མི་བསྒོམ་ཡེངས་དང་མ་ཡེངས་མེད། །མ་བསྒོམས་ལྷུག་པས་མང་པོ་གྲོལ་བ་ཡིན། །གྲོལ་དང་མ་གྲོལ་དོན་ལ་གཉིས་སུ་མེད། །གནས་ལུགས་ཤེས་ན་རྩོལ་ན་རྩོལ་མེད་བློ་བདེའོ། །རྟོག་མེད་འདོད་པའི་རྟོག་པས་བཅིངས་པ་ན། །རྣམ་རྟོག་ལངས་ན་ཕྱོགས་བཅུར་འགྲོ་བར་བསྒོན། །འགྲོ་འོང་མེད་པའི་རིག་པའི་གཞིས་ཐོག་ཏུ། །ཁ་ཡན་གློད་ནས་རང་ཡན་བཞག་པ་ན། །མི་གཡོ་རི་བོ་བཞིན་དུ་བརྟན་པར་གནས། །གོ་ལྡོག་འགྲོས་འདི་བུ་རྣམས་ཤེས་པར་གྱིས། །འདི་ལ་བསྒོམ་རྒྱུ་རྡུལ་ཙམ་མི་དམིགས་ཀྱང་། །ཡེངས་མེད་དྲན་པས་ཟིན་པ་རབ་ཏུ་གཅེས།། ༄ ཨེ་མ་ཧོ། ད་ཡང་སྐལ་ལྡན་བུ་རྣམས་ཚུར་ཉོན་དང་། །ཕྱི་ཡུལ་མེད་སྣང་སྟོང་པའི་རང་གཟུགས་འདི། །ཡེ་སྟོང་ཆུ་ཟླ་འདྲ་བས་སྤྱང་མི་དགོས། །ནང་གི་དྲན་རྟོག་རང་ཡལ་རྗེས་མེད་པས། །འབད་རྩོལ་གཉེན་པོ་དེ་ལ་འཇུག་མི་དགོས། །སྣང་སེམས་ཡེ་གྲོལ་ལྷུག་པའི་ཡེ་ཤེས་ལ། །སྤང་བླང་རེ་དོགས་གང་གིའང་སྒྲོ་མི་འདོགས། །རིག་པ་ཟང་ཀ་གཅེར་བུ་འདི་ཉིད་ལ། །ཡིད་དཔྱོད་སྦྱོས་པའི་གོན་པ་མ་བསྒོན་པར། །ཤིགས་སེ་ཁྲིས་སེ་བུན་ནེ་རྗེས་མེད་དུ། །རིས་མེད་མཉམ་པ་ཆེན་པོར་གློད་ལ་ཞོག །དེ་ཡི་ངང་ལ་དྲན་བསམ་ཅི་ཤར་ཡང་། །རིས་མེད་རང་བྱུང་རིག་པའི་རང་གདངས་སུ། །ཤེས་པར་གྱིས་ལ་རྗེས་ནི་མི་བསླེགས་པར། །སྣང་སེམས་ཁྲལ་མ་ཁྲོལ་དང་སངས་མ་སངས། །འལ་མ་འོལ་གྱི་ཆོས་ཉིད་ཡོ་ལངས་སུ། །རྒྱ་ཕྱམ་ཉིད་དུ་བཏང་ན་ཀུན་བཟང་གི །དགོངས་པའི་ཀློང་དུ་ད་ལྟ

སློབས་པ་ཡིན། །རྫོགས་པ་ཆེན་པོ་ཡེ་གྲོལ་ལྷུན་གྲུབ་ཀྱི། །སྣ་ཚོགས་རང་གྲོལ་རྣལ་འབྱོར་དེ་ལ་ཟེར། །མ་ཕྱིན་ན་ཡང་སངས་རྒྱས་ས་རུ་སླེབས། །མ་བསྒྲུབས་ན་ཡང་འབྲས་བུ་ལྷུན་གྱིས་གྲུབ། །མ་སྤངས་བཞིན་དུ་ཉོན་མོངས་རང་སར་དག །བླ་མ་དམ་པའི་དགོངས་པ་དང་མཉམ་མོ། །རྗེས་སུ་སློགས་སོ་ལས་རྣམས་ཟིན་པའོ། །གནད་འདི་ཡིན་པས་བུ་རྣམས་ཤེས་པར་གྱིས། །ཕ་རྒན་ཆོས་ཀྱི་རྒྱལ་པོའི་བཀའ་དྲིན་གྱིས། །བྱ་བྲལ་ལྷུན་གྱིས་གྲུབ་པའི་དགོངས་པ་རུ། །ཚོགས་དྲུག་རང་གྲོལ་ད་རེས་སླེབས་པའོ། །གནད་འདི་ཡིན་ཀྱང་ལ་ལས་མ་གོ་འདུག །ཐམས་ཅད་ཡེ་ཟིན་འདུག་སྟེ་ཡང་བྱེད་དོ། །ཡེ་གྲོལ་ཉིད་དུ་འདུག་སྟེ་ཡང་དགྲོལ་ལོ། །ཡེ་བཞག་ཉིད་དུ་འདུག་སྟེ་ཡང་འཛོག་གོ །ཡེ་སྒོམ་ཉིད་དུ་འདུག་སྟེ་ཡང་བསྒོམ་མོ། །ཡེ་ལྟོས་ཉིད་དུ་འདུག་སྟེ་ཡང་བལྟའོ། །ཡེ་བགྲོད་ཉིད་དུ་འདུག་སྟེ་ཡང་བགྲོད་དོ། །ཟེར་ནས་ཡིད་དཔྱོད་ལྟ་བར་རེ་བའི་མིས། །ཐོས་ཀྱང་ཚིག་རི་གོ་ཡང་རྣམ་རྟོག་གོ །རྟོགས་ཀྱང་པོ་ཚོད་བསྒོམས་ཀྱང་བློས་བྱས་སོ། །དཔྱད་ཀྱང་གཉིས་འཛིན་བསྒྲུབས་ཀྱང་འཁོར་བའོ། །ཆོས་ཉིད་ཡིད་དཔྱོད་མཁན་གྱི་མི་དེ་ལ། །རྫོགས་ཆེན་སྙིང་ཐིག་ལས་འབྲེལ་མེད་པར་ངེས། །བྱ་བྱེད་མི་དགོས་བྱས་པས་ཟིན་པ་མེད། །བྱ་དང་མི་བྱའི་རྩིས་ལས་འདས་པའོ། །བསྒོམ་མེད་བསྒོམ་པ་ལས་འདས་བསྒོམ་ཀྱང་འཕྱུང་། །བལྟར་མེད་ལྟ་བ་ལས་འདས་གང་ལ་བལྟ། །བཙལ་མེད་བཙལ་བ་ལས་འདས་རྙེད་པ་མེད། །འདི་ལྟར་རིག་པ་ཟང་མ་ཐལ་བྱུང་དུ། །འདུག་སྟེ་བཤད་ཀྱང་མི་ཉན་མི་དེ་ལ། །རྫོགས་ཆེན་ལས་འབྲེལ་མེད་པ་དགོད་རེ་བྲོ། །གང་ལ་བལྟས་ཀྱང་ཀ་དག་ཀློང་ཆེན་གྱི། །དགོངས་པར་ཤར་བས་འཁོར་འདས་གཉིས་སུ་མེད། །དེ་འདྲའི་དགོངས་པ་བླུ་རུ་བླངས་པ་ལ། །དུས་གསུམ་རྒྱལ་བ་དགྱེས་པར་གདོན་མི་ཟ། །འོ་ན་ཕྱི་རོལ་འཁྲུལ་པའི་སྣང་ཡུལ་དུ། །རང་སར་ཡན་དུ་བཅུག་ནས་སླར་ལ་ཡང་། །འཁྲུལ་པར་མི་འགྲོའམ་ཞེས་བརྗོད་གྱུར་ན། །ཐ་མལ་མི་ཡིས་བདག་ཏུ་བཟུང་བས་འཁྲུལ། །རྣལ་འབྱོར་པ་ཡིས་གཞི་མེད་རྩ་བྲལ་དུ། །ཤེས་པས་བཅོས་བསླད་

སྣང་ངོར་མི་བྱེད་པར། །རང་བབས་འཛིན་མེད་བཞག་པས་མི་འབྲལ་ལོ། །འདི་
ལ་གོལ་ས་ཨེ་ཡོད་བརྗོད་གྱུར་ན། །འདི་ལ་གོལ་ས་ནོར་ས་གཅིག་ཀྱང་མེད། །
གོལ་ས་ཞེན་ཅིང་ཆགས་ན་ཡོད་པ་ཡིན། །གང་ཤར་ཉིད་ལ་འཛིན་པ་མེད་པ་
ན། །གོལ་སར་ལྷུང་རྒྱུ་ཞིག་ནི་ག་ལ་འོངས། །འོན་ཀྱང་རིག་པ་ཡུལ་ལ་འཆར་
དུས་སུ། །གང་ཤར་རྣམ་པར་རྟོག་པའི་ངོ་བོ་ལ། །ལྟ་བ་དེ་ཉིད་བསྒོམ་དུ་འདོད་
པ་མིན། །དེ་ཡི་དུས་ཀྱི་རིག་པ་ས་ལེ་བ། །རྗེན་པའི་ཆ་དེ་ཕྲུལ་ལེ་སྐྱོང་
བའོ། །དེ་ཡང་རིག་པ་འཕྲོ་འདུ་མེད་པ་རུ། །གནས་པའི་དུས་ཀྱི་གནས་ཆའི་མི་
རྟོག་པ། །དེ་ཉིད་སྒོམ་གྱི་དངོས་གཞི་མ་ཡིན་ཏེ། །དེ་ཡི་དུས་ཀྱི་ཧྲིག་གེ་སང་ངེ་
བའི། །གསལ་དྭངས་ངར་ཆ་དེ་ཉིད་སྐྱོང་བའོ། །གནད་འདི་མ་གོ་འཆར་གནས་
གཉིས་ཀ་ལ། །བལྟ་བ་དེ་ཉིད་སྒོམ་པའི་ངོ་བོ་ཡིན། །སྙམ་ན་འཁྲུལ་པར་འགྱུར་
རོ་སྙིང་གི་བུ། །གནས་པ་ཙམ་ནི་བསམ་གཏན་ལྷ་དང་འདྲ། །འཆར་བ་ཙམ་ནི་
ཐ་མལ་རྟོག་པ་འདྲ། །དེ་ལ་བསྒོམས་ཀྱང་སངས་རྒྱས་འཐོབ་མི་འགྱུར། །
མདོར་ན་གང་གི་དུས་སུ་འང་རིག་པའི་ཆ། །རྗེན་པ་ཟང་ཐལ་ཤེལ་གོང་འདྲ་བ
དེ། །ཀློང་དུ་མ་གྱུར་བར་དུ་ས་ལེར་སྐྱོངས། །གྱུར་ནས་དེ་ཡི་ངང་ལ་འབྲལ
མེད་ཀྱིས། །ཁྲེགས་ཆོད་ལྟ་བའི་གནད་འགག་རིག་པ་ནི། །རྗེན་ལ་ཕྱུད་ནས་ས
ལེར་སྐྱོང་བ་ལ། །ཟེར་བས་གནད་འདི་ཁོ་ན་གལ་ཆེ་སྟེ། །འདི་ནི་ཐིག་བརྒྱའི
མདོ་འགགས་ཡིན་པས་ན། །སྐལ་ལྡན་སྙིང་གི་བུ་རྣམས་ཤེས་པར་གྱིས།། ༄
ཨེ་མ་ཧོ། ད་ཡང་སེམས་ཀྱི་བུ་རྣམས་གུས་པས་ཉོན། །ནོར་ས་མེད་པའི་ཐིག
ཆེན་བཞི་བསྟན་པས། །ལྟ་བ་ནོར་ས་མེད་པའི་ཐིག་ཆེན་ནི། །ད་ལྟའི་ཤེས་པ་ས
ལེ་འདི་ཀ་ཡིན། །གསལ་ལ་མི་ནོར་བས་ན་ཐིག་ཅེས་བྱ། །སྒོམ་པ་ནོར་ས་མེད
པའི་ཐིག་ཆེན་ནི། །ད་ལྟའི་ཤེས་པ་ས་ལེ་འདི་ག་ཡིན། །གསལ་ལ་མི་ནོར་བས
ན་ཐིག་ཅེས་བྱ། །སྤྱོད་པ་ནོར་ས་མེད་པའི་ཐིག་ཆེན་ནི། །ད་ལྟའི་ཤེས་པ་ས་ལེ
འདི་ཀ་ཡིན། །གསལ་ལ་མི་ནོར་བས་ན་ཐིག་ཅེས་བྱ། །འབྲས་བུ་ནོར་ས་མེད
པའི་ཐིག་ཆེན་ནི། །ད་ལྟའི་ཤེས་པ་ས་ལེ་འདི་ཀ་ཡིན། །གསལ་ལ་མི་ནོར་བས

ན་ཐིག་ཅེས་བྱ། །མི་འགྱུར་བ་ཡི་གཟེར་ཆེན་བཞི་བསྟན་པ། །ལྟ་བ་འགྱུར་བ་
མེད་པའི་གཟེར་ཆེན་ནི། །ད་ལྟའི་ཤེས་པ་ས་ལེ་འདི་ཀ་ཡིན། །དུས་གསུམ་
བརྟན་པའི་ཕྱིར་ན་གཟེར་ཞེས་བྱ། །སྒོམ་པ་འགྱུར་བ་མེད་པའི་གཟེར་ཆེན་ནི། །
ད་ལྟའི་ཤེས་པ་ས་ལེ་འདི་ཀ་ཡིན། །དུས་གསུམ་བརྟན་པའི་ཕྱིར་ན་གཟེར་ཞེས་
བྱ། །སྤྱོད་པ་འགྱུར་བ་མེད་པའི་གཟེར་ཆེན་ནི། །དེ་ལྟའི་ཤེས་པ་ས་ལེ་འདི་ཀ་
ཡིན། །དུས་གསུམ་བརྟན་པའི་ཕྱིར་ན་གཟེར་ཞེས་བྱ། །འབྲས་བུ་འགྱུར་བ་མེད་
པའི་གཟེར་ཆེན་ནི། ད་ལྟའི་ཤེས་པ་ས་ལེ་འདི་ཀ་ཡིན། །དུས་གསུམ་བརྟན་པའི་
ཕྱིར་ན་གཟེར་ཞེས་བྱ། །ལྟ་བ་མི་མཐུན་རྒྱ་ཆེ་གྲངས་མང་ཡང་། །ད་ལྟའི་རང་
རིག་རང་བྱུང་ཡེ་ཤེས་ལ། །བལྟ་བྱ་དང་ནི་ལྟ་བྱེད་གཉིས་སུ་མེད། །ལྟ་བ་མ་
བལྟ་ལྟ་བའི་མཁན་པོ་འཚོལ། །ལྟ་བའི་མཁན་པོ་བཙལ་བས་མ་རྙེད་ན། །དེའི་
ཚེ་ལྟ་བ་ཟད་སར་འཁྱོལ་བ་ཡིན། །ལྟ་བ་བལྟ་རྒྱུ་ཅི་ཡང་མེད་པ་ལ། །ཡེ་མེད་
སྟོང་ཆད་ཧད་པོར་མ་སོང་བར། །ད་ལྟའི་ཤེས་པ་མ་བཅོས་ས་ལེ་བ། །རྫོགས་པ་
ཆེན་པོའི་ལྟ་བ་དེ་ཀ་ཡིན། །སྒོམ་པ་མི་མཐུན་རྒྱ་ཆེ་གྲངས་མང་ཡང་། །ད་ལྟའི་
ཐ་མལ་ཤེས་པ་ཟང་ཐལ་ལ། །བསྒོམ་བྱ་དང་ནི་སྒོམ་བྱེད་གཉིས་སུ་མེད། །
བསྒོམ་པ་མ་སྒོམས་སྒོམ་པའི་མཁན་པོ་འཚོལ། །སྒོམ་པའི་མཁན་པོ་བཙལ་བས་
མ་རྙེད་ན། །དེའི་ཚེ་སྒོམ་པ་ཟད་སར་འཁྱོལ་བ་ཡིན། །སྒོམ་པ་བསྒོམ་རྒྱུ་ཅི་ཡང་
མེད་པ་ལ། །བྱིང་རྒོད་འཐིབས་རྨུགས་དབང་དུ་མ་སོང་བར། །ད་ལྟའི་ཤེས་པ་
མ་བཅོས་རང་གསལ་ལ། །མ་བཅོས་མཉམ་པར་འཇོག་པ་བསྒོམ་པ་ཡིན། །
སྤྱོད་པ་མི་མཐུན་རྒྱ་ཆེ་གྲངས་མང་ཡང་། །རང་རིག་ཡེ་ཤེས་ཐིག་ལེ་ཉག་གཅིག་
ལ། །སྤྱད་བྱ་དང་ནི་སྤྱོད་བྱེད་གཉིས་སུ་མེད། །སྤྱོད་པ་མ་སྤྱོད་སྤྱོད་པའི་མཁན་
པོ་འཚོལ། །སྤྱོད་པའི་མཁན་པོ་བཙལ་བས་མ་རྙེད་ན། །དེའི་ཚེ་སྤྱོད་པ་ཟད་སར་
འཁྱོལ་བ་ཡིན། །སྤྱོད་པ་སྤྱོད་རྒྱུ་ཅི་ཡང་མེད་པ་ལ། །བག་ཆགས་འཁྲུལ་པའི་
དབང་དུ་མ་སོང་བས། །ད་ལྟའི་ཤེས་པ་མ་བཅོས་རང་གསལ་ལ། །བཅོས་
བསླད་བླང་དོར་གང་ཡང་མི་བྱེད་པ། །དེ་ག་རྣམ་པ་དག་པའི་སྤྱོད་པ་ཡིན། །

འབྲས་བུ་མི་མཐུན་རྒྱ་ཆེ་གྲངས་མང་ཡང་། །རང་རིག་སྐུ་གསུམ་རྩོལ་མེད་ལྷུན་
གྲུབ་ལ། །བསྒྲུབ་བྱ་དང་ནི་སྒྲུབ་བྱེད་གཉིས་སུ་མེད། །འབྲས་བུ་མ་སྒྲུབས་སྒྲུབ་
པའི་མཁན་པོ་འཚོལ། །འབྲས་བུ་སྒྲུབ་མཁན་བཙལ་བས་མ་རྙེད་ན། །དེའི་ཚེ་
འབྲས་བུ་ཟད་སར་འཁྱོལ་བ་ཡིན། །འབྲས་བུ་སྒྲུབ་རྒྱུ་ཅི་ཡང་མེད་པ་ལ། །བླང་
དོར་རེ་དོགས་དབང་དུ་མ་སོང་བར། །ད་ལྟའི་ཤེས་རིག་རང་གསལ་ལྷུན་གྲུབ་
ཉིད། །མངོན་གྱུར་སྐུ་གསུམ་རང་གསལ་སྟོང་པ་ཉིད། །ཡེ་སངས་རྒྱས་པའི་
འབྲས་བུ་དེ་ཉིད་དོ།། ༄ ཨེ་མ་ཧོ། ད་ཡང་རིགས་ཀྱི་བུ་རྣམས་ལེགས་པར་
ཉོན། །དེ་ལྟར་དང་པོ་ཡེངས་མེད་བསྐྱངས་པ་ན། །བར་དུ་ཡན་པར་བཏང་ཡང་
དོན་ཐོབ་ནས། །ཐ་མལ་བཏང་ཡང་འགྲོ་འོང་མེད་པའོ། །སྣང་དང་སྟོང་པ་
གཉིས་ཀ་དབྱེར་མེད་ན། །དེའི་ཚེ་ལྟ་བ་ཀློང་དུ་གྱུར་པ་ཡིན། །རྨི་ལམ་ཉིན་པར་
གཉིས་ཀ་ཁྱད་མེད་ན། །དེའི་ཚེ་སྒོམ་པ་ཀློང་དུ་གྱུར་པ་ཡིན། །བདེ་དང་སྡུག་
བསྔལ་གཉིས་ཀ་ཁྱད་མེད་ན། །དེའི་ཚེ་སྤྱོད་པ་ཀློང་དུ་གྱུར་པ་ཡིན། །འདི་དང་
ཕྱི་མ་གཉིས་ཀ་ཁྱད་མེད་ན། །དེའི་ཚེ་གནས་ལུགས་ཀློང་དུ་གྱུར་པ་ཡིན། །
སེམས་དང་ནམ་མཁའ་གཉིས་ཀ་ཁྱད་མེད་ན། །དེའི་ཚེ་ཆོས་སྐུ་ཀློང་དུ་གྱུར་པ་
ཡིན། །རང་སེམས་སངས་རྒྱས་གཉིས་ཀ་ཁྱད་མེད་ན། །དེའི་ཚེ་འབྲས་བུ་ཀློང་
དུ་གྱུར་པ་ཡིན།། ༄ ཨེ་མ་ཧོ། ད་དུང་རིགས་ཀྱི་བུ་རྣམས་བདག་ལ་
གསོན། །གདོས་བཅས་ལུས་འདི་ཆུ་ཟླ་ལྟར་དུ་ལྟོས། །ངག་གི་སྨྲ་བརྗོད་བྲག་ཆ་
བཞིན་དུ་ཟློས། །སེམས་ཀྱི་རྟོག་ཚོགས་རང་སར་སངས་དུ་ཆུག །སྣང་གྲགས་
ཆོས་རྣམས་ཐམས་ཅད་སྒྱུ་མ་དང་། །སྨིག་རྒྱུ་རྨི་ལམ་གཟུགས་བརྙན་ཆུ་ཟླ་
དང་། །དྲི་ཟའི་གྲོང་ཁྱེར་མིག་ཡོར་སྤྲུལ་པ་དང་། །ཆུ་བུར་བྲག་ཆ་བཞིན་དུ་
འཛིན་མེད་སྤྱོད། །སྤྱོད་ལམ་ཐམས་ཅད་དེ་ཡི་ངང་ནས་ཀྱིས། །ཐུན་མཚམས་མ་
གཅོད་ཉིན་མཚན་འཁོར་ཡུག་སྤྱོད། །དྲན་བསམ་བཅོས་བསླད་མ་བྱེད་རང་བབས་
དང་། །རང་མདངས་རང་གྲོལ་འཛིན་མེད་མེད་གསལ་སྟོང་དུ། །བདེན་མེད་
བསྒོམ་མེད་རྩོལ་མེད་རྗེས་མེད་ཞོག །སྔར་འདས་རྣམ་པར་རྟོག་པ་ཐམས་ཅད

ཀྱང་། །བྱ་ལམ་ནམ་མཁར་རྗེས་མེད་ལྟར་དུ་ཞོག །ད་ལྟའི་ཤེས་པ་རྟུལ་བྲལ་བར་སྣང་ལྟར། །མ་འོངས་རྟོག་པ་རང་འཐག་ཆུ་བཅད་ལྟར། །ཁྲིག་གེར་གློད་ལ་བཟོ་བཅོས་མི་བྱེད་པར། །རང་བབས་རྒྱ་ཡན་ངང་དུ་ལྷུག་པར་ཞོག །ཕྲ་རགས་རྟོག་པ་དྲུག་གསུམ་དྲུག་ལྔ་སོགས། །ཁང་སྟོང་ཆུན་མ་སླེབས་པ་ལྟར་དུ་ཞོག །ཚོགས་དྲུག་ཡུལ་སྣང་ཐམས་ཅད་རྗེས་མེད་དུ། །སྒྱུ་མའི་གྲོང་ཁྱེར་ཞིག་པ་ལྟར་དུ་ཞོག །མདོར་ན་སྐྱེ་འགག་གནས་གསུམ་གཞི་ལམ་འབྲས། །ལྟ་སྒོམ་སྤྱོད་འབྲས་དུས་གནས་བརྗོད་ཚིག་དང་། །གཞག་བྱ་བཞག་བྱེད་དགྲོལ་བྱ་དགྲོལ་བྱེད་སོགས། །རང་གསལ་རེས་མེད་འཛིན་རྩོལ་སྤང་བླང་མེད། །རྒྱ་མཚོ་ཆེན་པོར་ཆུ་ཐྲན་ཐིམ་པ་ལྟར། །ཆོས་ཀུན་སེམས་ཀྱི་དབྱིངས་སུ་ཀ་དག་པར། །བློ་གདེང་བཅའ་ཞིང་འཛིན་མེད་ལ་ཟློའོ། །དེ་ལྟར་བསྒོམས་ཚེ་རྣམ་རྟོག་མང་འཕྲོས་ཀྱང་། །སྒོམ་ནི་མ་འོངས་སླམ་ནས་སྡུག་མི་དགོས། །སེམས་ནི་འཕྲོ་ཡང་སྟོང་ལ་གནས་ཀྱང་སྟོང་། །གང་ལྟར་ཤར་ཡང་རིག་པའི་ངང་ཡིན་པས། །དགག་སྒྲུབ་བླང་དོར་གང་ཡང་མི་བྱེད་པར། །མ་བཅོས་གཉུག་མའི་ངང་དུ་གློད་ལ་ཞོག །དེ་ཡིས་རྣམ་རྟོག་རང་སར་གྲོལ་བར་ངེས། །བློ་དམན་སྐྱེ་བོ་ངང་ལ་མི་གནས་ན། །ངོ་སྤྲོད་སྐབས་བཞིན་དཔྱད་འཛོག་སྤེལ་མ་གྱིས། ཡང་ན་འདི་བཞིན་རྣམ་རྟོག་ཨར་ལ་གཏོད། །དགོས་སམ་མི་དགོས་རྣམ་རྟོག་བསླང་ནས་ཀྱང་། །གཅིག་རྗེས་གཅིག་མཐུད་རྣམ་པ་སྣ་ཚོགས་པ། །རང་སེམས་སུན་རག་བར་དུ་སྤྲོས་ནས་ཀྱང་། །དེ་ནས་མི་འདོད་ཆེ་ན་གློད་ལ་ཞོག །ཡང་ན་སྙིང་དབུས་མཚན་ལྡན་བླ་མ་བསྒོམ། །དེ་ལ་སེམས་ནི་ཡུན་རིང་བཟུང་ནས་ཀྱང་། །དེ་རྗེས་འཛིན་མེད་རིག་པའི་ངང་ལ་ཞོག །ཡང་ན་སྙིང་གི་དབུས་སུ་ཐིག་ལེ་བསྒོམ། །དེ་ཉིད་མར་ལ་བབས་ནས་དབང་ཆེན་གྱི། །ས་གཞིར་ཐུག་རག་བར་དུ་སོང་བར་བསམ། །དེ་ཡི་འཕྲོ་རྒོད་ཐད་ཀྱིས་ཆོད་པར་ངེས། །རྒོད་པ་ཆོད་ཚེ་རིག་པའི་ངང་ལ་ཞོག །བྱིང་བ་ཆེ་ན་ལྟ་སྟངས་དར་བསྐྱེད་ལ། །རིག་པ་རྗེན་པ་ཕྱུད་ནས་ས་ལེར་སྐྱོངས། །ཡང་ན་རང་གི་སེམས་ཉིད་ཐིག་ལེ་རུ། །དམིགས་ལ་དངག་ནས་ཕཊ་སྒྲ

བརྗོད་མ་ཐག །ཚངས་བུག་ནས་འཐོན་དཔག་ཆེན་མདའ་འཕངས་ལྟར། །སོང་ནས་མཁའ་ལ་ཁྲུག་གིས་འདྲེས་པར་བསམ། །དེ་ནས་ནམ་མཁའི་མཚན་ཉིད་ཡིད་ལ་བྱིས། །དེ་ཡིས་བྱིང་བ་མི་སངས་མི་སྲིད་དོ། །བྱིང་བ་སངས་ཆེ་འཛིན་མེད་ངང་ལ་ཞོག །འདི་རྣམས་ཞལ་ཤེས་ཡིན་པས་ཤེས་པར་བྱིས། །རྟོག་མེད་འདོད་པའི་རྟོག་པས་མ་བཅིངས་པར། །རིག་པ་རྒྱ་བསྐྱེད་དཔངས་བསྟོད་ཕྱུལ་ཡས་སུ། །ཐོངས་ལ་གུ་ཡངས་ཡན་བ་བློ་བདེ་བྱིས། །དང་པོ་རྣམ་རྟོག་གཅོང་རོང་ཆུ་དང་འདྲ། །བར་དུ་ཆུ་བོ་གངྒཱ་དལ་བབས་འདྲ། །ཐ་མ་ཆུ་རྣམས་རྒྱ་མཚོ་རོ་གཅིག་ལྟར། །འོད་གསལ་མ་བུ་མཇལ་བའི་ངང་ལ་གནས། །ཁྱད་པ་ནད་གདོན་ཆེ་འཕྲུལ་ཅི་བྱུང་ཡང་། །བཅས་བཅོས་རིམ་གྲོ་གང་ཡང་མི་བྱེད་པར། །འདི་ལྟར་རོ་སྙོམས་ཐོག་བཟླས་སྤྱོད་པ་བྱིས། །ནགས་དང་དུར་ཁྲོད་མཚོ་གླིང་སྐྱེད་མོའི་ཚལ། །བྲག་ཕུག་ཁང་སྟོང་ཤིང་གཅིག་དྲུང་ལ་སོགས། །འཇིགས་ཤིང་ཉམ་ངའི་གནས་སུ་སོང་ནས་ཀྱང་། །རང་ལུས་སྟོད་བཅུད་སྣང་སྲིད་བདུད་རྩིར་བསྒྱུར། །ཕྱོགས་བཅུའི་རྒྱལ་བ་སྲས་བཅས་ཐམས་ཅད་མཆོད། །དེ་རྣམས་མཉེས་ནས་བརྩེ་བའི་རྣམ་འགྱུར་གྱིས། །འོད་དུ་ཞུ་ནས་འཁོར་འདས་ཐམས་ཅད་ཀུན། །འོད་གསལ་བདུད་རྩིས་ཡོངས་སུ་གང་བར་དམིགས། །ཡོན་ཏན་མགྲོན་གྱུར་དམ་ཅན་ཆོས་སྐྱོང་དང་། །སྙིང་རྗེའི་ཞིང་མཆོག་རིགས་དྲུག་སེམས་ཅན་དང་། །ལན་ཆགས་གདོན་བགེགས་འབྱུང་པོ་ཐམས་ཅད་དང་། །ནམ་མཁའི་མཐའ་དང་མཉམ་པའི་འགྲོ་བ་ཀུན། །མྱོང་གྲོལ་བདུད་རྩིས་ཚིམས་པར་བྱས་ནས་ཀྱང་། །འཁོར་འདས་རོ་གཅིག་སེམས་སུ་ཐག་བཅད་ལ། །སེམས་ཉིད་མ་བཅོས་ཆོས་སྐུའི་ངང་ཉིད་ནས། །འགྲོ་དང་འདུག་དང་མཆོངས་དང་རྒྱུག་པ་དང་། །སྨྲ་དང་དགོད་དང་ངུ་དང་གླུ་ལེན་དང་། །བཅགས་དང་དཀྲུག་ལོག་སྨྱོན་པའི་སྤྱོད་པ་བྱ། །མཐར་ནི་ཞི་ཞིང་བདེ་བའི་ངང་ལ་འདུག །མཚན་དུས་རང་བབས་བདེ་བར་ཉལ་ནས་ཀྱང་། །དྲན་བསམ་འཕྲོ་འདུའི་རྣམ་རྟོག་ཀུན་བྲལ་ཏེ། །སྐྱེ་མེད་དྲན་རྫོགས་གཉུག་མའི་ངང་ལ་ཉལ། །དེ་ལྟར་བྱས་ན་ནད་གདོན་

རང་ཞི་ནས། །ལྷ་སྒོམ་བོགས་འབྱིན་རྟོགས་པ་ནམ་མཁའ་འདྲ། །སྒོམ་པ་རང་
གསལ་སྤྱོད་པ་བུ་ཆུང་འདྲ། །གཟའ་གཏད་ཀུན་བྲལ་དང་གིས་སྨྱོན་པ་འདྲ། །
བདག་གཞན་གཉིས་མེད་འཕགས་པའི་གང་ཟག་འདྲ། །ཅི་སྨྲ་འཛིན་མེད་བྲག་ཆའི་
སྒྲ་དབྱངས་འདྲ། །ཁང་ལའང་ཆགས་མེད་འདབ་ཆགས་མཁའ་ལྡིང་འདྲ། །ཡ་
ང་བག་ཚ་མེད་པའི་སེང་གེ་འདྲ། །ཐམས་ཅད་ཡེ་གྲོལ་མཁའ་ལ་སྤྲིན་དྭངས་
འདྲ། །དེ་འདྲའི་རྣལ་འབྱོར་བདེ་གཤེགས་རིག་འཛིན་དངོས། །དད་བརྒྱའི་སྤྱི་
བོས་བཏུད་ནས་ཕྱག་བྱའི་འོས། །ཡིད་བཞིན་ནོར་བུ་བས་ཀྱང་ཆེས་ལྷག་གོ། ༔
ཨེ་མ་ཧོ། ད་ཡང་སྐལ་ལྡན་བུ་བཏང་གླུ་ལ་ཉོན། །རྣམ་སྣང་ཕྱི་ན་མེད་དེ་ནང་ན་
ཡོད། །སེམས་ཉིད་སྤྲོས་དང་བྲལ་བ་ཆོས་དབྱིངས་དང་། །གཏི་མུག་རང་སར་
དག་པའི་ངོ་བོ་ཉིད། །བཅོམ་ལྡན་རྣམ་པར་སྣང་མཛད་དངོས་ཡིན་ནོ། །རྡོར་
སེམས་ཕྱི་ན་མེད་དེ་ནང་ན་ཡོད། །རིག་རྩལ་འཆར་གཞི་མ་འགགས་མེ་ལོང་
དང་། །ཞེ་སྡང་རང་སར་དག་པའི་ངོ་བོ་ཉིད། །བཅོམ་ལྡན་རྡོ་རྗེ་སེམས་དཔའ་
དངོས་ཡིན་ནོ། །རིན་འབྱུང་ཕྱི་ན་མེད་དེ་ནང་ན་ཡོད། །བླང་དོར་དགག་སྒྲུབ་
མེད་པ་མཉམ་ཉིད་དང་། །ང་རྒྱལ་རང་སར་དག་པའི་ངོ་བོ་ཉིད། །བཅོམ་ལྡན་
རིན་ཆེན་འབྱུང་ལྡན་དངོས་ཡིན་ནོ། །འོད་དཔག་ཕྱི་ན་མེད་དེ་ནང་ན་ཡོད། །བདེ་
སྟོང་དབྱིངས་སུ་ནུབ་པ་སོར་རྟོག་དང་། །འདོད་ཆགས་རང་སར་དག་པའི་ངོ་བོ་
ཉིད། །བཅོམ་ལྡན་འོད་དཔག་མེད་པ་དངོས་ཡིན་ནོ། །དོན་གྲུབ་ཕྱི་ན་མེད་དེ་ནང་
ན་ཡོད། །རིག་པ་ཐལ་བྱུང་རང་གྲོལ་བྱ་གྲུབ་དང་། །ཕྲག་དོག་རང་སར་དག་
པའི་ངོ་བོ་ཉིད། །བཅོམ་ལྡན་དོན་ཡོད་གྲུབ་པ་དངོས་ཡིན་ནོ།། ༔ ཨེ་མ་ཧོ།
ད་ཡང་སྐལ་ལྡན་སེམས་ཀྱི་བུ་གཅིག་པོ། །དགའ་ཞིང་སྤྲོ་བས་རྡོ་རྗེའི་གླུ་ལ་
ཉོན། །དེ་ལྟར་རྟོགས་ན་སྣང་སྲིད་ཐམས་ཅད་ཀུན། །གདམས་ངག་དཔེ་ཆ་དོན་
གྱི་དཀྱིལ་འཁོར་ཡིན། །སྣང་བ་དཀར་དམར་སྣ་ཚོགས་ཤོག་བུ་ལ། །རང་བྱུང་
ཡེ་ཤེས་རིག་པའི་སྨྱུ་གུ་ཡིས། །གཞི་མེད་ཡེ་གྲོལ་འཛིན་མེད་ཡི་གེ་བྲིས། །སྣང་
སྟོང་གཉིས་མེད་དང་དུ་དཔེ་བལྟ་བྱས། །སྟོང་གསུམ་ཐམས་ཅད་ལྷུན་གྲུབ་དཀྱིལ་

འཁོར་ལ། །ཆར་རྒྱུ་རང་བབས་རྒྱུ་ཡིས་ཆག་ཆག་གདབ། །ལམ་སྣང་རང་
བཞིན་ཐིག་ཆེན་གདབ་པ་དང་། །རྐང་པའི་རྗེས་ནི་ཁ་དོག་རྡུལ་ཚོན་རིས། །རང་
ལུས་སྣང་སྟོང་ཡི་དམ་ལྷ་ཡི་སྐུ། །སྨྲ་བརྗོད་གྲགས་སྟོང་རྡོ་རྗེའི་བཟླས་པ་
དང་། །དྲན་བསམ་འཛིན་མེད་རང་གྲོལ་ལྷ་ཡི་ཐུགས། །ཡན་ལག་འགུལ་
བསྐྱོད་ཐམས་ཅད་ཕྱག་རྒྱའོ། །བཟའ་དང་བཏུང་བ་ཆོས་ཉིད་མཆོད་པ་དང་། །
གཟུགས་སུ་སྣང་བ་ཐམས་ཅད་ལྷ་ཡི་སྐུ། །སྒྲ་ཆེན་བརྗོད་པ་ཐམས་ཅད་རོལ་མོ་
ཉིད། །བསྲུང་མེད་ཉམས་མེད་རང་བབས་དམ་ཚིག་གོ །དེ་འདྲའི་རྣལ་འབྱོར་པ་
ཡིས་ཅི་བྱས་ཀྱང་། །འོད་གསལ་ཆོས་ཉིད་ངང་ལ་གདམས་ངག་དང་། །བསྐྱེད་
རིམ་དམ་ཚིག་དང་བཅས་རྫོགས་པས་ན། །འབད་རྩོལ་རྒྱུ་འབྲས་ཆོས་ལ་བརྟེན་མི་
དགོས། །འབད་མེད་དངོས་གྲུབ་ཡ་མཚན་རྨད་པོ་ཆེ། །སྒྱུར་དུ་ཐོབ་པ་རྫོགས་པ་
ཆེན་པོ་ཡི། །ཁྱད་ཆོས་ཡིན་ནོ་སྐལ་ལྡན་སྙིང་གི་བུ། །དེ་ལྟར་ངེས་པར་ཉམས་
སུ་བླང་གྱུར་ན། །སྤྲིན་རྣམས་ནམ་མཁའི་ངང་ལ་ཡལ་བ་བཞིན། །འཁོར་
འདས་རྟོག་ཚོགས་གདོད་མའི་གཞི་ལ་དག །ཉི་མའི་དཀྱིལ་འཁོར་སྒྲིབ་མེད་
གསལ་བ་བཞིན། །རང་རིག་འོད་གསལ་ཆོས་སྐུ་མངོན་གྱུར་ནས། །བསད་པ་
གསོ་ནུས་གསང་བ་གོ་ནུས་ཞིང་། །རྫུ་འཕྲུལ་སྣ་ཚོགས་བསྟན་ནས་འགྲོ་བ་
འདུལ། །ས་ལམ་ཡོན་ཏན་མ་ལུས་རབ་རྫོགས་ནས། །གང་ཟག་དབང་པོ་རབ་
རྣམས་ཚེ་འདིར་གྲོལ། །འབྲིང་ནི་འཆི་ཀ་ཐམ་བར་དོ་རུ། །ཀ་དག་གཞི་ལ་གྲོལ་
ནས་ནང་དབྱིངས་སུ། །སྐུ་གསུམ་ཡེ་ཤེས་འབྲལ་མེད་རྟག་བཞུགས་ནས། །
གང་ལ་གང་འདུལ་སྤྲུལ་པ་བཀྱེ་ནས་ཀྱང་། །འགྲོ་དོན་རྒྱུན་མི་འཆད་པར་མཛད་
པའོ། །ཚིག་དོན་འདི་རྣམས་ཡིད་ལ་ཟུངས་ཤིག་དང་། །སྐྱེད་པའི་ཉི་མ་ནང་ནས་
འཆར་བར་ངེས། །དེ་འདྲའི་དགོངས་པ་བླུ་རུ་ལེན་མཁན་དེ། །བྱ་བཏང་ཚོགས་
དྲུག་རང་གྲོལ་ཡིན་པར་སྣང་། །དགེ་འདིས་སྐལ་ལྡན་གདུལ་བྱ་མང་པོ་ཡིས། །
མ་རིག་ཉོན་མོངས་རྟོག་པའི་དྲི་མ་ཀུན། །ཀ་དག་གདོད་མའི་དབྱིངས་སུ་སྒྱུར་དག་
ནས། །འབྲས་བུ་ཚེ་འདི་ཉིད་ལ་ཐོབ་པར་ཤོག། །ཅེས་འོད་གསལ་རྫོགས་པ་

ཆེན་པོའི་ཁྲེགས་ཆོད་ལྟ་བའི་གླུ་དབྱངས་ས་ལམ་མྱུར་དུ་བགྲོད་པའི་རྩལ་ལྡན་མཁའ་ལྡིང་གཤོག་རླབས་ཞེས་བྱ་བ་འདི་ནི། ཨོ་རྒྱན་རིན་པོ་ཆེས་མཛད་པའི་རིག་པ་གཅེར་མཐོང་གི་ངོ་སྤྲོད། ཀུན་མཁྱེན་མཛོད་བདུན་དང་ཤིང་རྟ་གསུམ། རྫོགས་ཆེན་རྒྱབ་ཆོས་ནམ་མཁའ་སྐོར་གསུམ། ཟབ་དོན་རྒྱ་མཚོའི་སྤྲིན་ཕུང་། རྫོགས་ཆེན་མཁའ་འགྲོའི་སྙིང་ཐིག །སངས་རྒྱས་ལག་བཅངས་སོགས་གཏེར་ཁ་དུ་མའི་རྫོགས་ཆེན་མང་པོ་ལ་གཞི་བྱས། བླ་མའི་མན་ངག་དང་རང་གི་ཉམས་མྱོང་གིས་ཟུར་བརྒྱན་ཏེ་དད་ལྡན་གྱི་སློབ་མ་མང་པོ་ལ་ཕན་ཕྱིར་༧བྱ་བཏང་ཚོགས་དྲུག་རང་གྲོལ་གྱིས་སྦྱར་བའོ། །འདི་ཀྱང་བསྟན་པ་དང་སེམས་ཅན་ལ་ཕན་པ་དཔག་ཏུ་མེད་པ་ཐོགས་པའི་རྒྱུར་གྱུར་ཅིག །རྡོ་རྗེའི་གླུ་འདི་ནི་ཐར་པ་དོན་དུ་གཉེར་བའི་སྐལ་ལྡན་ཀུན་ལ་ཕན་ཕྱིར་གླངས་པ་ཡིན་པས། ལེན་པའི་དུས་ནི་རྣལ་འབྱོར་པས་ལྟ་བ་སྐྱོང་བའི་དུས་སུ་ལེན་པའོ། །ལེན་ལུགས་ནི་རིག་འཛིན་ཤྲཱི་སིང་ཧའི་ཞལ་ནས། སངས་རྒྱས་ཀྱི་ཐུགས་ཁྱབ་གདལ་དུ་གནས། སེམས་ཅན་གྱི་རིག་པ་དུམ་བུར་གནས། ནམ་མཁའ་ལྟར་རྒྱ་བསྐྱེད་པ་བོགས་ཆེའོ། །ཞེས་གསུངས་པ་ལྟར་རིག་པ་ནམ་མཁའ་ལྟར་རྒྱ་ཆེར་བསྐྱེད་དཔངས་བསྟོད་ཁྱུལ་ཡས་སུ་བཏང་ནས་སེམས་ཉིད་ཁྱབ་གདལ་ཡངས་པའི་ངང་ནས་རྡོ་རྗེའི་གླུ་འདི་འཐེན་དང་ལྟ་སྒོམ་བོགས་འཐོན་པའོ།། །།

༄༅། །ཁྲེགས་ཆོད་ལྟ་བའི་ཁྲིད་ཡིག་མཁའ་ལྡིང་གཤོག་རླབས་
ཀྱི་བསྡུས་དོན་བརྒྱུད་གསུམ་གདམས་མཛོད་དགྲོལ་བའི་ལྡེའུ་མིག་
ཅེས་བྱ་བ་བཞུགས།།

༄༅། །དེ་ལ་འདིར་གྲུབ་དབང་ཞབས་དཀར་རིན་པོ་ཆེས་མཛད་པའི་འོད་གསལ་རྫོགས་པ་ཆེན་པོའི་ཁྲེགས་ཆོད་ལྟ་བའི་གླུ་དབྱངས་ས་ལམ་མ་ལུས་མྱུར་དུ་བགྲོད་པའི་

རྒྱལ་ལྡན་མཁའ་ལྡིང་གཤོག་རླབས་ཞེས་བྱ་བ་འདི་ཉིད་འཆད་པར་བྱེད་པ་ལ་ཐོག་མར་
དགེ་བ་གླད་ཀྱི་དོན། བར་དུ་དགེ་བ་གཞུང་གི་དོན། ཐ་མར་དགེ་བ་འཇུག་གི་
དོན་དང་གསུམ་ལས། དང་པོ་ལ། ཐ་སྙད་རྟོགས་པའི་སྙད་དུ་དཔེ་དོན་འབྲེལ་
བའི་མཚན་བསྟན་པ། བར་ཆད་ཞི་བའི་ཆེད་དུ་དངོས་བརྒྱུད་ཀྱི་བླ་མ་རྣམས་ལ་
མཆོད་པར་བརྗོད་པ། བརྗོད་བྱ་མན་ངག་གི་ཁྱུངས་བསྟན་པའི་སྒོ་ནས་སྐལ་བཟང་
གི་སློབ་ཚོགས་སྤྲོས་གཞུང་འདི་ལ་ཡིད་ཆེས་དགོས་པར་གདམས་པ། རྗོད་བྱེད་
བསྟན་བཅོས་ཀྱི་ཆེ་བ་བསྟན་ཏེ་རྩོམ་པ་མཐར་ཕྱིན་པའི་རྒྱུ་དམ་བཅའ་ཞིང་འདིའི་ཆེད་དུ་
བྱ་བའི་གདུལ་བྱ་ལ་ཉན་པར་བསྐུལ་བ། ངོ་མཚར་བའི་ཚིག་གིས་བརྗོད་བྱའི་ངོ་བོ་
བསྟན་ཏེ་སྤྲོ་བ་བསྐྱེད་པ་དང་ལྔ་ལས། དང་པོ་ནི། འདོ་གསལ་རྫོགས་པ་ཆེན་པོ༔
ཞེས་པས་བསྟན། གཉིས་པ་ནི། ན་མོ་གུ་རུ༔ སོགས་ཚིགས་བཅད་གསུམ་
གྱིས་བསྟན། གསུམ་པ་ནི། དེ་གསུམ་མཁྱེན་བརྩེ་ཧྲ་བདུན༔ སོགས་
ཚིགས་བཅད་གཉིས་ཀྱིས་བསྟན། བཞི་བ་ནི། ཨེ་མ་ཧོཿ བྱ་བཏང་གུ་
ཡངས་༔ ཞེས་ཚིགས་བཅད་གཅིག་གིས་བསྟན། ལྔ་བ་ནི། འཁོར་འདས་༔
སོགས་ཚིགས་བཅད་བཞི་འོ། །གཉིས་པ་བར་དུ་དགེ་བ་གཞུང་གི་དོན་ལ་བཞི།
ལྟ་བས་གཏན་ལ་ཕབ་པ་དང་། སྒོམ་པས་ཉམས་སུ་བླང་པ། སྤྱོད་པས་རྒྱལ་
སྦྱོང་བ། འབྲས་བུ་མངོན་དུ་གྱུར་ཚུལ་ལོ། །དང་པོ་ལ་གཉིས། སེམས་ཀྱི་
རྩ་བརྡར་བཅད་པ་དང་། རིག་པ་ངོ་སྤྲད་པའོ། །དང་པོ་ལ་ལྔ། ལོ་རྒྱུས་
བརྗོད་པ་དང་། རྩད་བཅད་པ། སེམས་མེད་པའི་གནས་ལུགས་རྟོད་པ།
འཁོར་འདས་གྲོལ་འཁྲུལ་གྱི་ཚུལ་རྒྱས་པར་བསྟན་པ། གྲུབ་མཐའི་མིང་གིས་
བརྗོད་ཚུལ་ལོ། །དང་པོ་ལ་བཞི། མདོ་སྔགས་ཀྱི་ཆོས་ཐམས་ཅད་ཀྱི་དོན་གནད་
འདུ་ཚུལ་དང་། སེམས་ཀྱི་གཞིས་ལ་དྲི་མ་བྲལ་བར་བསྟན་པ། འོན་ཀྱང་ཉམས་
སུ་མ་བླངས་ན་མི་གྲོལ་ཚུལ་དང་། དབང་པོ་རྣོ་རྟུལ་མེད་པར་ཀུན་གྱིས་རྟོགས་པར་
བསྟན་པའོ། །དང་པོ་ནི། ཨེ་མ་ཧོཿ སྐལ་ལྡན་༔ སོགས་ཚིགས་བཅད་
གསུམ་དང་རྐང་པ་གཉིས། གཉིས་པ་ནི། གསལ་དྭངས་ཉི་མའི་༔ སོགས་

ཚིགས་བཅད་གཉིས། གསུམ་པ་ནི། དཔེར་ན་འོ་མ༔ སོགས་ཚིགས་བཅད་གཅིག །བཞི་པ་ནི། འདི་ཉིད་ཉམས་སུ་བླང་ན༔ སོགས་ཚིགས་བཅད་བཞིས་བསྟན། གཉིས་པ་རྒྱུད་བཅད་པ་ལ་གཉིས། སེམས་ཀྱི་རྒྱུད་མ་ཆོད་ན་གནད་ཡང་དག་ཏུ་མི་འགྲོ་བར་བསྟན་པ་དང་། བྱུང་གནས་འགྲོ་གསུམ་གྱིས་རྒྱུད་བརྡར་བཅད་པའོ། །དང་པོ་ནི། ཨེ་མ་ཧོཿ ད་ཡང་སྐལ་ལྡན་བུ་མཆོག༔ སོགས་ཚིགས་བཅད་གཉིས་དང་རྐང་པ་གསུམ། གཉིས་པ་ནི། དེས་ན་རང་གི༔ སོགས་ཚིགས་བཅད་བཅུ་གཅིག་དང་རྐང་པ་གསུམ་གྱིས་བསྟན། གོང་གི་གསུམ་པ་སེམས་མེད་པའི་གནས་ལུགས་ལྷེད་པ་ནི། ཨེ་མ་ཧོཿ ད་ཡང་སྐལ་ལྡན་བུ་རྣམས༔ སོགས་ཚིགས་བཅད་དྲུག་གིས་བསྟན། གོང་གི་བཞི་པ། འཁོར་འདས་གྲོལ་འཁྲུལ་གྱི་ཚུལ་རྒྱས་པར་བསྟན་པ་ནི། ཨེ་མ་ཧོཿ ད་ཡང་སྐལ་ལྡན་སེམས་ཀྱི༔ སོགས་ཚིགས་བཅད་བཅུ། གོང་གི་ལྔ་པ། གྲུབ་མཐའི་མིང་གི་བརྗོད་ཚུལ་བཤད་པ་ནི། ཨེ༔ ད་ཡང་སྐལ་ལྡན་སྙིང་གི༔ སོགས་ཚིགས་བཅད་ལྔའོ། །གོང་གི་ས་བཅད་གཉིས་པ་རིག་པ་ངོ་སྤྲོད་ཚུལ་ལ། མདོར་བསྟན་པ་དང་། རྒྱས་པར་བཤད་པ་གཉིས་ལས། དང་པོ་ནི། ཁྱོད་རྣམས་སེམས་ཉིད་རང་སར༔ སོགས་ཚིགས་བཅད་བཞི་དང་རྐང་བ་གསུམ་མོ། །གཉིས་པ་ངོ་སྤྲོད་རྒྱས་པར་གདབ་པ་ལ་ས་བཅད་རྣམ་པ་དགུ་ལས། དང་པོ་རིག་པ་སྐུ་གསུམ་དང་སྐུ་ལྔ་ཡེ་ཤེས་ལྔར་ངོ་སྤྲོད་པ་ནི། ཨེ༔ ད་ཡང༔ ད་ལྟའི་རང་རིག་རང་གསལ༔ སོགས་ནས་འདི་ལ་མི་ཤེས་བྱ་བ་ཅི་ལ་ཟེར་ཞེས་པའི་བར་རོ། །གཉིས་པ་སྟོང་གསལ་བརྗོད་མེད་ཀྱི་རིག་ཆ་རྗེན་པར་ངོ་སྤྲོད་དེ་སྣང་ཆ་ཐམས་ཅད་དེའི་རྩལ་དང་རོལ་བར་ངོ་ཤེས་ནས་ལྟ་སྒོམ་སྤྱོད་འབྲས་ཐམས་ཅད་རིག་པ་གཅིག་པུར་ངོ་སྤྲོད་པ་ནི། ཨེ༔ ད་ཡང༔ རང་སེམས་དངོས་མེད་ནམ་མཁའ༔ སོགས་ནས་ཞེན་ཆགས་འཁྲུལ་བ་ཆོད་ཅིག་སྙིང་གི་བུ་ཞེས་པའི་བར་རོ། །གསུམ་པ་སྣང་བ་སེམས་སུ་ངོ་སྤྲོད་པའི་ཐབས་མདོར་བསྟན་པ་ནི། ཨེ་མ༔ སྐལ་བར་ལྡན༔ ལྷུག་གིས་མ་བརྒྱབ༔ ཞེས་ནས། དེ་བཞིན་ཇི་ལྟར་སྣང་ཡང་སྟོང་

པའོ། །ཞེས་པའི་བར་གྱིས་བསྟན། བཞི་བ་རིགས་དྲུག་སེམས་ཅན་རྣམས་ཀྱི་
བལྟ་བྱ་མི་མཐུན་པ་ཐམས་ཅད་རང་གི་སེམས་ཀྱིས་བྱས་པ་དང་། གང་སྣང་ཐམས་
ཅད་སེམས་སུ་ངོ་སྤྲོད་པའི་ཐབས་རྒྱས་པར་བཤད་པ་ནི། ཨེ་མ༔ སྐལ་བར༔
སྣང་བ་ཐམས་ཅད༔ སོགས་ནས། འདི་ནི་རྣམ་རྟོག་སེམས་སུ་ངོ་སྤྲོད་དོ། །
ཞེས་པའི་བར་རོ། །ལྔ་བ་དེ་ལྟར་བྱེད་མཁན་གྱི་སེམས་དེ་ཉིད་ཀྱང་སྣང་སྟོང་གཉིས་
མེད་དུ་ངོ་སྤྲོད་པ་ནི། ཨེ་མ༔ ད་ཡང༔ དེ་ལྟར་བྱེད་མཁན༔ སོགས་
ནས་འདི་ནི་གཉིས་མེད་རང་གྲོལ་ངོ་སྤྲོད་དོ། །ཞེས་པའི་བར་རོ། །དྲུག་པ་
གཞིའི་རིག་པ་དང་། གཞི་སྣང་དུས་ཀྱི་རིག་པ་གཉིས་ཀ་སྐུ་གསུམ་དབྱེར་མེད་དུ་ངོ་
སྤྲོད་པ་ནི། ཨེ༔ ད་ཡང་བྱ་བཏང་བདག་གི༔ སོགས་ནས། རྒྱུན་མི་
ཆད་པའོ། །ཞེས་པའི་བར་རོ། །བདུན་པ་དུག་ལྔ་ཡེ་ཤེས་ལྔར་ངོ་སྤྲོད་པ་ནི།
ཨེ༔ ད་ཡང༔ ཁྱེད་རང་རྣམས་ལ༔ སོགས་ནས་དུག་ལྔ་རང་གྲོལ་ངོ་སྤྲོད་
དོ། །ཞེས་པའི་བར་རོ། །བརྒྱད་པ་ཚོགས་དྲུག་གི་ཡུལ་བཟང་ངན་རོ་མཉམ་ཆེན་
པོར་ངོ་སྤྲོད་པ་ནི། ཨེ༔ ད་ཡང་སྙིང་དང་འདྲ་བའི༔ སོགས་ནས།
ཚོགས་དྲུག་རང་གྲོལ་ངོ་སྤྲོད་དོ། །ཞེས་པའི་བར་གྱིས་བསྟན། དགུ་བ་གནས་
འགྱུ་རིག་གསུམ་གཅིག་ཏུ་ངོ་སྤྲོད་པ་ནི། ཨེ༔ ད་ཡང༔ ཁྱེད་རྣམས་རང་
སེམས་གློད་ལ༔ སོགས་ནས། འཕྲོ་གནས་གཉིས་སུ་མེད་པར་ངོ་སྤྲོད་དོ། །
ཞེས་པས་བསྟན་ཏོ། །དེ་ཡན་གྱིས་གཞི་ལྟ་བ་གཏན་ལ་ཕབ་ཚུལ་སོང་ངོ་།། ༄
ད་ནི་སྒོམ་པས་ཉམས་སུ་ལེན་ཚུལ་བཤད་པ་ལ་ལྔ། མ་བཅོས་ཡེ་བབས་ཀྱི་སྒོམ་པ་
བཤད་པ་དང་། བསམ་གཏན་སྐྱེ་བའི་གནས་ནས་ལྟ་སྒོམ་སྤྱོད་འབྲས་ཡ་མ་བྲལ་
བར་སྒོམ་པས་སྐྱོང་ཚུལ་བསྟན་པ། སྤང་བླང་དགག་སྒྲུབ་དང་བྲལ་བའི་མ་བཅོས་
རང་བབས་གཤིས་ཀྱི་སྒོམ་པ་བསྟན་པ། སྒོམ་པའི་སྐབས་ལྟ་སྒོམ་སྤྱོད་འབྲས་མི་
ནོར་བའི་གནམ་ཐིག་དང་མི་འགྱུར་བའི་གཟེར་བུ་གདབ་པ། མཐར་ཐུག་སྒོམ་པ་
ཚད་དུ་འཁྱོལ་བའི་རྟགས་ལྟ་སྒོམ་སྤྱོད་འབྲས་ཀློང་དུ་གྱུར་ཚུལ་བསྟན་པའོ། །དང་
པོ་ལ་གཉིས་ལས། དང་དངོས་དང་། ཞར་བྱུང་ངོ་། །དང་པོ་ལ་གཉིས།

འཁོར་འདས་ཀྱི་ཆོས་ཐམས་ཅད་ཡེ་མཉམ་རིག་སྟོང་ཆེན་པོར་རོ་གཅིག་པར་རྟོགས་པའི་སྒོམ་པ་དང་། རྫོགས་ཆེན་ལྟ་བའི་ངང་ལ་བཟང་ངན་རེ་དོགས་སྤྲོས་མཚན་ཀུན་དང་བྲལ་བའི་སྒོམ་མེད་ཀྱི་སྒོམ་པ་བསྟན་པའོ། །དང་པོ་ནི། ཨེ་མ༔ སྐལ་ལྡན་ཁྱོད་རྣམས་མ་ཡེངས་དལ་ལེར༔ སོགས་ཚིགས་བཅད་གསུམ་དང་རྐང་པ་གཅིག །གཉིས་པ་ནི། རྫོགས་ཆེན་ངང་ལ༔ སོགས་ཚིགས་བཅད་གཉིས། གཉིས་པ་ཞར་བྱུང་བཤད་པ་ལ་གསུམ། སྒོམ་པ་ཡང་དག་པའི་ལམ་གྱི་རྟགས་ཚད་བཟུང་བ། སྒོམ་པ་ལོག་ལམ་དུ་གོལ་བའི་ལོག་རྟོག་དགག་པ། ངོ་སྤྲོད་གནད་དུ་ཁེལ་མ་ཁེལ་གྱི་སྐྱོན་ཡོན་དང་ལྟ་བའི་ངེས་ཤེས་སྐྱེས་པའི་ཚད་བསྟན་པའོ། །དང་པོ་ནི། དེ་འདྲའི་རྫོགས་ཆེན༔ སོགས་ཚིགས་བཅད་གཉིས་དང་རྐང་པ་གཅིག །གཉིས་པ་ནི། ཐམས་ཅད་སྟོང་པ༔ སོགས་ཚིགས་བཅད་གཅིག་དང་རྐང་པ་གཅིག །གསུམ་པ་ནི། ངོ་སྤྲོད་འདི་རྣམས༔ སོགས་ཚིགས་བཅད་བདུན་ནོ། །གོང་གི་གཉིས་པ། བསམ་གཏན་སྐྱེ་པའི་གནས་ནས་ལྟ་སྒོམ་སྤྱོད་འབྲས་ཡ་མ་བྲལ་བར་སྒོམ་པས་སྐྱོང་ཚུལ་བསྟན་པ་ལ་བདུན། བསམ་གཏན་སྐྱེ་བའི་གནས་བསྟན་པ། སྒོ་གསུམ་གློད་ལ་རང་བབས་ཀྱི་བཞག་ཐབས་བཤད་པ། གློས་བྱས་མཚན་འཛིན་དང་བྲལ་དགོས་པར་བསྟན་པ། ལྟ་སྒོམ་སྤྱོད་འབྲས་ཐམས་ཅད་ཀྱི་མཆོག་དང་ཡང་རྩེ་དང་སྙིང་པོ་དང་རྒྱལ་པོ་ལྟ་བུའི་ཐ་སྙད་སྦྱར་བ། དོན་ལ་རིག་པ་སྤྲོས་བྲལ་ཟང་ཀ་གཅིག་པུ་ལས་གཞན་དུ་ལྟ་སྒོམ་སྤྱོད་འབྲས་སོ་སོར་དབྱེར་མེད་པར་བསྟན་པ། དུས་གསུམ་གྱི་རྟོག་ཚོགས་ཐམས་ཅད་བྱ་ལམ་རྗེས་མེད་ལྟ་བུར་བསྟན་པ། ལྟ་སྒོམ་སྤྱོད་འབྲས་ཐམས་ཅད་ནན་ཏན་བྱས་ནས་བསྒྲུབ་ཏུ་མེད་ཅིང་། མ་བསྒོམས་རང་བབས་ལྷུག་པར་བཞག་པའི་གྲོལ་བས་གནད་བསྟན་པའོ། །དང་པོ་ནི། ཨེ༔ ད་ཡང༔ དེ་ལྟར་ལྟ་བའི༔ སོགས་ཚིགས་བཅད་གཅིག །གཉིས་པ་ནི། ལུས་ཀྱི་བྱ་རྩོལ༔ སོགས་ཚིགས་བཅད་གསུམ་དང་རྐང་བ་གཅིག །གསུམ་པ་ནི། བློ་ཡི་ཆོས་ཀྱི༔ སོགས་ཚིགས་བཅད་གཅིག །བཞི་བ་ནི། གཟུང་འཛིན་ཀུན་བྲལ༔ སོགས་ཚིགས་བཅད་

དྲུག་དང་ཆད་བ་གཉིས།   ལྔ་བ་ནི།   བལྟ་རུ་མེད་ཀྱི༔   སོགས་ཚིགས་བཅད་བཞི།   དྲུག་པ་ནི།   རྣལ་འབྱོར་ཤེས་པ༔   སོགས་ཚིགས་བཅད་གཉིས་དང་ཆད་པ་གསུམ།   བདུན་པ་ནི།   གང་ལྟར་ཤར་ཡང་༔   སོགས་ཚིགས་བཅད་བདུན་དང་ཆད་པ་གསུམ།   གོང་གི་གསུམ་པ།   སྤྱང་བླང་དགག་སྒྲུབ་དང་བྲལ་བའི་མ་བཅོས་རང་བབས་གཞིས་ཀྱི་སྒོམ་པ་བསྟན་པ་ལ་བདུན།   ཕྱི་སྣང་བ་ཡེ་སྟོང་དང་ནང་འཛིན་པ་ཡེ་གྲོལ་ཏུ་ཤེས་ནས་སྤྱང་བླང་མེད་པར་རིག་ཆ་རྗེན་པའི་ངང་དུ་རང་བབས་སུ་བཞག་པའི་སྒོམ་པ།   སྣང་སེམས་ཡེ་གྲོལ་ཆོས་སྐུའི་ཀློང་དུ་གདེང་ཟིན་པའི་ཚད་མངོན་དུ་གྱུར་བ།   གཞུང་རྩོམ་པ་པོ་རང་ཉིད་དེ་འདྲའི་གདེང་ཚད་ལ་ཐོན་ཡོད་པར་བསྟན་པ།   ཆོས་ཉིད་ཡིད་དཔྱོད་ཀྱིས་དཔོག་ཏུ་མེད་པའི་ཚུལ་བཤད་པ།   གང་སྣང་ཆོས་སྐུར་རྟོགས་པའི་རྣམ་འབྱོར་གྱི་ཁྱད་ཆོས།   སྒོམ་པའི་གེགས་དང་འཕྲང་བསལ་བ།   གོལ་ཤོར་དང་བྲལ་བའི་གཉུག་མ་གཞིས་ཀྱི་བཞུགས་ཚུལ་བཤད་པའོ།   །དང་པོ་ནི།   ཨེ་༔   ད་ཡང་༔   ཕྱི་ཡུལ་མེད་སྣང་༔   སོགས་ཚིགས་བཅད་གཉིས་དང་ཆད་པ་གསུམ།   གཉིས་པ་ནི།   དེ་ཡི་ངང་ལ༔   སོགས་ཚིགས་བཅད་གཉིས་དང་ཆད་པ་གཅིག   །གསུམ་པ་ནི།   མ་ཕྱིན་ན་ཡང་༔   སོགས་ཚིགས་བཅད་གཉིས་དང་ཆད་པ་གཅིག   །བཞི་བ་ནི།   གནད་འདི་ཡིན་ཀྱང་༔   སོགས་ཚིགས་བཅད་ལྔ་དང་ཆད་པ་གཅིག   །ལྔ་བ་ནི།   གང་ལ་བལྟས་ཀྱང་༔   སོགས་ཚིགས་བཅད་གཅིག   །དྲུག་པ་ནི།   འོ་ན་ཕྱི་རོལ༔   སོགས་ཚིགས་བཅད་བདུན།   བདུན་པ་ནི།   མདོར་ན་གང་གི་སོགས༔   ཚིགས་བཅད་གཉིས་དང་ཆད་པ་གཅིག་གོ   །དེ་ནི་གོང་གི་ས་བཅད་བཞི་པ་སྒོམ་པའི་སྐབས་ལྟ་སྒོམ་སྤྱོད་འབྲས་མི་ནོར་བའི་གནམ་ཐིག་དང་།   མི་འགྱུར་བའི་གཟེར་བུ་གདབ་པ་ལ་གསུམ་ལས།   ནོར་ས་མེད་པའི་ཐིག་ཆེན་བཞི་དང་།   འགྱུར་བ་མེད་པའི་གཟེར་ཆེན་བཞི།   ལྟ་སྒོམ་སྤྱོད་འབྲས་ཟད་སར་འཁྱོལ་ཚུལ་ལོ།   །དང་པོ་ནི།   ཨེ་༔   ད་ཡང་༔   ནོར་ས་མེད་པའི་སོགས་ཚིགས་བཅད་གསུམ་དང་ཆད་པ་གཉིས།   གཉིས་པ་ནི།   མི་འགྱུར་བ་ཡི༔   སོགས་ཚིགས་བཅད་གསུམ་དང་

རྐང་པ་གཅིག །གསུམ་པ་ནི། ལྟ་བ་མི་མཐུན༔ སོགས་ཚིགས་བཅད་བཅུ་
དང་རྐང་པ་གཉིས། གོང་གི་ལྟ་བ་མཐར་ཐུག་སྒོམ་པ་ཚད་དུ་འཁྱོལ་བའི་རྟགས་ལྟ་
སྒོམ་སྤྱོད་འབྲས་ཀློང་དུ་གྱུར་ཚུལ་བསྟན་པ་ནི། ཨེ༔ ད་ཡང༔ དེ་ལྟར་
དང་པོ་ཡེངས་མེད༔ སོགས་ཚིགས་བཅད་བཞིས་བསྟན། ༈ དེ་ནི་རྩ་བའི་
ས་བཅད་གསུམ་པ། སྤྱོད་པས་རྩལ་སྦྱོང་བ་ལ་བདུན་ལས། དང་པོ་སྒོ་གསུམ་
གྱི་སྤྱོད་པ་མ་བཅོས་རང་བབས་སུ་འཇོག་པ་དང་། སྣང་གྲགས་ཐམས་ཅད་སྒྱུ་མའི་
དཔེ་བཅུ་ལྟ་བུར་ངོས་བཟུང་ནས་སྤྱོད་ལམ་ཐམས་ཅད་དུ་དེའི་ངང་སྐྱོང་བ། ལས་
དང་པོ་བའི་རྣམ་རྟོག་འཕྲོ་རྒོད་ཐམས་ཅད་རང་ཡལ་དུ་འགྲོ་བའི་ཐབས་སྣ་ཚོགས་ཀྱི་
སྤྱོད་པ་བསྟན་པ་དང་། བྱིང་རྨུག་འཐིབས་གསུམ་རང་ཡལ་དུ་འགྲོ་ཚུལ་གྱི་སྤྱོད་པ་
བསྟན་པ། རྐྱེན་སྣང་གང་ཤར་ཀྱང་རོ་སྙོམས་ཐོག་བརྫིས་ཀྱི་སྤྱོད་པ་ལ་བརྟེན་ནས་
གེགས་སེལ་ཚུལ། རྨི་ལམ་འོད་གསལ་དུ་བསྲེ་ཚུལ། རྟོགས་པའི་གདེང་ཚད་
ཟིན་པའི་གང་ཟག་གི་སྒོ་གསུམ་གྱི་སྤྱོད་པའི་ཁྱད་ཆོས་བཤད་པའོ། །དང་པོ་ནི།
ཨེ༔ ད་དུང་རིགས་ཀྱི༔ སོགས་ཚིགས་བཅད་གཅིག །གཉིས་པ་ནི།
སྣང་གྲགས་ཆོས་རྣམས༔ སོགས་ཚིགས་བཅད་དྲུག་དང་རྐང་པ་གཉིས། གསུམ་
པ་ནི། དེ་ལྟར་སྒོམ་ཆེ༔ སོགས་ཚིགས་བཅད་ལྔ་དང་རྐང་པ་གཉིས། བཞི་
པ་ནི། བྱིང་བ་ཆེ་ན༔ སོགས་ཚིགས་བཅད་བཞི་དང་རྐང་པ་གཅིག །ལྔ་པ་
ནི། ཁྱད་པར་ནད་གདོན༔ སོགས་ཚིགས་བཅད་ལྔ་དང་རྐང་པ་གཉིས།
དྲུག་པ་ནི། མཚན་དུས་རང་བབས༔ སོགས་རྐང་པ་གསུམ། བདུན་པ་ནི།
དེ་ལྟར་བྱས་ན༔ སོགས་ཚིགས་བཅད་གསུམ་མོ། ༈ དེ་ནི་གོང་གི་རྩ་བའི་
ས་བཅད་བཞི་པ་འབྲས་བུ་མངོན་དུ་གྱུར་ཚུལ་ལ་གཉིས་ལས། རིག་པ་རང་གི་ངོས་
ལ་སྐུ་དང་ཡེ་ཤེས་ལ་སོགས་འབྲས་བུའི་ཆོས་རྣམས་རང་ཆས་སུ་ཡོད་པར་བསྟན་པ་
དང་། སྣང་སྲིད་དག་པ་རབ་འབྱམས་ཇི་ལྟ་བ་བཞིན་མངོན་དུ་གྱུར་ཚུལ་ལོ།
དང་པོ་ནི། ཨེ་མ༔ ད་ཡང༔ རྣམ་སྣང་ཕྱི་ན་མེད་དེ༔ སོགས་ཚིགས་
བཅད་ལྔ་དང་རྐང་པ་གཅིག །གཉིས་པ་ལ་གསུམ། རིག་རྩལ་རོལ་བ་གང་ཤར་

ཐམས་ཅད་དབྱིངས་ཀྱི་རྒྱན་དང་དག་པ་རབ་འབྱམས་འབབ་ཞིག་ཏུ་ཤར་བ་དང་། སྐྱེ་འཆི་བར་དོ་གསུམ་གང་རུང་དུ་གྲོལ་ཚུལ་དང་། གྲོལ་ནས་འགྲོ་བ་སེམས་ཅན་གྱི་དོན་མཛད་ཚུལ་ལོ། །དང་པོ་ནི། ཨེ་༔ ད་ཡང་༔ དགའ་ཞིང་སྤྲོ་བས༔ སོགས་ཚིགས་བཅད་དྲུག་དང་རྐང་པ་གསུམ། གཉིས་པ་ནི། དེ་ལྟར་ངེས་པར་༔ སོགས་ཚིགས་བཅད་གསུམ། གསུམ་པ་ནི། གང་ལ་གང་འདུལ་༔ སོགས་ཚིགས་བཅད་གཅིག་དང་རྐང་པ་གཉིས་སོ།། ༈ ད་ནི་ཐ་མར་དགེ་བ་མཇུག་གི་དོན་བཤད་པ་ལ་གཉིས། དགེ་བ་གཞན་དོན་དུ་བསྔོ་བ་དང་། མཛད་བྱང་བསྟན་པའོ། །དང་པོ་ནི། དགེ་འདིས་སྐལ་ལྡན༔ སོགས་ཚིགས་བཅད་གཅིག །གཉིས་པ་ནི། ཅེས་འོད་གསལ་རྫོགས་པ་༔ སོགས་ཀྱིས་བསྟན་ཏོ། །ཞེས་པའང་རང་གཞན་ལ་ཕན་པའི་སེམས་ཀྱིས་བསྟན་མིང་པས་ཀ་དག་སྤྲོས་བྲལ་གླིང་ནས་བྲིས་སོ། །དགེའོ།། དགེའོ།། དགེའོ།། །།

INDEX